British and Commonwealth
WARSHIP
CAMOUFLAGE
of WWII

Volume II

British and Commonwealth
WARSHIP
CAMOUFLAGE
of WWII

Volume II

MALCOLM WRIGHT

Battleships and Aircraft Carriers

Seaforth
PUBLISHING

DEDICATION

This volume is dedicated to the memory of my father, Albert William George Wright, who trained as a wireless operator with the RANVR before World War II. But, when the call to duty came, he was declared as being in a reserved occupation and sent home. It broke his heart to see his fellow reservists go while he stayed home and he always regretted not being allowed to go with them. He built aircraft as his part of the war effort but his heart was always with those at sea.

CONTENTS

INTRODUCTION

This work was inspired by friends and readers of my World War II *Convoy* series of wargame books who felt I should publish the hundreds of colour drawings of ships that I have made over the years, as well as my maritime paintings and cover art. They were gathered together over the past fifty years, sometimes from descriptions given by veterans, museum models, works of art, etc. Where I have remembered the sources, these have been included in the bibliography. Many were taken from a study of war art that I did some decades ago. There are some which, across half a century, I have simply forgotten the origin of. In these cases, where mistakes occur in the drawings I have produced, I accept full blame.

One of the first occasions on which I recall realising the importance of paint schemes used in war was when, as a boy and, later, as a young man, I spent many hours in the company of various naval veterans of several nations, particularly British and Australian. Of great value was that I was able to meet two men who had served in naval dockyards. One of the two worked in Sydney, Australia, and the other worked at three dockyards in the UK from slightly before the war to just after it. It was fortunate that I met these men in the prime of their lives with memories still fresh and not distorted or dulled by age and the years in between.

These hours were many decades ago and the veterans having sadly all passed on. How I wish they were still here so I could clarify some things with them. They were kind enough to help me match colours on various model ships I built and with some of my early artwork. There were colours that I found hard to imagine being used in my young days but, of course, since then there have been publications showing the paint schemes for a whole range of ships. Today we know much more about them but, even so, many records were destroyed or lost. I remember one ex-sailor laughing that HMAS *Hobart* arrived in Fremantle from the Mediterranean painted pink. In his story, he said he thought it was because they had mixed undercoat into grey because they were short of paint and, as soon as the ship arrived in Sydney, they painted it grey again. He had obviously never heard of the famous Mountbatten Pink scheme, and nor had I, so I was unsure if he was just telling a tall tale. In later years, I realised what he had seen was a well-used camouflage scheme in the Mediterranean theatre of war up until late 1942.

An analysis of colour photographs is helpful, but the film used in World War II is not necessarily true to shade, with many colours appearing darker or lighter than in real life due to poor-quality film or just tricks of the light. But black and white photographs can be quite helpful if you have access to the shades that were available and which were probably used on the ship in question. Distorting the shades of a black and white photograph will often reveal areas that were too light to see in the original and, with patient research, it is possible to reconstruct schemes. In this manner, and with a lot of detective work, I have assembled line drawings of the hundreds of ships that appear in this series. If any are wrong, then I accept responsibility but would point out that in some cases there are no hard references and therefore my deductions are probably as good as any. In some instances, I was able to use the work of earlier authors as reference or to check my own research against theirs. I have not always totally agreed with some and, if my drawings vary from other sources, it is because that is my opinion based on the research of many decades. Sometimes, the difference may be merely the size and shape of a squiggle or triangle or the exact tint of the shade.

This book is intended as a quick reference source for people wanting to paint model ships as a hobby, for wargaming or art. Where possible, I have shown both sides of a ship if the camouflage differed and more than one illustration if armament and equipment changes made the ship's appearance change. I have not listed them by camouflage scheme, rather by ship type. This should enable the reader to go straight to the ship type wanted and find an appropriate scheme. They are also listed by name and, while not all the ships of each class are always shown, I have nonetheless included a lot of them, so the reader can also often chose by name when painting a model.

Overhead views are included for some ships, as concealment from aircraft was important for much of World War II. However, where not shown, it was common to paint upper surfaces grey or, in the case of Cemtex, to leave it in its natural grey. Some camouflage schemes were carried across the deck but, by and large, the easiest way was to use grey, even if it meant painting over wooden decks that had been kept holystoned for years by the sweat of sailors.

One of the very important issues for those of you painting models to remember is that sometimes there is no exact shade. There may well be a recommended shade, and even a paint guide with colour chips to go with it, but you must place yourself in the shoes of the sailors of the day. Imagine you have been at sea with a convoy for a week or two; you arrive back in harbour exhausted and in need of rest. While half the ship is sent off for a few quick days leave, the others remain behind to carry out minor maintenance. This usually meant either touching up the paintwork or preparing it for the half on leave to tackle when they returned. Laid out in front of you is a sort of cookbook telling you to add this much of a certain pigment to that much white or grey and the result will be the shade specified for a particular scheme. But you are tired, or perhaps the ship is on standby to leave harbour on yet another mission. So your level of care when told to add a cup of this to a tin of that can be rather less than ideal. The famous 'TLAR' comes into effect. The buffer puts in the pigment, a seaman stirs it, and they look at the result and say "That looks about right" – hence the abbreviation TLAR.

Veteran after veteran told me how arduous the task of chipping rust and re-painting was. It was hated. Even more so by tired men waiting for the rest of their shipmates to get back so they could get a few days leave themselves. So, up until 1943, we must take some of the official Admiralty shades with a pinch of salt. Even they accepted that a ship may not have the right amount of paint and recommended a scheme be as near as possible. In some cases, this meant the colours might not even be the same; in which instance, the recommendation was that they should be of similar shade tone. Hence, pale blue was often used instead of pale green and vice versa. No ship was going to be held back from her vital role in war just because the paint scheme was not exact.

From 1943 onward, this was eased; never fully overcome, but eased. That was because the Admiralty started to issue ready-mixed paint to the ships along with full instructions for specific schemes. Thus, in late war photography, we are more likely to see ships looking much the same shade when wearing various regulation schemes. Also, new ships coming from the shipyard would have been painted in the yard using paint delivered for the purpose.

But I state never fully overcome because there were often shortages and a ship might have to make do with what was available to the crew to use. There were instances of there being insufficient amount of a particular shade to cover the area intended, so that area was either made smaller than specified, or often the problem was solved by mixing some other spare paint to eke out the shade that was running out. Therefore, you should never assume a ship is exactly one shade or another, regardless of what official records might state.

Even shipyards ran short of paint and, rather than hold a vessel up from

entering service, it would be sent to sea with whatever was available. This explains why the reader will see ships of exactly the same class, but which, although painted similarly, the colours may not necessarily be the same.

A gentleman I met years ago, who had worked in Royal Dockyards, told me that, when he started work there a few years before World War II, they had a plentiful stock of paint on hand. But they were limited to specific colours: primrose, buff, MS4a grey, 507c grey and white with black. Sometimes, there was a quantity of Brunswick green and there was sure to be some 507a, too. Also in plentiful supply was lots and lots of red lead undercoat. Therefore, when a ship required painting, or its paint locker refilled, they were the only ones that could be supplied. It should therefore be no surprise that early schemes, which were worked out by the officers of the ship, would be based around what they had or what they could mix with those shades.

Other issues affected how a ship looked. The sudden demand for masses of paint was a crisis for all the nations involved. Even the USA, with its vast resources, ran short from time to time. This meant that sometimes the pigments accepted were below standard and faded very quickly. Those who have looked at photographs of US warships in dark navy blue will realise how quickly that faded, often in patches. US shipyards were churning out ships at a prodigious rate and rather than delay, the new ships would be painted in what was available and the task of providing the correct shades left to the dockyard where the ship had its first refit, or the crew to alter during the working-up period. Getting the ships completed and at sea was more important than the exact shade of paint.

In addition to poor quality pigments fading, there were at times great difficulties in supplying particular colours. Green, for example, was in high demand by the Army and the Air Force as part of their camouflage schemes. Many shades of khaki required green pigment too, as did olive drab. For this reason, green was often not available for warships and other colours had to be substituted. Blue was in less demand by the other services and therefore pale blue often stood in for pale green in naval schemes. Indeed, there were many shades of blue and blue grey used, although the designer of a particular scheme may have specified green of various hues.

Lastly, not only were paint schemes affected by shortage of pigments, the TLAR system, fading and wrong colours available, there was also the effect of seawater on the paint itself. Ships spending lots of time at sea suffer salt corrosion and become rusty. Paint can bubble up in rust patches and flake off, exposing previous paint colours underneath. It often came about because paint was applied and the ship then put to sea before it had time to sufficiently dry and fix. Readers will almost certainly have seen photographs of ships with whole sections of paint missing. This was usually due to allowing insufficient time to dry and fix or poor quality paint. For some paint schemes, this effect was very bad. White and other pale shades became much less effective once they became rusty. For larger ships, with more crew available, touching up was much easier but still affected by the TLAR principle.

It is up to the person painting a model as to how specific they are but, when using reference sources, just keep in mind that the very neat-looking ship in a photograph has probably just come from a refit or dockyard job. The ship that looks rather scruffy has probably been worked hard and had little time for the fancy touch-up jobs. I recall years ago seeing a photograph in a book, with a caption that referred to a particular destroyer returning to harbour with its paint scheme in a 'disgraceful condition'. A veteran World War II sailor looking at the book was quite derisive of the caption. It was a case, he said, of the person writing it having no consideration or understanding of what that ship must have been through in the weeks preceding the photograph for it to be in that state. No doubt he was quite correct.

So if your model painting skills are not the best, you can always claim your model ships have seen a lot of sea time. If you are a very discerning model painter that strives for total accuracy in shade, spare a thought that perhaps you may not be producing a realistic model after all, simply one that looks perfect. A more genuine approach would be to deliberately alter shades, change patterns slightly and add a rust streak or two here and there. Then you can truly claim you model is very accurate. There could be an area that has been cleaned of rust and touched up, but the new paint is not exactly the same shade. Close, but darker or lighter!

A final point: when working on this book, I deliberately made contact with some ex-naval veterans and asked them their opinion of the TLAR attitude. Most responded that it was by far the most common way of mixing paint, especially when in a hurry. One pointed out, and then just recently yet another, that, even in peacetime, when ships were painted to regulation and by crew who had time to do it, there was nothing at all unusual in seeing a group of sister ships tied up together, all resplendent in new paint straight out of the regulation tins, and all still somewhat different. In the case of flotilla craft, this could even have been deliberate to enable individual ships to be recognised while operating together.

SCALE
DRAWINGS ARE NOT TO SCALE. In order to give the reader a good view of the drawings, they have not been produced to a comparative scale, rather they are to the best size for viewing in the format of this book.

PHOTOGRAPHIC ANALYSIS
Black and white film varies in quality and did so even more during World War II with the shortage of quality film stock. The armed services used vast quantities, which left civilian photographers, and even military ones, at the mercy of what they could obtain. As a result, true shade is not always present. A scheme can look lighter or darker than it really was. Pale blue can come out quite dark grey and give the wrong impression of the real shade. Similarly, it can fade almost to nothing and look like there is no camouflage at all.

With diligent research, one can sometimes be lucky enough to come up with multiple photographs of the same ship, from different sources and angles. Some may be in sepia and others a variety of faded or under-exposed film. But, if one knows what the colour was supposed to be, it is possible to take these, analyse them and come to a fairly reasonable conclusion as to the pattern and the depth of shade. This is helped if the collection includes the ship from different angles and one can work out the depth of shade from the sun etc. It is not perfect but, in some cases where records have been lost, it is our best way of working out what a particular ship looked like.

I have used that technique many times. It is a case of using some detective work to gather a whole range of evidence and then, from that, come to a reasonable conclusion. It is something that requires great patience in finding the different sources to compare but, in this day of the internet, that has become much easier. With patience, one can look up the memories posted online, either by the veteran or his family, along with some Box Brownie photographs those people took, and compare them with more official sources.

I have touched on issues here that I have used for fifty years of my life during research. I have, of course, referred to official sources too - the Imperial War Museum sources in London are excellent. That was the easiest research of all and produced lots of 'what should have been' as well as a lot of 'what actually was' instances. But I am firmly of the belief, based on personal interviews over many decades, that what was supposed to be and what actually was, has not been recorded.

ACKNOWLEDGEMENTS

The author was greatly assisted in the completion of this book through the editing and research assistance of Dave Schueler, my chief editing assistant; Andy Doty, proof-reader and monitor of accuracy, plus Ian Thompson, Adam Jones, Jim Bryce and Sam Smith, all of whom were kind enough to be proof-readers.

The members of the Shipbucket website proved to be of a great help. The knowledge of the members and their ability to come up with difficult to find information from obscure sources is very impressive. Of great value in double checking the pennants of Royal Navy ships was the unpublished PDF: *Ships Pennant Numbers: The Royal Navy Pennant Numbering System* by Jim Bryce.

The champion sources of them all, over years of research, were the veterans to whom we owe so much for the sacrifice they made fighting World War II. They often lost their health and suffered the pain of friends killed. I deliberately sought many out over the past five decades and am so glad that I did so while they were young and vital, and able to call on clear memories. They were an inspiration to me and so many were always happy to tell proud stories of their beloved ships. It is sad that all those I consulted over the years have passed on, taking their memories with them. May they rest in peace.

Mal Wright
2014

REFERENCE SOURCES

Numerous paintings by war artists. Some were actually 'there' and I place a higher reliance on their work than some who painted later.

Breyer, Siegfried, *Battleships and Battlecruisers*, (MacDonald and Jane's, 1973).

Brown, David, *Carrier Operations of WWII*, Volumes I and II, (Ian Allen, 1974).

Brown, David, *Warship Profiles* series, (Profile Publications, 1971-74). A large number of these older booklets are very helpful.

Burt, R. A., *British Battleships of World War One*, (Arms and Armour Press, 1986).

Gillett, Ross, *Australian and New Zealand Warships 1914-45)*, (Doubleday Books, 1987).

Gooden, Henrietta, *Camouflage and Art, Design for Deception in World War 2*, (Unicorn Press, 2007). Some good technical discussion on the how and why.

Hodges, Peter, *Royal Navy Warship Camouflage 1939–1945*, (Almark Publications, 1973). Long out of print but an invaluable work.

Hreachmack, Patrick, *The Painter's Guide to World War Two Naval Camouflage*, (Clash of Arms, 1996). A useful guide.

Jane's Fighting Ships, (Jane's, numerous editions).

Lenton, H.T., & Colledge, J.J., *Warships of WWII*, (Ian Allen, 1964)

Raven, Alan, *Warships Perspectives*, (WR Press, 2000-3). Four volumes. I have been a great admirer of his work for years going back to early magazine articles. His volumes on Royal Navy warships are highly recommended.

Raven, Alan, *Ensign* series, also produce some years ago now.

Raven, Alan, and Roberts, John, *Man O' War* series, Arms and Armour Press 1978-80)

Royal Navy, *Confidential Admiralty Fleet Orders*, 1943 – 45. Various RN Fleet Instructions.

Whitley, M.J., *Battleships of World War Two*, (Arms and Armour Press, 1978)

Williams, David, *Naval Camouflage 1914-1945*, (Naval Institute Press, 2001). A most brilliant book but with sadly far too few colour illustrations.

Various Authors, *Camera At Sea,* (Bay Books, 1980). Compiled by the staff of *Warship.*

Warship, A Quarterly Journal of Warship History, across many editions 1978-79. Particularly the articles by Robert Dumas, which were invaluable for the *King George V* class details year for year.

There are numerous other books not specifically related to camouflage but which contain colour photographs and illustrations, as well as those that show good quality black and white illustrations.

RECOMMENDED ONLINE RESOURCES

The-Blueprints.com (http://www.the-blueprints.com/blueprints/ships/)

Old Ship Picture Galleries (http://www.photoship.co.uk/Browse%20Misc%20 Galleries/)

Naval Weapons of the World From 1880 to Today (http://www.navweaps.com/ Weapons/index_weapons.htm)

Finewaterline.com (http://www.finewaterline.com/pages/gallery/modelgallery. htm**)**

The U-Boat Net (http://www.uboat.net/allies/warships/)

Tworzymy najlepsze plany okrętów dla modelarzy [Ship plans for modellers] (http://profilemorskie.home.pl/PlanyPDF.htm#RZP)

Axis History Forum (http://forum.axishistory.com/index)

PAINT REFERENCE SOURCE

Snyder & Short Enterprises. This company produces paint chips of RN hues and those other nations for WWII. I have used them extensively and commend them to the reader. What they cannot provide are examples of sub-standard paint and consequent fading. These paint chips are what the shades should have been but, for all the reasons mentioned above, what was actually available, or what paint looked like after being exposed to seawater and sunlight cannot be so easily reproduced.

PAINT TYPES AND SCHEMES

At the commencement of World War II, there were no official Admiralty-approved designs for the camouflage of a warship. The commanding officers of ships were left to decide if this would be done and how, depending on the available paint supply. On occasion, they may have consulted the senior officer of the squadron or fleet to which the ship was attached. In some areas, ships thus applied quite similar schemes, even though they were actually unofficial. Examination of photographs from the era can therefore mislead modern researchers into thinking there was a standard scheme when, it fact, it was just ships' crews applying similar ideas; perhaps copying others. Such schemes used the paint that was available to each ship. It requires a lot of paint to repaint an entire ship and this was not usually available on board as it would not only require a lot of room but would also be a fire hazard.

UNOFFICIAL CAMOUFLAGE SCHEMES

In the pre-war era, major warships were painted when in dock and ships only carried enough paint in their lockers as would be required during the removal of rust and general touch up work in between refits. Therefore, if a ship was to be camouflaged, she was limited to what was available. That could be black, white and the two main shades of the fleet: MS4a Home Fleet grey and 507c Mediterranean grey. 507a dark grey was another shade commonly available. There may have been a small amount of primrose, Brunswick green or buff carried by a ship on some stations and, as quartermasters do not like throwing things away, ships that had previously been on those stations may still have some stashed away in their paint lockers. Naturally, this meant that the range of shades able to be produced by an individual ship would be limited. Captains might also resort to paint available for purchase from sources ashore. These were referred to by the Admiralty as 'local procurement shades'.

The examination of early schemes leaves little doubt that local procurement was understandably common under the pressure of war. Indeed, for some ships it may have been the easiest source of supply. The large monitor HMS *Terror*, operating in support of the British Army along the coast of North Africa, was constantly targeted by enemy aircraft and, being limited to what was available from Alexandria, managed to obtain quantities of British Army Sand and Stone. The scheme was particularly good for a ship operating near the coast on bombardment duty. Therefore, local procurement was not always from naval or maritime sources.

In all cases, a scheme not designed by the Admiralty but worn by a warship of the Royal Navy would be referred to as 'unofficial' even *if* the Admiralty had given approval to actually camouflage the ship. However, as it was realised that the war was likely to drag on for years, the wheels of the Admiralty turned toward some official schemes which would use certain colours, thus providing a predictable supply requirement. Green was always in short supply during the early years as priority for its use was, understandably, given to the army and for use on aircraft.

Once a range of suitable colours had been designed, based around pigments that could be reliably obtained, it made supply to ships much easier. Repair ships, depot ships, dockyards and naval stores dumps could be stocked accordingly. The Admiralty could then also issue instruction books on how to apply these paints and provide designs drawn up for specific ships.

ADMIRALTY SCHEMES

To suit this supply situation, the Admiralty devised three basic disruptive designs. These were Light, Intermediate and Dark. The Intermediate was often referred to as Medium. They were designed to meet the average light conditions in the various operational zones. The intent in all instances of disruptive schemes was to break up the normal view of the ship; in other words, to disrupt what the eye was seeing.

ADMIRALTY LIGHT DISRUPTIVE

The tones of these designs were best suited to dull conditions where direct sunlight might be less common. Pale shades have a tendency to blend in with a light background and, with a mix of colours, the blend can make a ship almost invisible. It did require careful counter-shading. There are always areas of overhang that provide shadow and the use of high gloss instead of matt in the shade meant a greater reflection of light and, thus, such an area may match that in full light. This type of scheme was favoured for the North Atlantic, convoys to Russia, etc. The colours used were often quite close to each other in shade and only a certain amount of high contrast would be present. It was not unusual for several colours to be applied, even as many as six on some ships, but this was unpopular because of the amount of touch up paint that needed to be carried and also because it took a lot of work to keep each shade up to standard.

ADMIRALTY INTERMEDIATE OR MEDIUM DISRUPTIVE

Naturally, not all areas suited the light schemes. The central and southern Atlantic, for example, tended toward much brighter conditions. Therefore, the shades chosen were stronger even though the actual pattern of the camouflage in layout and style may resemble the lighter type. The number of shades used was usually less but, as all things were continually experimented with, it was not always the case. Achieving an intermediate scheme could be simply a matter of applying new medium shade paint over a light one. Ships often changed stations and this would require the camouflage to be suited to the new area. Adjusting the intensity of colour was easier than repainting the entire ship and photographic evidence would seem to suggest that many ships changed back and forth between the grades of disruptive colours.

ADMIRALTY DARK & ADMIRALTY DARK DISRUPTIVE

Bright sunlight can cause highly contrasting shades to confuse the eye. In the Eastern Mediterranean, the Red Sea and the Indian Ocean, black and white can very effectively break up the outline of a ship and, while the viewer can clearly see that it is indeed a ship, the confusion of light reaching the eye will hinder observing exactly what ship is being seen, its size and type etc.

Therefore, in this instance, disruption to the eye is important, resulting in the use of darker shades upon very light. Matt white areas would become detached from areas of black. Counter-shading light or white areas in high gloss was important. For dark colours, countershading was less important because shade simply added to the contrast. With such a scheme, very dark grey on pale grey would be successful - as would black on white. If an intermediate colour was used, this might spoil the effect of contrast.

THE WESTERN APPROACHES SCHEME

Although one of the most widely-adopted for ships operating on the North Atlantic convoy runs, this was not used on capital ships. The Peter Scott design was for small ships engaged in anti-submarine warfare. Some ideas were taken from it for larger ships, but the design remained a feature of escorts.

MOUNTBATTEN PINK

Lord Louis Mountbatten, commanding the 5th Destroyer flotilla in the Mediterranean, designed a camouflage which ultimately used three shades of a pinkish grey. It required the mixing of Red Lead undercoat with various shades of grey. It was not used on capital ships, but it is probably the most argued-over and contentious of all shades, as there seems to be many opinions about its actual colour.

ADMIRALTY STANDARD LIGHT SCHEME

From the mid-war period onward, the increasing use of radar meant that ships were often detected at long range, regardless of camouflage. Once detected by radar, a keen observer would soon see through the effects of schemes intended to confuse and thus be able to use those contrasting shades to identify the target. The solution was to make it very hard to distinguish details of the ship. The scheme was only effective in areas of bright light and was therefore most commonly found on ships sent to the Indian Ocean or the Pacific. The idea was to take a leaf from the Western Approaches book and paint the ship overall in very pale grey with heavy counter-shading of shade areas. This made it difficult for an observer to pick out specific details so, although the ship could be seen, it was not always possible to identify it. To increase the problem of observation, a blue panel was added on the hull. This was instructed to be painted from the forward breakwater to the end of the muzzles of 'Y' gun/mount but, in practice, varied a lot. Its intent was to give an illusion of the ship being shorter than it actually was and thus probably further away. There were instructions for the forward edge of the panel to be sloped forward at the top, to create a false bow, but this too was often ignored. For the British Eastern Fleet, mostly operating in the Indian Ocean, the blue panel was to be a very pale blue. For the British Pacific Fleet, it was to be dark blue. However, once again, there was considerable variation, especially as ships often changed station.

ADMIRALTY SPECIAL SCHEMES

From time to time, the Admiralty camouflage department issued designs of a specific type, for particular ships. These were often experimental and exclusive to that vessel. A vessel may have a scheme applied; then other ships that went to sea in company were requested to put in a report on its effect. This came about because it was not possible for the Admiralty's own designers to go to sea and actually observe the value, or lack thereof, of the many ideas they came up with.

By the end of World War II, other Admiralty schemes were being issued and these included a darker version of the Light scheme discussed for the Indian Ocean and Pacific theatres. Various colours were now available and tried out experimentally, although, by this time, they were no longer unofficial, being instead applied to see how various things worked. Hence, duck egg green and duck egg blue appeared, along with various combinations of green which was now, finally, in plentiful supply. There were so many of these experiments that it is not possible to sort them into any specific recognisable group.

ADMIRALTY STANDARD SCHEME

This was introduced in mid-1944 and was intended to replace all other camouflage schemes. However, the influence of war meant this never happened. It was intended to limit the colours to only two. A dark shade was applied as a panel, or to the whole hull, with a lighter shade for the rest of the ship. Masts were usually white.

MISTAKES

The demands of war meant that many dockyards not normally given naval work had to be used. But even naval dockyards could suffer manpower short-ages or have to use less-skilled workers than they may normally have done. When a camouflage scheme was applied, a plan was supplied to the dockyard and, under the supervision of a foreman painter, it would be marked out in chalk on the side of the ship. The measurements could vary according to the skill of those doing the work; hence a patch of a particular colour could be applied in a proportion not part of the plan, or to a wrong shape and so on. These variations of official patterns were merely mistakes due to human error. The reader should not necessarily conclude the Admiralty intended it that way.

PENNANT NUMBERS

Most aircraft carriers and battleships had a number without a flag superior but most of the war-built escort carriers were allocated flag superior D. Exceptions were HMS *Hermes*, HMS *Argus*, HMS *Iron Duke* and some seaplane tenders that used the letter I, but all these changed to the letter D in 1940.

DECK LETTERS

Letters identifying aircraft carriers from each other were sometimes displayed on the flight deck and sometimes not. Most remained constant but some were changed when ships operated in the Pacific

BRITISH AND COMMONWEALTH WARSHIP PAINTS DURING WWII

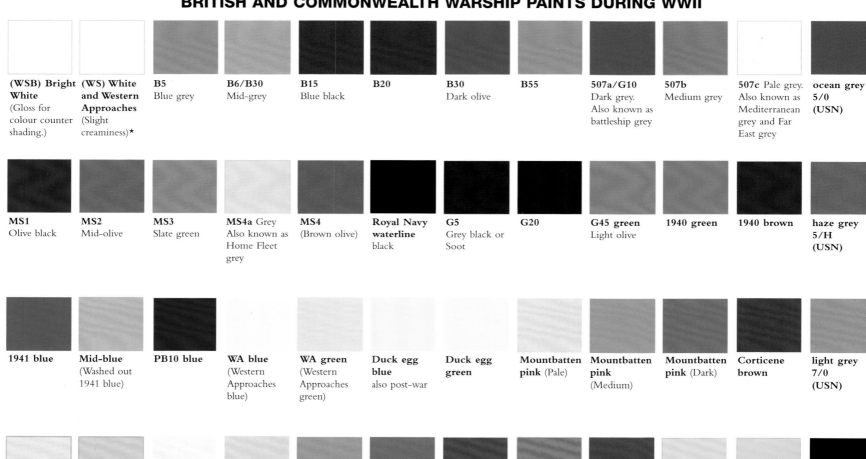

(WSB) Bright White (Gloss for colour counter shading.)

(WS) White and Western Approaches (Slight creaminess)★

B5 Blue grey

B6/B30 Mid-grey

B15 Blue black

B20

B30 Dark olive

B55

507a/G10 Dark grey. Also known as battleship grey

507b Medium grey

507c Pale grey. Also known as Mediterranean grey and Far East grey

ocean grey 5/0 (USN)

MS1 Olive black

MS2 Mid-olive

MS3 Slate green

MS4a Grey Also known as Home Fleet grey

MS4 (Brown olive)

Royal Navy waterline black

G5 Grey black or Soot

G20

G45 green Light olive

1940 green

1940 brown

haze grey 5/H (USN)

1941 blue

Mid-blue (Washed out 1941 blue)

PB10 blue

WA blue (Western Approaches blue)

WA green (Western Approaches green)

Duck egg blue also post-war

Duck egg green

Mountbatten pink (Pale)

Mountbatten pink (Medium)

Mountbatten pink (Dark)

Corticene brown

light grey 7/0 (USN)

Sand

Dark sand

Sand stone (pale)

Light stone

Mid-stone

Dark stone

Red lead Undercoat and hull below the waterline

Bright red Peacetime Waterline

Brunswick green (Peacetime)

Buff (Peacetime)

Primrose (Peacetime)

navy blue 5/N (USN)

AIRCRAFT SYMBOLS used in this book (markings and colours may vary)

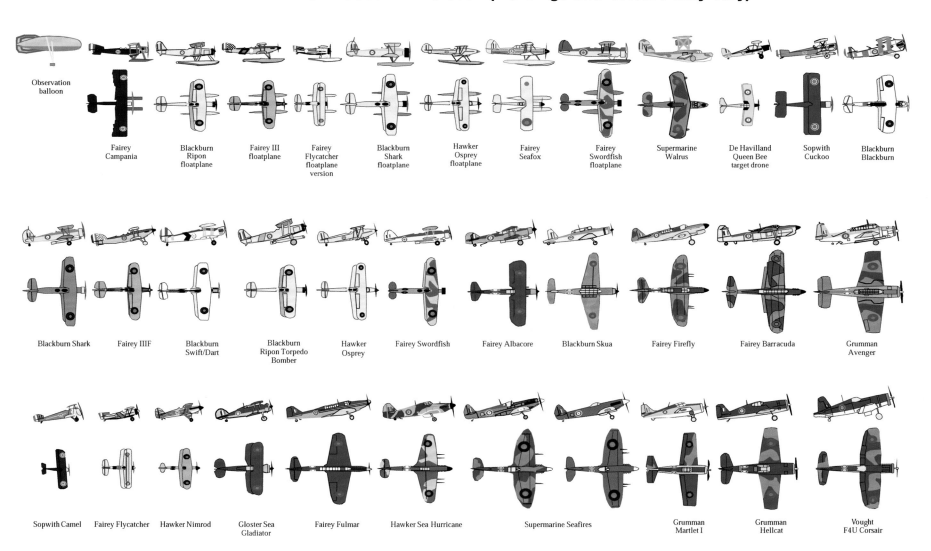

Observation balloon

Fairey Campania

Blackburn Ripon floatplane

Fairey III floatplane

Fairey Flycatcher floatplane version

Blackburn Shark floatplane

Hawker Osprey floatplane

Fairey Seafox

Fairey Swordfish floatplane

Supermarine Walrus

De Havilland Queen Bee target drone

Sopwith Cuckoo

Blackburn Blackburn

Blackburn Shark

Fairey IIIF

Blackburn Swift/Dart

Blackburn Ripon Torpedo Bomber

Hawker Osprey

Fairey Swordfish

Fairey Albacore

Blackburn Skua

Fairey Firefly

Fairey Barracuda

Grumman Avenger

Sopwith Camel

Fairey Flycatcher

Hawker Nimrod

Gloster Sea Gladiator

Fairey Fulmar

Hawker Sea Hurricane

Supermarine Seafires

Grumman Martlet I

Grumman Hellcat

Vought F4U Corsair

SYMBOLS USED FOR WEAPONS AND ELECTRONICS IN THIS VOLUME

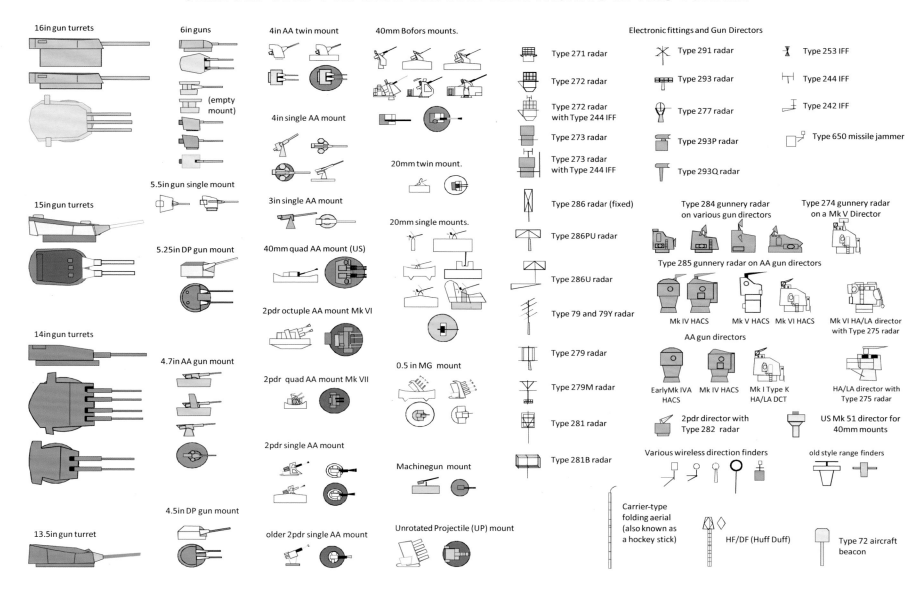

16in gun turrets

6in guns

(empty mount)

5.5in gun single mount

15in gun turrets

5.25in DP gun mount

14in gun turrets

4.7in AA gun mount

13.5in gun turret

4.5in DP gun mount

4in AA twin mount

4in single AA mount

3in single AA mount

40mm quad AA mount (US)

2pdr octuple AA mount Mk VI

2pdr quad AA mount Mk VII

2pdr single AA mount

older 2pdr single AA mount

40mm Bofors mounts.

20mm twin mount.

20mm single mounts.

0.5 in MG mount

Machinegun mount

Unrotated Projectile (UP) mount

Type 271 radar

Type 272 radar

Type 272 radar with Type 244 IFF

Type 273 radar

Type 273 radar with Type 244 IFF

Type 286 radar (fixed)

Type 286PU radar

Type 286U radar

Type 79 and 79Y radar

Type 279 radar

Type 279M radar

Type 281 radar

Type 281B radar

Electronic fittings and Gun Directors

Type 291 radar

Type 293 radar

Type 277 radar

Type 293P radar

Type 293Q radar

Type 253 IFF

Type 244 IFF

Type 242 IFF

Type 650 missile jammer

Type 284 gunnery radar on various gun directors

Type 274 gunnery radar on a Mk V Director

Type 285 gunnery radar on AA gun directors

Mk IV HACS   Mk V HACS   Mk VI HACS

Mk VI HA/LA director with Type 275 radar

AA gun directors

Early Mk IVA HACS   Mk IV HACS   Mk I Type K HA/LA DCT

HA/LA director with Type 275 radar

2pdr director with Type 282 radar

US Mk 51 director for 40mm mounts

Various wireless direction finders

old style range finders

Carrier-type folding aerial (also known as a hockey stick)

HF/DF (Huff Duff)

Type 72 aircraft beacon

HMS IRON DUKE Pennant 18
Iron Duke class battleship 1918 and 1939

Iron Duke was flagship of the fleet when the Battle of Jutland in World War I was fought and remained in service after the war. However, under the terms of the 1930 London Naval Treaty, the ship was required to be disarmed as a battleship. As such, she became a training ship with her side armour removed along with 'B' and 'Y' turrets. The three remaining main gun turrets were fully operable but she also carried a range of other weapons. A platform was built alongside the original 'Y' turret base on which a 5.25in twin turret was placed, but fitted with 4.5in guns. This was apparently to perform a dual teaching role. There were various other AA weapons, but these had changed over a period of time to suit requirements. There had been two 4.7in AA guns aft of similar type to those on *Rodney* and some other ships. At least one was removed for the 5.25in turret. The armament included a quad 2pdr, some single 2pdrs of different patterns and a quad 0.5in MG mount of the type common to the fleet. At one time, it had been intended to fit an octuple 2pdr mount aboard for training but these were in very short supply. At the outbreak of World War II, *Iron Duke* was at Scapa Flow acting in her training role and for testing new weapons, as well as flagship for the Admiral Commanding the Orkney and Shetlands, Admiral Sir William

French. She was also a base accommodation ship for transit crew and the Royal Navy Post Office of the fleet. The ship was heavily bombed by the Luftwaffe on 17 October 1939. Fortunately, some of the salvage crews working on the vessels of the German High Seas Fleet scuttled in 1919 were present to assist. Tugs took her in tow and, to avoid sinking, the ship had to be beached. Later, she was moved to a flat, shallow area where she could be allowed to settle on the bottom but remain mostly above water. Concrete was poured into many of the breached areas and it was obvious she would never put to sea again.

The main and secondary guns were removed for coastal defence. However, the ship remained at Scapa as a depot and base defence ship. As such, her AA changed many times according to availability and the training duty she could still provide. It is difficult to find detailed information, but she appears to have commenced the war in 507a battleship grey with scrubbed, unpainted wood decks. However, there are some hints that she may have been camouflaged against air attack after the October 1939 raid. The grand old ship was eventually sold for scrapping, which took place on site from March 1946.

HMS CENTURION Pennant I 50
WWI King George V class battleship 1927-40

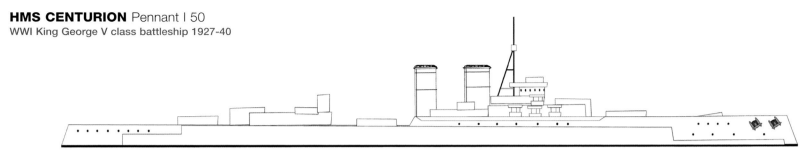

Centurion is included here because of her unique role in World War II. She was a unit of the World War I *King George V* class and served with the Grand Fleet during the war. Because of post-war treaties and financial issues, the class was disposed of in the mid to late 1920s. However, *Centurion* was selected to act as a radio-controlled target ship for fleet gunnery exercises. All her armament was stripped away, but armour was retained and many of the interior watertight compartments were sealed as a ship would be in battle stations. The destroyer *Shikari* controlled her and all crew were, of course, removed from the ship before gunnery shoots commenced. At the end of a shoot, her crew, which included damage repair specialists, would return aboard. Although disarmed, the ship was quite functional and between shoots her crew steamed her to wherever she was needed. This included ranging as far afield as the Mediterranean so that the fleet there could also practice with her. As a target ship, she would only be fired on by 8in and smaller guns and, with her battleship armour still protecting her, it was expected that she would be immune to cruiser gunfire. However, during the working up of new County class cruisers, it was found that their new 8in guns could inflict very serious damage and she almost sank after one exercise. The ship was repaired but future exercises limited the number of hits she could take. When war approached, she was busy performing her target duties and continued to do so until the end of 1940, when another role was envisaged for her.

HMS CENTURION Pennant I 50
WWI King George V class battleship 1942

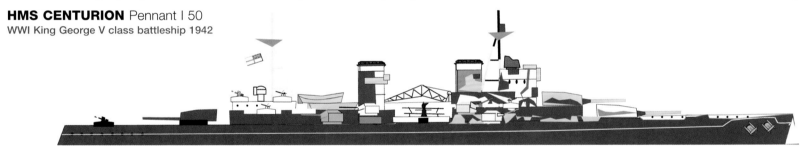

During April 1941, a plan was devised to convert *Centurion* into a dummy version of HMS *Anson*. She would sail to the Mediterranean to make Axis intelligence believe the fleet there had been reinforced with a new battleship. The dummy *Anson* sailed from the UK in May, after a hasty conversion. The aft funnel was removed entirely and a dummy erected on the old 'P' mount amidships. Various materials from metal to wood and even canvas were used to build a false superstructure and hangar. Dummy turrets were fitted with long, round logs as barrels! Wood tripod masts and fake cranes were also added. The area amidships, where a battleship such as *Anson* would have had a catapult and aircraft, was painted white and onto this a fake Walrus was added in black paint. It proved impossible to produce fake 5.25in turrets within the short time given for the conversion, so instead these were painted onto the side of the superstructure. The ship was given a very dark paint scheme, onto which various areas of greys and white were applied. All in all, it was confusing and intended to be so. Because *Centurion* was not flush-decked, the scheme was applied in a manner that would make her look like she was. Degaussing cables were prominent on many ships at that time, so one was applied to the hull and painted in a lighter colour to give the impression of following a flush-decked warship hull. There are only a few photographs of the ship taken after her conversion but, as the whole thing was top secret, that is hardly surprising. The illusion of being a battleship would have been spoilt if she was attacked by enemy aircraft and was unable to reply, so the only real weapons aboard were two 2pdr and eight 20mm AA guns. Internal areas such as the former magazines were converted into extra fuel tanks to increase her range. In view of a plan then being considered to sink her as a block-ship at Tripoli, eight large containers were fitted in the bottom of the ship and filled with explosives so she could be remotely scuttled if the operation went ahead. As it happened, she did apparently fool Axis intelligence services but to have sailed from Gibraltar to Alexandria direct would have resulted in them spotting that she was a fake, so she took passage via Cape Town. However, she encountered heavy seas and the fake 'A' turret was lost overboard and, on arrival at Aden, a false story was put about that she had lost the forward turret in an engagement with an enemy raider! Nine months were spent in Bombay before she returned to Aden in 1942 with a new fake turret and light AA increased to four 2pdr and seventeen 20mm guns. She took part in the Malta convoy Operation Vigorous, when she was hit by enemy bombs, and was kept at Alexandria as a potential block ship for the Suez Canal. After the victory at El Alamein, she spent some time on anti-aircraft duty on the Great Bitter Lake section of the Suez Canal. In 1944, she sailed for the UK, reaching Devonport on 12 May. She was then prepared for what would be her last operation. On 6 June 1944, she was scuttled as part of the breakwater off the Normandy beachhead. Unfortunately, the troops were not told and there were reports some were discouraged to see a supposedly modern battleship sunk by the enemy. The German gunners who fired on her also claimed to have sunk her with massive loss of life – as so few of her crew abandoned ship – but, of course, they were simply the final few who ran her in and set off the demolition charges. No doubt it sounded good in Nazi propaganda.

QUEEN ELIZABETH CLASS BATTLESHIPS

HMS QUEEN ELIZABETH Pennant 00
Queen Elizabeth class battleship 1915

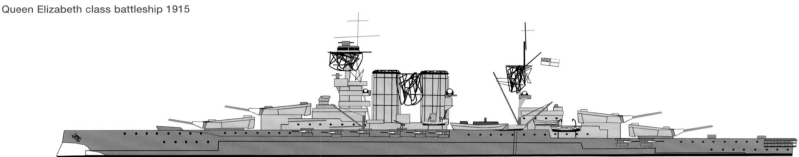

Queen Elizabeth as built. This illustration shows her on bombardment duty at Gallipoli, where it was thought that her powerful 15in guns would prove extremely effective. As she came under fire from Turkish batteries, there was an attempt to confuse the rangefinders of those guns by hanging nets and ropes from the upper areas and between the funnels – precursors to the canvas baffles later worn by many British ships. A false bow wave was painted on and the upper works rendered a few shades lighter than the hull. Note that she was the only ship of the class to complete with the aft-facing 6in gun batteries. These were removed when the ship returned to the UK since they were quite useless. The guns were mounted so low that their range of vision was small and, at speed, they were unworkable because they were so close to the water that they were continually swamped. The ship was recalled from Gallipoli as the danger from mines, torpedo boats and submarines was considered to be greater than the value of her bombardments. She was hit several times by enemy fire, although without serious damage.

HMS QUEEN ELIZABETH Pennant 00
Queen Elizabeth class battleship 1936

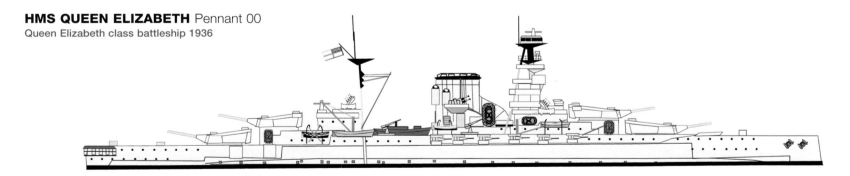

This illustration shows *Queen Elizabeth* after she had been refitted from 1926-8. The funnels were trunked and the number of searchlights reduced. She remained with this appearance until 1936 when she had two octuple 2pdr pom-poms added on either side of the funnel. There were quad 0.5in MG mounts side by side on the aft superstructure and two more abreast the bridge. The following year, she returned home to the UK for a major rebuild which took from 1937-41, producing a very modern ship that was hardly recognisable from the above two images.

HMS QUEEN ELIZABETH Pennant 00
Queen Elizabeth class battleship 1941

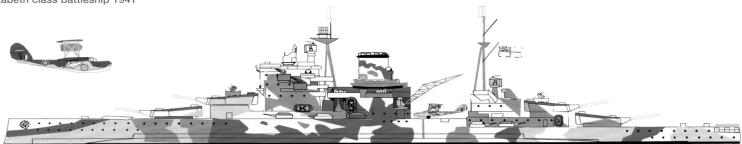

Queen Elizabeth went in for a major rebuild three years after *Warspite* and World War II commenced while it was underway. German aircraft bombed the dockyard at Portsmouth, which delayed her completion. Eventually, she was transferred to Rosyth in December 1940 and the work finished there. As a result, she did not return to service until 21 February 1941. The scheme shown is a complicated 'first Admiralty disruptive scheme' using B5, M570c, B55 and G5. The decks were wood but possibly over-painted in grey. The main armament remained the same, but all the original 6in secondary guns were removed, along with their casemates. The entire area was plated over and high quality steel replaced the original armour. The new secondary armament comprised ten twin 4.5in DP mounts of the same type mounted on the newer British fleet carriers. These weapons were slightly countersunk into the deck. Because of the urgency to complete her and move her

away from the threat of bombing, some of the 4.5in mounts were taken from the incomplete carrier *Indomitable* and the Mk IV gun directors from the cruiser *Fiji*, also under construction. Four octuple 2pdr pom-poms were fitted either side of the hangar. Directors for each were placed on the sides of the bridge. Four quad 0.5in MG mounts were fitted, two on 'A' turret and two on 'X' turret. For a battleship leaving the yard in 1941, the light AA was surprisingly limited. She was issued with a Walrus aircraft and had the capacity to carry four if needed. The catapult was athwartships. Type 273 radar was fitted to the foremast, Type 279 radar on the tripod mainmast and Type 285 on the secondary directors. The main gun directors were given Type 284. At this time, it was possible to distinguish this ship from her very similarly-rebuilt sister, *Valiant*, due to both masts being tripods, while *Valiant* only had the foremast as a tripod.

This illustration shows *Queen Elizabeth* from the starboard side at the completion of her rebuild. This was the first official Admiralty Disruptive Scheme issued. Complicated camouflage schemes, such as this, were popular for a while, but it was soon found that they required a lot of upkeep to maintain. Against all the sensible rules of camouflage, it was not uncommon for battleships to retain a black waterline. However, in some photographs of the ship in this particular scheme, the camouflage has been taken right down to the waterline. During the rebuild, the ship received six new boilers, rather than the four fitted to *Warspite*, and was thus able to maintain a good speed for the rest of her service. There were four AA directors set side by side with one in each pair slightly elevated to give coverage over the other. As rebuilt, these were formidable AA ships in comparison to other British battleships prior to the *King George V* class. Although sent to join the Home Fleet, her services were

urgently required elsewhere and within a short time the ship transferred to the Mediterranean to become flagship of the 1st Battle Squadron. She was present for the convoy known as Operation Tiger, the evacuation of Crete and then operations in support of convoys at the Eastern end of the Mediterranean. Type 282 radar for close-range barrage fire was fitted in June. On 19 December 1941 she was at anchor in Alexandria Harbour when Italian two-man underwater chariots launched by the submarine *Scire* carried out an attack. Limpet mines attached to the hull caused massive damage and the ship sank in very shallow water. Her decks were above water and British intelligence tricked the Italians into believing the attack was not a success. In fact, the ship had been so badly damaged that she was under repair for a year, and thus out of action for the whole of 1942. After difficult on-site repairs, the ship was refloated and sent to the USA for major repairs.

HMS QUEEN ELIZABETH Pennant 00
Queen Elizabeth class battleship 1943

Queen Elizabeth started repairs in the USA in September 1942, during which her paint scheme was completely changed to a simpler style. 507a/G10 was used with MS3 slate green on a base of MS4a. It is most probable that these were mixed in the US or were adapted from USN supplies and thus the shade may not have been exactly that specified by the Royal Navy. The shade 507a, for example, is described in some cases as being bluer than Royal Navy paint. Green was in extremely short supply in the UK and was certainly locally supplied, even though as close to specification as possible. The decks were painted dark grey. Turret tops were dark grey except for 'A' and

'B', which were green. Some of the green camouflage was carried up onto the decks and these turret tops matched. Note that the colour of the 4.5in AA turrets also complied with the nearest colour. With US assistance, the light AA was greatly augmented. The quad machine gun mounts were removed and replaced by twin 20mm. Fourteen single 20mm were also fitted. Type 279AW (air warning) radar aerials are carried at both mastheads, as was required with that set. IFF sets Type 242, Type 244, Type 253 are carried.

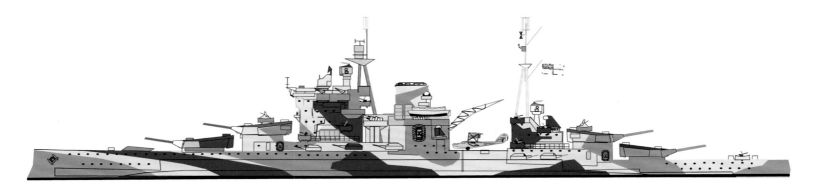

This illustration shows the port side of *Queen Elizabeth* in the camouflage scheme at end of her USA repairs. The areas are larger and clearer cut, making it easier to maintain. A large box has been placed around the legs of the forward tripod, with the legs passing through it, which provided additional strength. Radar fit on the forward tripod has been upgraded to Type 273Q closed-box

lantern radar. There is a Type 650 missile jammer on the aft mast. The rest of her radar fit remains the same as before. Aircraft facilities are still carried. The ship returned to the UK in this form and joined the Home Fleet to work up.

HMS QUEEN ELIZABETH Pennant 00
Queen Elizabeth class battleship 1943-4

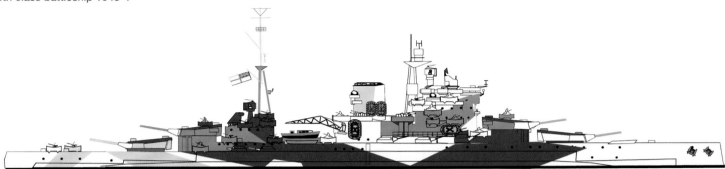

After working up with the Home Fleet, *Queen Elizabeth* was painted in a new Admiralty scheme thought to be suited to hot climates, where heat haze made light areas hard to see and dark areas stand out, thus creating a distorted view of the ship. The ship was painted in overall 507c pale grey, with areas of B6/B30, MS4a and B15 blue black. The decks were painted grey and some camou-flage was carried up onto them. The Type 273Q radar lantern had a Type 244 IFF aerial added to the top. The Type 279 radar was replaced by a Type 279M set on the head of the mainmast. Type 650 missile jammers are on the aft tripod legs. She was transferred to the Indian Ocean as flagship of the British Eastern Fleet and arrived at Colombo on 30 January 1944.

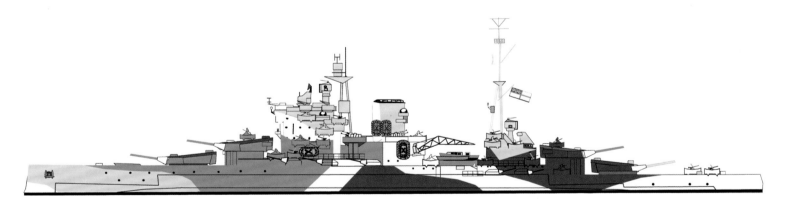

At the time of her service in the Indian Ocean, the light AA of *Queen Elizabeth* consisted of thirty-two 2pdr pom-poms, sixteen twin 20mm and fourteen single 20mm. This was a substantial arma-ment, considering that she had only four quad machine gun mounts after her reconstruction only three years earlier. Aircraft facilities were removed, as there were now a considerable number of aircraft carriers operating with the British Eastern Fleet. The aircraft catapult area had a boat house built onto it and the launches and boats previously carried on top of the hangar were now moved down to there. After her massive rebuild and then repairs in the USA, this period was her most active in World War II. She took part in numerous operations against Japanese bases in Burma, the Andaman Islands and Dutch East Indies (Indonesia). She usually provided AA cover for carrier groups but used her 15in guns on enemy targets at Sabang (twice), Car Nicobar and Port Blair. Gunnery support was also provided to cover landings during the Arakan campaign.

HMS QUEEN ELIZABETH Pennant 00
Queen Elizabeth class battleship November 1944-5

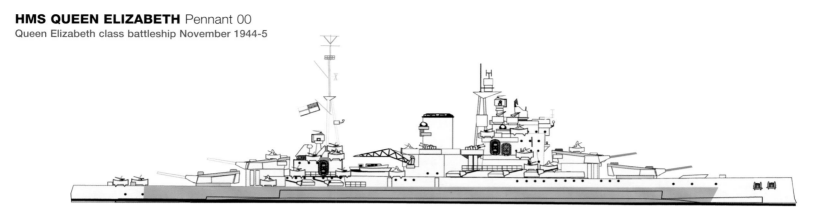

Queen Elizabeth after her refit in Durban, October to November 1944. The ship has been painted overall in 507c pale grey and has a panel on the hull using mid-blue to provide a shortening effect. This scheme was common to most ships that served with the British Eastern Fleet and was much easier to maintain than the earlier multi-colour types with extensive patterns. The decks were mid-grey MS4a, as were the turret tops. There were no changes to armament during the brief refit and the ship was back with the fleet in time for the attacks on Sabang, carried out from 17 to 23 November 1944.

HMS QUEEN ELIZABETH Pennant 00
Queen Elizabeth class battleship November 1944-5

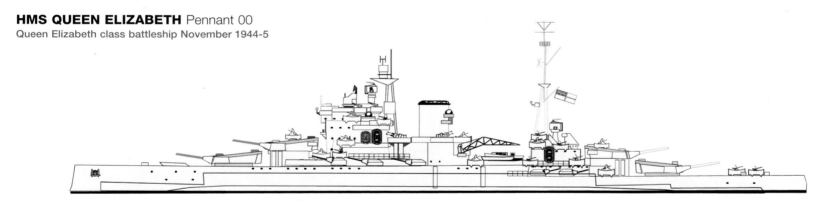

This illustration shows the port side of *Queen Elizabeth* after the Durban refit. The ship has a much cleaner look with the boats moved from the top of the hangars and confusion camouflage removed. She covered the capture of Rangoon before being relieved as flagship by the battleship *Nelson*, which, with the war in Europe over and being too slow for the British Pacific Fleet, was sent to the Indian Ocean. *Queen Elizabeth* then returned home, arriving on 7 August, just as the war with Japan was ending. With no foreseeable requirement for older battleships, this ship was paid off into reserve at Rosyth later the same month. Due to her many rebuilds and work carried out, she was in relatively good condition, unlike some of her sister ships, but in 1948 she was sold for scrap.

HMS WARSPITE Pennant 03
Queen Elizabeth class battleship 1918

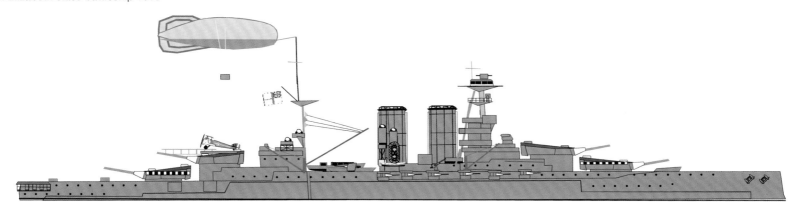

Warspite as she appeared near the end of World War I. Although references say there was a flying-off platform on 'X' turret, there is no evidence of this in photographs taken between the start of 1918 and early 1919. She was one of two ships of the class fitted to carry a kite balloon for gunnery observation. Deflection scales have been added to 'A' and 'Y' turrets. Ships varied these locations to assist recognition. Note that the ship was not bulged at this time. The designed 6in casemate guns facing aft were never fitted, after trials with *Queen Elizabeth* showed them to be useless. Instead, she has single guns fitted with shields on the upper deck amidships. Single 12pdr AA guns are carried port and starboard of the fore funnel. Her very dark scheme approximates 507a. Turret tops were dark Brunswick green. The decks are holystoned wood.

HMS WARSPITE Pennant 03
Queen Elizabeth class battleship 1927

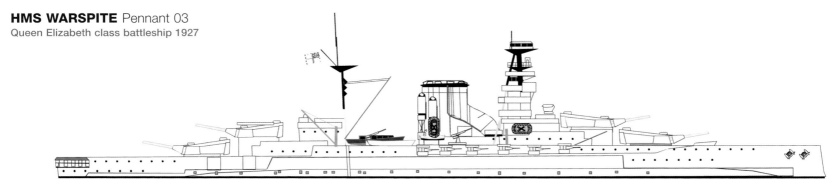

Warspite went to be rebuilt in 1924 and emerged in 1926 when she went to the Mediterranean as flagship of the C-in-C, and is shown here in overall 507c. As the flagship, all decks would have been thoroughly holystoned and all brass would be shiny. The slightest sign of rust would have been immediately dealt with. The flying-off platform remains on top of 'X' turret, but the rest of her appearance has been radically altered. The original two funnels were trunked into one and the original 12pdr AA guns were exchanged for 4in single AA guns, but without directors (they were locally controlled). Her boat deck 6in guns were also removed and the ship was given anti-torpedo bulges. There were no light AA weapons mounted at this time.

HMS WARSPITE Pennant 03
Queen Elizabeth class battleship January 1938

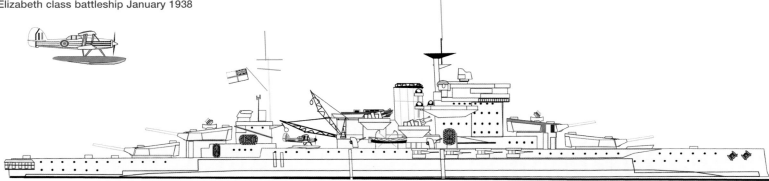

Warspite was stationed with the Mediterranean fleet during the Spanish Civil War and is shown here with neutrality markings on 'B' turret. The ship is in overall 507c grey, but the top of 'B' turret was painted dark grey, probably to make the white of the national markings stand out. Decks would have been very pale wood. Having just completed a major rebuild, she was, at this time, the most powerful battleship in the Royal Navy after the *Nelson* class. During the rebuild, she was virtually gutted and nearly all the superstructure removed. New boilers and new turbines were fitted, internal subdivision improved and armour increased over the magazines, machinery spaces and barbettes. The 6in battery was reduced to eight guns and the old AA guns were replaced by four twin 4in

mounts. Light AA was also added in the form of four octuple 2pdr pom-poms and four quad 0.5in MG mounts. The 2pdrs formed a group around the funnel, with two per side, while the quad 0.5in MGs were placed two per turret on 'B' and 'X' main gun turrets. For the period, this was a very heavy AA armament. She received two Blackburn Shark aircraft, both of which were accommodated in the hangars added during the rebuild. Technically, two more could be carried with deck stowage areas provided, but this was not usually done. The old main gun director, which had been on the conning tower forward, was moved aft and a new director fitted on top of the new block bridge. Mk IV HACS directors for the 4in AA guns were fitted either side of the bridge.

HMS WARSPITE Pennant 03
Queen Elizabeth class battleship 1940

At the time of the Battle of Narvik, *Warspite* was in 507b grey or an unofficially mixed shade very close to that. The decks were still natural wood, but were no longer holystoned to a fresh wood-look each day and were instead allowed to fade to a natural pale greyish wood. The turret tops were a darker grey. Any signs of peacetime fanciness had gone and the ship was painted to look as dull as possible. Note that although there were few changes to the 1938 view, the very dark shade gave her a much more warlike look. Two Fairey Swordfish floatplanes replaced the Sharks and,

being far more capable, were able to be used for ASW patrols and even limited air strikes. The small aerial added to the front of the bridge was not radar, but was used to detect enemy wireless transmissions. At this point, *Warspite* had no radar fitted. There were no changes to the AA, but large Carley floats had been provided. The position of the ensign was lowered. The protection of this class proved effective in World War I, but was further increased before World War II.

HMS WARSPITE Pennant 03
Queen Elizabeth class battleship 1941

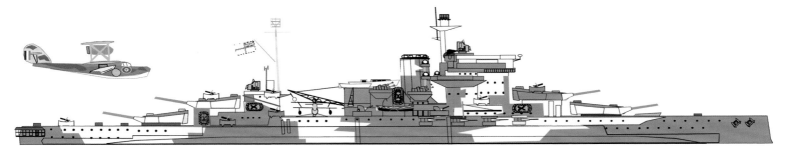

Warspite adopted a camouflage scheme of two colours in late 1940 or early 1941. The colours used were probably 507c and 507b, but local procurement is also a possibility as it takes a lot of paint to cover a battleship and shortages were common in wartime. The decks remained unpainted wood that was permitted to fade to grey with the effect of salt water. This starboard pattern remained much the same for the rest of her career and was only altered slightly during touch ups. The ship now carried a Walrus amphibian, with there usually being one or two aboard. The ship was damaged during the battle for Crete and went to the USA for repairs where Type 281 radar was fitted on the main mast and Type 284 radar to the main gun directors. Type 285 radar was fitted to the 4in AA directors and those guns protected with zareba-type splinter shelters. Very unusually, there was a small ship Type 271 radar fitted on the top of the foremast. Presumably this was because a Type 283 set, normally carried by large ships, was not available. The light AA was improved by removing the quad 0.5in MG mounts from 'A' and 'X' turrets and replacing them with single 20mm AA. Nine other 20mm were fitted at this time.

HMS WARSPITE Pennant 03
Queen Elizabeth class battleship 1942-3

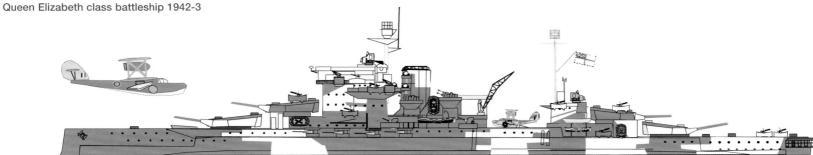

Warspite port side view. The scheme does not appear to be an Admiralty type and was probably unofficial. But it was retained because it was effective and for economic reasons, as paint was not only expensive but in very short supply due to other war demand. In 1942, the Type 271 radar lantern was removed and a Type 273 installed. Type 282 radar for the 2pdr directors is also fitted. The number of 20mm guns has also been increased.

HMS WARSPITE Pennant 03
Queen Elizabeth class battleship 1943-4

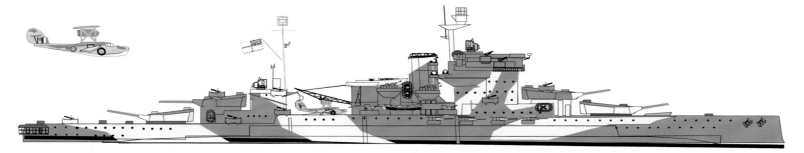

By 1943, the square edges of the camouflage were smoothed out, but the areas covered remained almost the same, as did the shades of grey. There was a further increase in the number of 20mm Oerlikon guns. 'X' turret was badly damaged when the ship was hit by a German guided bomb off Salerno in September 1943 and was inoperable. *Warspite* was one of those ships that seemed to be everywhere the fighting was toughest and, as a consequence, suffered damage many times. The accumulation of repaired areas was such that it seemed there was nowhere on the ship that had not been repaired or replaced. Her speed had dropped off but she was still in demand, being especially refitted to provide gunfire support for the Allied landings in Europe. The latter part of the war was a busy time, with the ship being on call for her heavy guns to lay down devastating barrages against German land forces.

HMS WARSPITE Pennant 03
Queen Elizabeth class battleship 1944-5

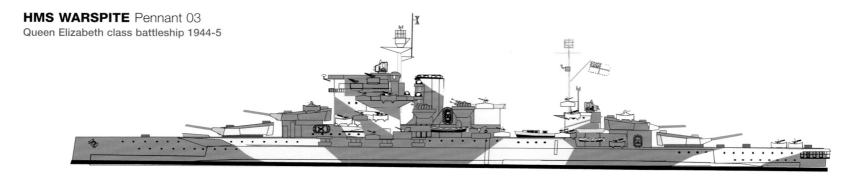

Warspite is shown at the end of her career. As with the starboard side, her port side pattern has not changed much from the time it was applied. Sharp edges were removed, but the areas covered and two shades of grey were much the same, with only touch ups creating slight changes. By June 1944, all the remaining 6in casemate guns had been removed and the 20mm on 'A' and 'X' turrets replaced by twin mounts. The final total of 20mm rose to thirty-five. It was decided not to repair 'X' turret as the war, and *Warspite*'s service, were both obviously coming to an end. However, the main battery radars were updated for her bombardment duties. A Type 244 IFF interrogator was fitted at the top of the Type 273 radar lantern with a Type 253 hourglass-type IFF on the foremast. There was a Type 650 missile jammer on the main mast. *Warspite* had a long and distinguished career since the Battle of Jutland in World War I, where she was hit 29 times, through Norway in 1940, to the Mediterranean. At Punto Stilo, she struck the Italian battleship *Guilio Cesare* at a range of approximately 26,000 yards, the longest range hit ever achieved by any battleship in history. *Warspite* served in the Indian Ocean fleet as well, becoming one of the busiest capital ships in the Royal Navy during World War II.

HMS VALIANT Pennant 02
Queen Elizabeth class battleship 1933

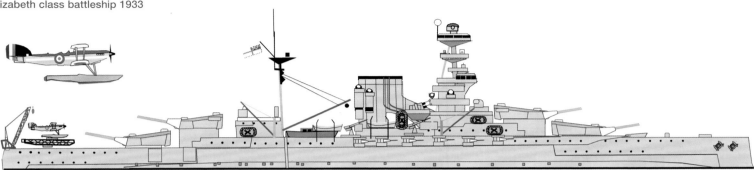

Valiant is shown here in 1933 after her major reconstruction of 1929-30, when, as with her sister ships, the two funnels originally carried were trunked into one. Although very similar to *Queen Elizabeth*, her funnel was a little lower and flatter on top. A lack of funds meant she was fitted with only one of the two octuple 2pdr pom-poms intended. A Fairey IIIF floatplane was supplied, along with a catapult on the stern and a handling crane. Experience at sea showed that the aircraft facilities were impractical and they were removed in 1933. The Fairey IIIF had proved too flimsy for such an exposed position as no hangar was provided. Note, where possible, catapult aircraft were normally turned toward the bow when the ship was moving for aerodynamic reasons. In heavy weather, they could be struck down to the deck and lashed securely. But the lessons learnt

before World War II were that aircraft were flimsy and easily damaged. Hence, later ships were provided with hangars for storage. At this time, the ship was part of the Home Fleet, which had been renamed from the 'Atlantic Fleet' in 1932. She is shown dressed all-over in MS4a, which at that time was also renamed Home Fleet grey. Decks were wood and heavily scrubbed to a pale straw in colour. Her previous 3in AA guns had been replaced with single 4in AA guns during the major rebuild but the aft gun was a little more forward than those carried on her sisters, thus providing less obstruction to the boat deck. Her bridge structure differed a little from her sisters and she was also able to be distinguished from them by the rather large number of Carley floats carried.

HMS VALIANT Pennant 02
Queen Elizabeth class battleship 1936

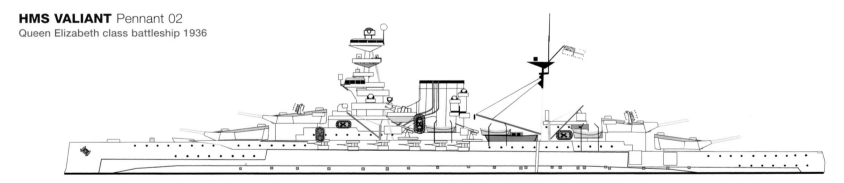

Valiant was ordered to join the Mediterranean fleet in July 1935 and remained on that station until 1937. The ship is now illustrated in overall 507c. Turret tops were MS4a, but may have been Brunswick green at some point. On deployment to her new station, the second octuple 2pdr pom-pom mount was fitted and she was given quad 0.5in MG mounts side by side on 'A' and 'X' 'turrets. Note that there was only a single HACS director on the fighting top with none aft. For some reason, the Carley float just aft and below 'B' turret was moved from on its side to standing

upright – one of those mysterious little things, the reasons for which will probably remain unknown. There was an additional, rather square, wireless locator on the front of the bridge. This was the final appearance of the ship prior to the major rebuild scheduled from 1937-9 at Devonport. Her sister ship, *Queen Elizabeth*, did not start her rebuild until August and was delayed by bombing when World War II started, but *Valiant* was already at sea, working up, by then.

HMS VALIANT Pennant 02
Queen Elizabeth class battleship September 1939

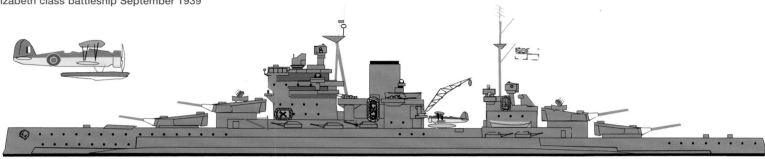

Valiant is shown on re-entering service after her massive rebuild in overall 507b medium grey, probably an easy way to make use of paint stocks already available in quantity. The decks were initially holystoned wood but were soon painted in the same shade. Turret tops also appeared to be 507b. This ship could be differentiated from *Queen Elizabeth* by the superstructure on top of the hangar being one level lower and by the different searchlight arrangements on the funnel. Additionally, the forward mast was a tripod, but the mainmast was a simple pole, the aircraft cranes were also of a different pattern and the funnel tops differed. There were also minor differences to the bridge. *Valiant* was also fitted with a Type 79Y AW radar on the maintop during her rebuild,

but no other types of radar were added at that time. The Type 79Y was not a very reliable set but nonetheless was useful when it worked and did have some capacity to detect large surface targets. The rebuild resulted in all the original 6in secondary guns being removed. In their place, were ten twin 4.5in AA mountings countersunk into the deck. Quad 0.5in MG mounts were placed side by side on 'B' and 'X' turrets to supplement the octuple 2pdr mountings which were placed two per side grouped around the hangar. *Valiant* sailed for the West Indies to work up, returning in time for the Norway campaign as part of the 2nd Battle Squadron, Home Fleet.

HMS VALIANT Pennant 02
Queen Elizabeth class battleship January 1941

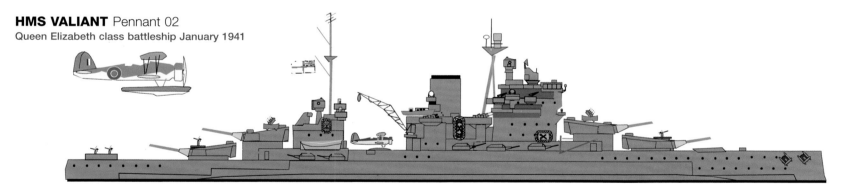

Valiant joined Force H based at Gibraltar at the end of 1940 and was part of the attack on the French fleet at Mers el-Kebir. Her colour scheme remained the same but the outward appearance was changed by the addition of a Type 273 radar lantern at the top of the forward tripod mast and a larger radio direction finder stationed behind it. Gunnery radar Type 284 was fitted for the main armament. The Type 79Y AW radar was upgraded to Type 79B; a small improvement only, but capable of picking up a low flying aircraft at six nautical miles, plus higher level aircraft and formations at between eighty and ninety nautical miles. Additionally, it was able to pick up surface ships from large down to small. The early Type 273 could only detect surface ships, but had a range out to 36,000 yards against large vessels. It was limited to about 3,000 yards for detection of a surfaced

submarine. Despite limitations, radar was rare in the fleet and this made her very valuable during 1940-1. Unusually, for British battleships, she had single 20mm guns added on top of 'A' and 'Y' turrets. The port quad 0.5in MG mount on 'B' turret was replaced by a single 20mm AA at some point but the starboard one remained, as did those on 'X' turret. This could have been because of a shortage of 20mm Oerlikon guns, which were in strong demand. A zareba has been placed well aft on the quarterdeck to accommodate four single 20mm guns. As a concession to camouflage, the previously white canvas gun shrouds have been painted grey. The aircraft type carried was the Swordfish floatplane, two of which were usually carried.

HMS VALIANT Pennant 02
Queen Elizabeth class battleship July 1942

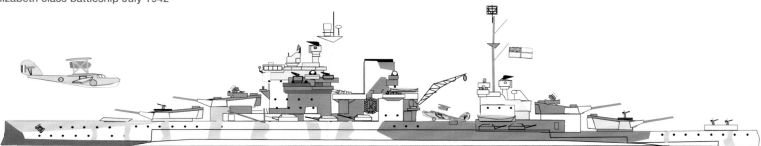

Valiant is shown here after July 1942 with her original solid 507b grey converted into a disruptive pattern of unofficial design. The repainting was probably carried out at Durban, but possibly Alexandria, in late 1941. There is some doubt when this repainting was carried out and it could have been as early as mid-1941. The scheme utilised colours that were available in sufficient quantity. 507c pale grey was applied over the existing paint, along with MS4a, to create a disruptive scheme. A false clipper bow was a feature of both sides of the ship and, as the colours were somewhat raised up, it might have been intended to give the impression of a smaller ship, further away. The decks were painted grey as before. Type 281 radar had replaced the older Type 79B set on the mainmast. This was a more reliable set with longer range, but no surface capability. The HACS directors had Type 285 radar added and could fix on an air target at around nine miles. However, weather conditions affected this range. The Swordfish aircraft previously carried were replaced with Walrus amphibians. On top of 'B' mount, a 20mm single still occupied the port position and there was a quad 0.5in MG mount on the starboard for a time but for how long is not recorded.

HMS VALIANT Pennant 02
Queen Elizabeth class battleship July 1942

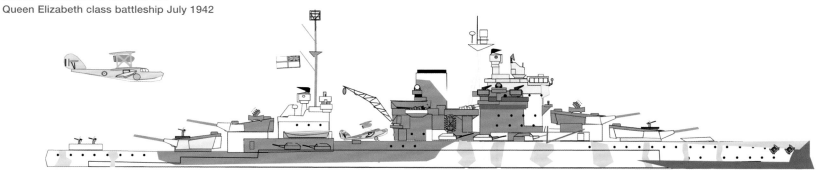

This is a starboard side view of *Valiant* in her disruptive scheme. She was ordered to join the Mediterranean fleet at Alexandria after operating with Force H out of Gibraltar. The ship was very active in that theatre of operations, including taking part in the Battle of Cape Matapan where she engaged the Italian heavy cruiser *Zara*, and took part in several shore bombardments. Although hit by two bombs during the evacuation of Crete, she was easily repaired. She also set off a mine, but the damage was not serious and repaired at Alexandria. Her light AA was increased by ten 20mm Oerlikon guns and the quad 0.5in MG mounts were retained. It is not known when the port side 20mm mount on top of 'B' turret was replaced with a multiple machine gun mount, but it does not appear after this period. Having avoided serious damage previously, the hull was badly breached and the ship bottomed in a daring attack by Italian frogmen on 19 December 1941. The damage was so severe that it was May 1942 before the ship could be made seaworthy enough to sail to Durban for major repairs.

HMS VALIANT Pennant 02
Queen Elizabeth class battleship August 1942

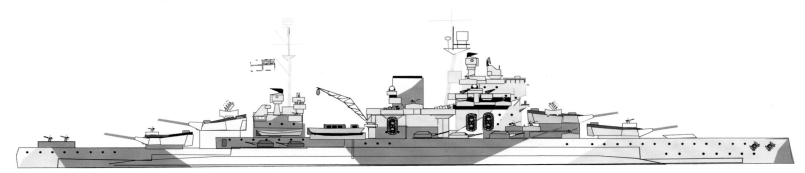

Valiant is shown here shown here from the starboard side after August 1942, following her repairs at Durban. The colours used were 507c pale grey, with MS4a and 507b. While in dockyard hands, her previous disruptive scheme was simplified using the same paints. In some cases, such as the bow and other areas, parts of the previous scheme were retained or simply modified. For most of her time after repair the ship remained very inactive as part of the South Atlantic area command. This possibly reflects that it was not possible to complete the repairs to full satisfaction. Whatever the reason, she saw little sea time between August 1942 and February 1943. The decks were painted in some sort of mid-grey, but due to weathering an exact shade was hard to maintain and no record remains. It is also possible that the decks had simply weathered grey as the earlier paint wore off.

HMS VALIANT Pennant 02
Queen Elizabeth class battleship August 1942

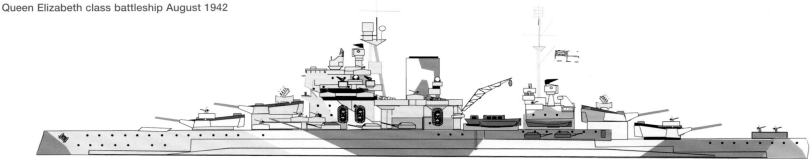

A port side view of *Valiant* after repairs at Durban. During this period, additional 20mm Oerlikon guns were fitted, raising the 20mm AA total to twenty single mounts. However, the quad 0.5in MG mounts were retained until she returned to the UK for further work in February 1943, by which time they must have been among the very few such mountings to be found on a large warship in the fleet. She sailed via Gibraltar in this scheme and that it was only a temporary measure is shown by the fact that the next camouflage pattern is far more elaborate and of Admiralty design.

HMS VALIANT Pennant 02
Queen Elizabeth class battleship May 1943

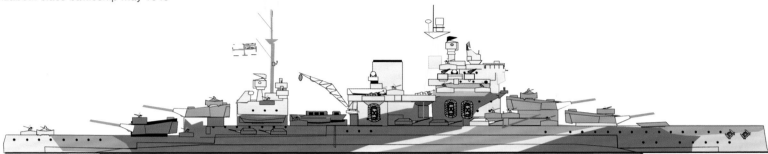

Having returned to the UK, *Valiant* was given another refit and was ready for active service again by May 1943. After a working up period, she was to have been sent to the Far East Fleet, but instead was ordered to the Mediterranean to cover landings on Sicily, then Calabria, and bombardment duty at Salerno. The scheme worn during that time is shown here and was an Admiralty design similar to many provided for ships in the mid-war period. The colours were G5 dark grey, MS3 slate green, WS white and MS4a grey. The pattern was of a type intended to concentrate dark colour in the central area of the ship when seen at a distance, thus producing a shortening effect. The decks were painted MS4a but, due to weathering, there were areas of aged timbers showing through. The light AA has been altered to six twin 20mm and twenty-five single 20mm. The 20mm tubs on 'A' and 'Y' turrets were removed at some time during this period.

HMS VALIANT Pennant 02
Queen Elizabeth class battleship May 1943

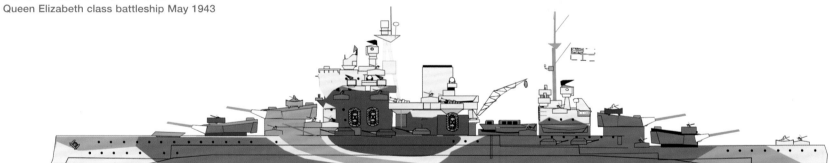

Valiant's port side after her 1943 UK refit. The two sides of the ship were quite different, although the same colours were employed for the pattern that was designed particularly for *Valiant*. Although smaller ships might have standard schemes adopted by whole groups or classes, it was more usual for capital ships to have camouflage patterns that were different on both sides and specific to that ship. Type 281 radar on top of the mainmast was replaced by a Type 281B, which, while having a shorter detection range for aircraft, was more reliable and also had the ability to detect surface craft. It also only required one aerial instead of two. The 2pdr pom-pom directors had Type 282 radar installed on them and Type 650 missile jammers were added to the mainmast. On the starboard side, a large Carley float was placed on the side of the hangar and two more on the bridge. For reasons unknown, *Valiant* seemed to have one on the rear superstructure for at least a time, rather than on the hangar side.

HMS VALIANT Pennant 02
Queen Elizabeth class battleship 1944

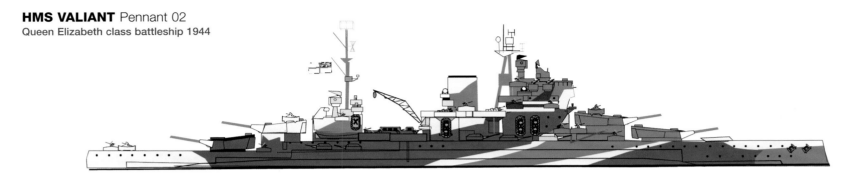

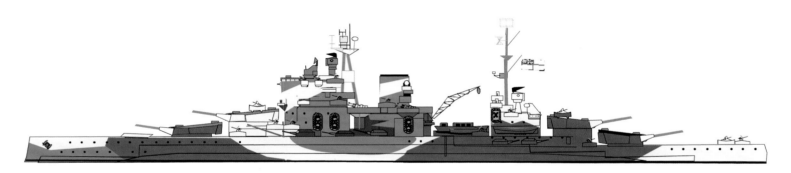

Valiant is shown here with the previous scheme modified for service in the British Eastern Fleet. The ship was now in overall 507c with areas of B5 blue grey and G5 grey black. The contrast was strong and in a region notorious for heat haze would probably have been very effective. The reduction of the number of shades to three would have reduced maintenance. The Type 284 gunnery radar was replaced with Type 274, which enabled blind fire to be used for the main armament. Type 244 IFF was added to the top of the Type 273 lantern, which itself was upgraded. Thirty-five single 20mm were fitted along with six twin 20mm. In this state, *Valiant* sailed to the Indian Ocean, where she participated in the operations against Sabang and Surabaya from April to July 1944. On 8 August 1944, the floating dry dock she was in at Trincomalee collapsed after being improperly flooded. *Valiant* was fully laden and had an estimated 37,400 tons displacement. The fall caused

massive damage to her hull, which was torn open in many places, both inner propeller shafts severed and the port rudder damaged. There were indentations in the hull up to eighteen inches deep, with some extending almost the length of the vessel. The incident was put down to unrepaired damage to the dry dock caused by a Japanese air attack in 1942. The ship had to return to the UK for major repairs, was patched up and sent to limp home. On arrival at Suez, her unrepaired areas and leaks had increased the draught so much that she grounded, remaining stuck for six hours. As she could not pass through the Suez Canal, the only alternative was to make the long passage around South Africa, stopping at Cape Town and Durban for further temporary repairs. This delayed her arrival back in the UK until 1 February 1945 and, of course, she had to be heavily escorted as, at her slower speed, she would have been a juicy target for a U-boat.

WORLD WAR I ERA BATTLESHIPS AND BATTLECRUISERS
35

HMS VALIANT Pennant 02
Queen Elizabeth class battleship 1945

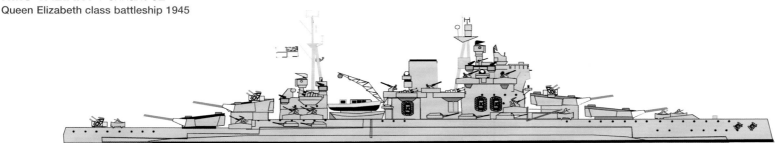

Valiant is shown in 1945 after repairs in the UK. It was uncertain how long the war with Japan would last, although it was quite obvious that Germany would soon collapse. War damage had left the ship in a very battered state. It was considered that if she returned to duty at all, it would be with the British Eastern Fleet with the Japanese as the enemy. Malaya may have to be taken by an amphibious landing, followed by Borneo and the Dutch East Indies. The lost propellers and shafts were repaired, along with as much of the hull damage as was feasible without completely rebuilding the ship. If she was to support landings, the same Kamikaze attacks the American fleet was undergoing were likely, therefore the AA armament was massively increased. The octuple pom-pom mounts were increased to six, plus two quad 2pdr each on 'B' and 'X' turrets, and sixteen

single 40mm Bofors were fitted along with seven twin 20mm and two singles. The work was reaching its completion when the war against Japan ended suddenly. She was finished after the Japanese capitulation, re-commissioned and carried out trials, but with reduced crew. *Valiant* was then paid off into the reserve fleet in June 1946, but was attached to the training establishment HMS *Impériuse* where she performed duties as a sea-going training ship. In January 1948, she was put up for disposal. Note that during the final repair, her pole mainmast was converted to a tripod. The reader can be confident of telling her and her sister ship *Queen Elizabeth* apart in photographs as only the *Queen Elizabeth* carried a tripod mainmast during hostilities. *Valiant* was given an all-over coat of MS4a Home Fleet grey, which she carried until scrapped.

HMS BARHAM Pennant 04
Queen Elizabeth class battleship 1918

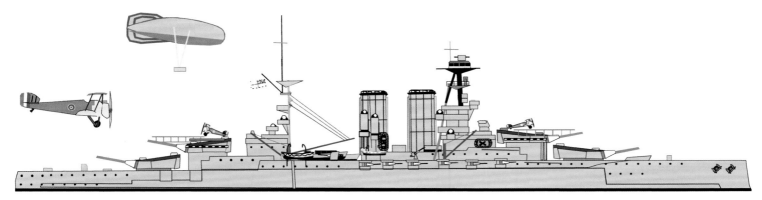

Barham is shown here in what would become known as Home Fleet grey, MS4a, at the end of 1918. Deflector scales were painted on 'B' and 'X' turrets. This ship was fitted to tow a kite balloon for observation, as was her sister *Warspite*. Anti-torpedo bulges have not yet been fitted, which allows a good view of the extensive side armour carried by these ships. Although never actually fitted, the positions for 6in casemate guns facing aft remain abreast the after turrets. A single 6in gun was carried on the boat deck but this was removed as it provided little protection for the crew.

Two single 12pdr AA were carried, one each side of the fore funnel. Flying-off platforms were fitted to 'B' and 'X' turrets. The ship carried a large number of searchlights as a result of lessons learnt during the night phase of the Battle of Jutland. During that battle, she engaged the *Von Der Tann* at 19,000 yards, scoring several damaging hits. She then went on to engage the *Seydlitz* and *Derfflinger*, causing considerable damage to both. *Barham* herself was hit six times but none caused sufficient damage to impair her fighting power. In 1918, two Sopwith Camel fighters were carried.

HMS BARHAM Pennant 04
Queen Elizabeth class battleship 1935

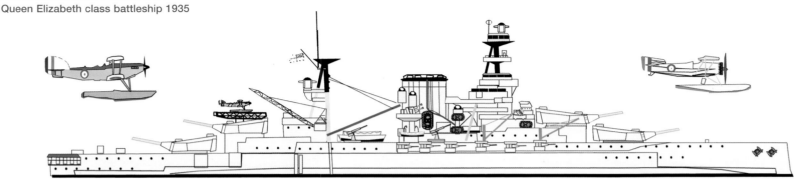

Barham underwent a major reconstruction during the late 1930s and emerged with the original two funnels trunked into one. A SIIT-type catapult was fitted on 'X' turret, along with a large crane at the mainmast to handle aircraft. The mainmast itself was turned into a tripod with a director for secondary guns and the 4in AA guns fitted to it. Another such director was fitted on top of the forward fighting top. Many changes were made to the layout of the bridge and searchlight arrangements. Light AA was increased to two octuple 2pdr pom-poms, one each side of the funnel. Quad 0.5in MG mounts were fitted either side of the conning tower. The ship served with the Mediterranean fleet from late-1935 and is shown painted in overall 507c for that region.

HMS BARHAM Pennant 04
Queen Elizabeth class battleship 1939-40

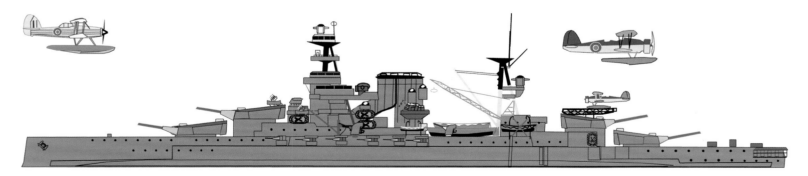

Barham was with the Mediterranean fleet at the outbreak of war but, by December, had been transferred to the Home Fleet and was painted overall in 507b, except for the decks which remained as in peacetime. The earlier aircraft carried on the catapult was replaced by a Swordfish floatplane. AA armament had been increased slightly by the addition of an extra quad 0.5in MG mount on 'A' turret, giving her a total of three such mounts. There were Mk IV HACS directors for the 4in guns on the platform at the rear of the bridge. She had a bad start to the war when she rammed and sank the destroyer HMS *Duchess* on arriving home, and then was torpedoed in the bow by U-boat *U-30*.

HMS BARHAM Pennant 04
Queen Elizabeth class battleship mid-1940

Barham was given an unofficial camouflage scheme in mid-1940, but it was worn for only a few months before being painted out by the end of the year. The above illustration is based on unclear photographic evidence and can only be considered as being as near as possible. Repairs after her disastrous return home took some time, but she returned to duty in time for the abortive Dakar campaign as part of Force H, where she was hit by two shells from shore batteries. In December 1940, she was transferred to the Mediterranean fleet and the scheme shown here was replaced by one which she carried until her loss. Note that another quad 0.5in MG mount had been added on the aft superstructure. No radar was fitted.

HMS BARHAM Pennant 04
Queen Elizabeth class battleship 1941

Barham's starboard side showing the unofficial scheme she adopted when sent to join the Mediterranean fleet. It was described as being black and white; however, this may be in error as photographs suggest something lighter. Nonetheless, black and white schemes were popular in the eastern Mediterranean fleet at the time and I have shown how she would look if those colours were correct. AA armament had been increased by giving her two quad 0.5in MG mounts on 'B' turret, arranged at different levels. Another was placed on 'X' turret, to the starboard of the catapult.

A further position was prepared on 'Y' turret, but it is uncertain if she actually had a mounting fitted before her loss. However, I have shown the mount in this illustration. The quad 0.5in MG was considered too light to be effective against the latest aircraft of the period and generally replaced by 20mm as soon as possible. *Barham* does not seem to have received any 20mm and the concentration of seven quad 0.5in MG mounts must have been unique within the fleet. There was no radar fitted.

HMS BARHAM Pennant 04
Queen Elizabeth class battleship late 1941

Barham's port side, showing the unofficial scheme she wore while with the Mediterranean fleet. Although described as a black and white scheme, it appears grey in most photographs. So I have shown her in contrasting 507a and 507c, which was popular and available from standard paint stores. Although old black and white photographs do fade and have exposure problems, my inclination is to accept dark grey on light as her true scheme. Decks remained unpainted wood but were no longer holystoned. *Barham* did not receive radar. *Barham*'s arrival in the Mediterranean was as

inauspicious as her return home in 1939. She was hit by Ju-87 Stukas during the Crete campaign, which damaged 'Y' turret, set the ship on fire and caused some serious flooding. After repairs at Durban, *Barham* returned to the Mediterranean fleet, but, on 24 November 1941, was torpedoed by U-boat *U-331*. Three hits were scored, which overwhelmed the torpedo bulges. As the ship capsized, its magazines detonated causing a huge loss of life.

HMS BARHAM Pennant 04
Queen Elizabeth class battleship 1941

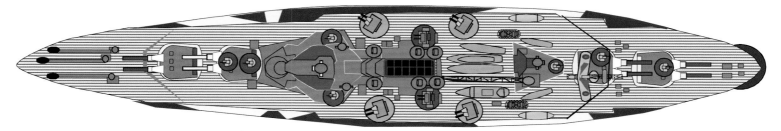

This illustration is an overhead view of *Barham* at the time of her loss. The wood decks were unpainted, but other metal areas were painted in the same shades as the camouflage. An area of Corticene remained on the bridge where crew stood for long periods of time. The AA armament of four twin 4in gun mounts was well spaced and protected by anti-splinter protection. The octuple 2pdrs abreast the bridge and the seven sets of quad 0.5in MG mounts are also obvious. The quad machine guns would undoubtedly have been due for replacement with 20mm, but her loss in late-

1941 meant this never happened. While considered an excellent weapon in the 1930s, war experience, particular with dive bomb attacks, showed that the machine gun lacked the hitting power to deter such attackers and required a larger crew than a single 20mm Oerlikon, which had greater hitting power while taking up only the same amount of space. The previously-carried Swordfish was replaced prior to *Barham*'s loss by a Walrus which could be placed on deck by the crane and the ships boats arranged to make room for it.

HMS MALAYA Pennant 01
Queen Elizabeth class battleship 1917

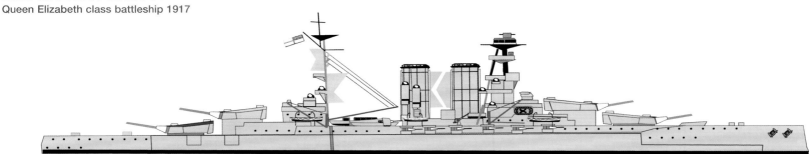

Malaya is shown wearing a World War I measure intended to confuse enemy rangefinders through the use of baffles. These were usually canvas and placed as shown. The Royal Navy used a rangefinder that measured the known distance between objects on an enemy ship to estimate its range via triangulation. It was thought that baffles made the parts of a ship look closer together and therefore further away. However, it was later found that German rangefinders did not use the same method and the baffles were therefore a waste of time. They did make a brief reappearance in the Mediterranean in World War II, but were soon abandoned. While not intended to hide the ship, this was, nonetheless, a form of camouflage, as it was an attempt to confuse an observer as to the vessel's appearance and size. The ship ws painted in overall medium grey MS4a. No bulges were fitted and this enables a good view of the extensive area of side armour these ships had. The ship is shown with single 3in AA guns and, although the permanent fitting of light AA was years away, these ships carried a large number of medium and light machine guns that could be deployed with landing parties or used against low-flying aircraft. The ship carried an Admiral's stern walk for a short time and later had flying off platforms fitted.

HMS MALAYA Pennant 01
Queen Elizabeth class battleship 1937

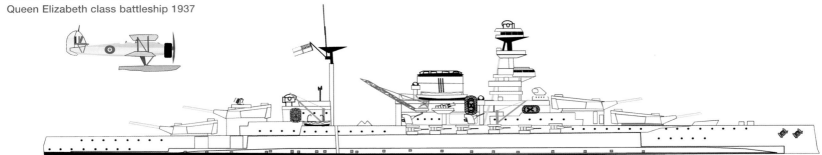

In the late 1920s, *Malaya* had her two funnels trunked into one and torpedo bulges added, along with various other modifications. Her old AA guns were removed and replaced by four single 4in AA. Then, from 1934-7, she was extensively refitted to provide her with aircraft facilities, which included a hangar that could accommodate two aircraft. Technically, four could be carried, with two on deck if required, but this was not normally done. The catapult was placed athwartships and, at first, Shark floatplanes were carried but were replaced by Swordfish in 1938. Her AA arma- ment was improved with the fitting of an octuple pom-pom mount either side of the funnel and two quad 0.5in MG mounts on 'X' turret. Note that these mounts were very exposed and without splinter protection. Mk IV HACS directors were fitted to the fighting top and the aft deckhouse. For the late 1930s, this armament was considered quite adequate for anti-aircraft protection. The ship is shown here in pale grey 507c while she was part of the Mediterranean fleet.

HMS MALAYA Pennant 01
Queen Elizabeth class battleship late 1940

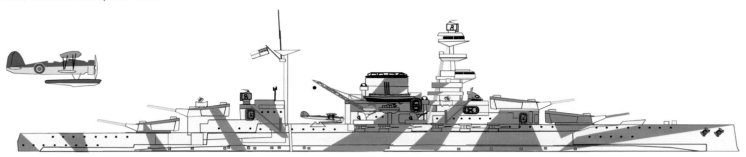

Malaya is shown wearing a scheme of overall 507c grey with areas of darker 507b added to break up her outline. The only light AA addition at this time was quad 0.5in MG mounts either side of the bridge. The mounts on 'X' turret had been given splinter protection for the crew. At this time, Type 284 radar had been fitted for main armament and Type 285 for the Mk IV HACS directors.

Search radar was not fitted until 1941. The realities of war can be seen through the addition of extra Carley floats. The wood decks were painted dark grey and this appears to have applied to the turret tops as well. With her single central funnel, that appeared somewhat lower due to the hangars, the *Malaya* was a handsome ship with a look of power.

HMS MALAYA Pennant 01
Queen Elizabeth class battleship March 1941

The port side view of *Malaya* was similar to the starboard, but with minor differences. The ship joined Force H based on Gibraltar due to the activities of German ships attempting to raid Atlantic convoys, but she also took part in Western Mediterranean operations. In March 1941 she was with Convoy SL1 when the German battleships *Scharnhorst* and *Gneisenau* attacked, but they broke off and withdrew rather than risk engaging *Malaya*. Type 281 radar had just been fitted when the ship

was torpedoed by U-boat *U-106*, which was attacking Convoy SL68 off the Cape Verde Islands. *Malaya* was able to steam to Trinidad and then went on to the USA for more extensive repairs, the first such work carried out under Lend-Lease. *Malaya* was a very active battleship and her return to the fleet was urgently required. Prior to this scheme being painted out, and the Admiralty disruptive scheme being added, the ship spent a short period during which she was painted 507b overall.

HMS MALAYA Pennant 01
Queen Elizabeth class battleship late 1943

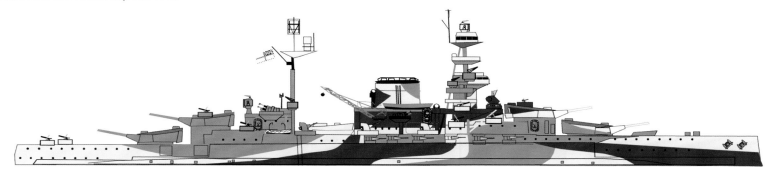

Malaya is shown wearing an official Admiralty disruptive camouflage scheme. It is unclear what the lightest colour was, but it was certainly similar to WA blue. The other shades were B15 blue black and B5 blue grey. By this period of World War II, dockyard-applied paint schemes were more likely to use the designated shades on a ship such as this, rather than the closest thing available. To completely repaint a battleship, the correct pigments and mixes would have to be specifically ordered. The wood decks and turret tops remained dark grey during this period. The AA was considerably increased by adding a pair of octuple pom-poms to the aft superstructure and the addition of a large number of single 20mm Oerlikon guns. The quad 0.5in MGs were completely removed. The radar fit was enhanced with the placement of a Type 273 lantern on top of the main-mast. Aircraft were no longer carried and some of the boats previously carried on the top of the hangar were moved down to the main deck.

HMS MALAYA Pennant 01
Queen Elizabeth class battleship September 1944

This port side view of *Malaya* depicts her as she appeared at the end of her war service. The Admiralty disruptive scheme was the same as applied in 1943 and used the same colours. The ship had been deactivated on 3 December 1943 due to manpower shortages, but was kept in a state of readiness for shore bombardment, including a refit from March to May 1944, which included updating electronics, adding Type 650 missile jamming gear and IFF. After other ships were damaged off Normandy, she was returned to service in support of Allied troops ashore in France. In October, she was no longer required and once again passed into reserve, this time for the final time. After a period as an accommodation ship, she was sold for scrap in 1948. *Malaya* had a very active career from World War I through World War II and can be considered a very successful ship.

ROYAL SOVEREIGN CLASS BATTLESHIPS

HMS ROYAL OAK Pennant 08
Royal Sovereign class battleship 1937

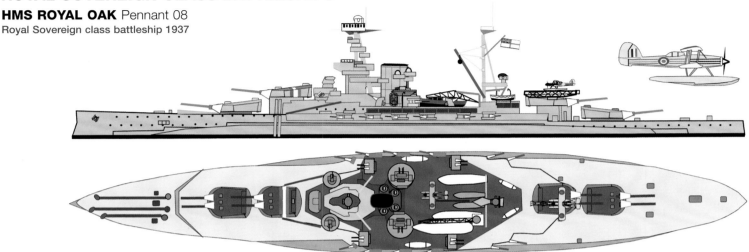

This shows the ship while on neutrality duty during the Spanish Civil War. The overall colour was Home Fleet grey MS4a but she displayed peacetime features such as white canvas, polished wood, Admiral's launch and other boats in white. The fighting tops were also white. 'B' turret was painted with red, white and blue identification markings. The turret top was painted dark grey to offset the colours. From 1923-4, she was given extensive anti-torpedo bulges which extended almost to the 6in secondary battery. From 1934-6, additional armour was added, the bridge modified and a SIIT-type catapult was fitted to the top of 'X' turret. This required an aircraft crane to be fitted. When not stowed on the turret top, the aircraft could be placed on the boat deck. Although she was fitted with four 4in AA twins during the refit, the only light AA comprised a pair of Mk VII octuple

2pdrs each side of the funnel and quad 0.5in machine guns either side of the DCT. Note the doors in the hull forward. These covered twin torpedo tubes that were mounted above the water as an experiment. Her armament is the same as she carried at the time of her sinking. In peacetime, it was the practice to holystone the wood decks almost white as part of the daily routine of her crew. The overhead view shows the anchor handling areas in Brunswick green, a common 'tidy ship' feature on ships that were kept smart-looking, along with one winch top in red and one in green, marking port and starboard, a feature designed to help new recruits and reservists. Areas of brown Corticene saved weight and were easier on the feet of crew members than plain steel. There is a single Mk IV HA/LA director aft and another on top of the fighting top.

HMS ROYAL OAK Pennant 08
Royal Sovereign class battleship 1939

Royal Oak is shown at the start of World War II having been over-painted in a much darker shade of grey, probably 507b or a similar on-board mix of paints. Her decks were natural wood which had been holystoned to keep it new-looking. Although this was discontinued on the outbreak of war, it is unlikely that the decks had time to fade prior to her loss. Turret tops were dark grey. The ship took part in a sweep against enemy merchant shipping during the first week of the war as part

of the Home Fleet and had little time to make other changes. Although often played down as completely worn out and a unit of little fighting value, to minimise the propaganda value of her loss to U-boat *U-47*, *Royal Oak* was actually the most extensively-refitted and up to date unit of the *Royal Sovereign* class battleships. Had she survived longer, there is no doubt she would have played an active role in the war. There was no radar fitted at the time of her sinking.

HMS REVENGE Pennant 06
Royal Sovereign class battleship 1917-8

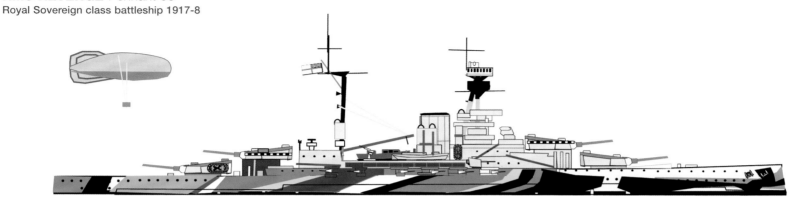

Revenge was one of two ships of the *Royal Sovereign* class to carry camouflage in World War I, but in her case it was mostly only applied to the hull, not the upper works. Dazzle camouflage required the colours to heavily contrast with each other to give a false impression of the ship's size, type and speed. The scheme was applied after her role in the Battle of Jutland in 1916. She was also fitted to tow an observation balloon – an attempt to give spotting information to the gunnery officers, from above the mass of smoke that so often obliterated visibility of the enemy. The range marks on her 'A' and 'X' turrets were to help other ships to see in which direction they were aiming, which was

found to be of great help in the poor visibility typical of the North Sea. There was a profusion of searchlights around the bridge, funnel and even the main mast. *Revenge* was present at the Jutland, where she engaged the German battleship *König*, expending 105 15in rounds and a torpedo. She also engaged the Zeppelin *L11* and four destroyers, successfully evading at least four torpedoes. She also tried to finish off the German battlecruiser *Seydlitz* without success. *Revenge* took over as flag-ship of the 1st Battle squadron when *Marlborough* was torpedoed. In addition to the casemate 6in guns, there was also a mount on the main deck. 3in AA guns were carried port and starboard.

HMS REVENGE Pennant 06
Royal Sovereign class battleship Early 1939

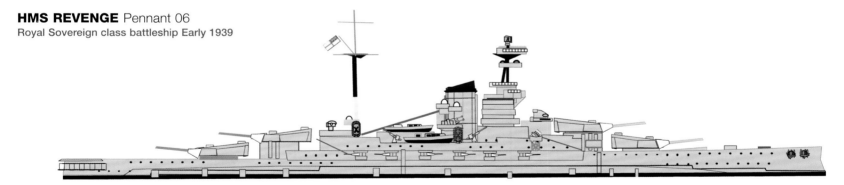

Immediately after World War I, *Revenge* had an Admiral's stern walk added, the only one of her class to be so fitted. It makes her easy to spot in photographs of the class. As a ship of the Home Fleet, she was painted in overall drab grey MS4a. Decks were still timber. By 1939, her funnel had been capped to help keep smoke away from the bridge and fighting top. There were only four single 4in

AA carried but these were soon replaced by twin mounts. Pre-war, she had been fitted with octuple 2pdr pom-pom mounts either side of the funnel and quad 0.5in MG mounts each side of the forward director. It requires a lot of paint to cover a battleship and until 1940 she remained in dull grey.

HMS REVENGE Pennant 06
Royal Sovereign class battleship 1939-40

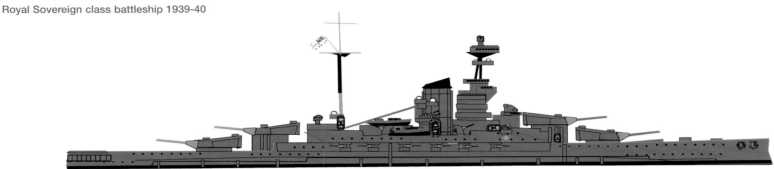

As war loomed, this ship was part of the Home Fleet and then sent to join the Channel Force. She is shown here with vertical surfaces in overall 507a Home Fleet grey. Horizontal surfaces are not known but probably still peacetime-style as the threat of air attack was not yet appreciated. The deck was most likely still holystoned wood.

HMS REVENGE Pennant 06
Royal Sovereign class battleship mid-1940

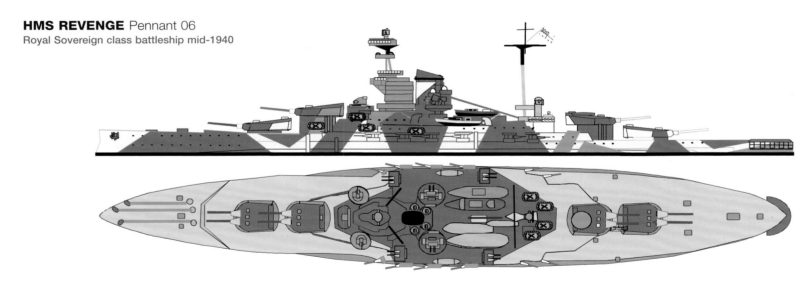

Revenge is shown in mid-1940 wearing a scheme she was to carry for much of her war service with only a few alterations. The port side pattern is shown here. For such a large ship, the three shades scheme relied on paint that was immediately available. 507a formed the darker shade of grey, MS4a was the middle shade and the overall grey was 507c. The wood decks have been allowed to fade and were soon to be painted grey. The metal horizontal decks are all 507a. Canvas has been painted grey but, of course, it always shows a slightly different colour than the same paint applied to metal or wood surfaces. The Admiral's barge was still stained wood, but all other boats were grey. More life rafts were added. The Admiralty had not issued formal instructions for paint schemes, their only comment (CFAO69) was to warn that, while different patterns might be used on each side, this could make ship recognition difficult. Note that in this illustration the 4in guns do not have splinter protection around their mounts. A base was added to the top of 'X' turret for a quad 2pdr, which had not yet been fitted. Her light AA therefore remained two octuple 2pdr mounts and two quad 0.5in MG mounts.

HMS REVENGE Pennant 06

Royal Sovereign class battleship mid-1941-2

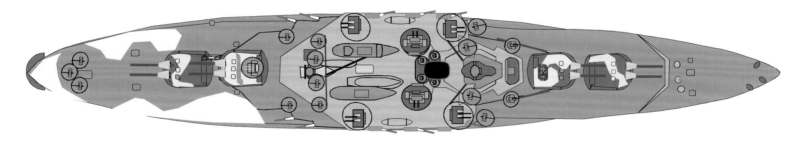

Revenge displays her starboard side camouflage pattern that was carried 1940-3. The port side still used the previously shown pattern; however this shows changes in equipment by mid-1941. The decks have been over-painted in mid-grey that is possibly 507b, but more likely paint mixed on board from the paint locker or local procurement shades. The intent of the scheme on both sides was to confuse the observer and also make the ship look shorter. Because of the air threat, nearly everything possible was dulled down. Only some Corticene remained on the bridge, where it protected the feet of those on watch. The threat from aircraft also resulted in the addition of a quad

2pdr mount on 'X' turret and ten 20mm Oerlikon guns. Two replaced the quad 0.5in MG mounts previously carried. The 4in gun mounts were given protection in the form of splinter shields around them to protect the gun and ammunition handlers from bullets and splinters. Type 279 radar was over the forward fighting top and Type 285 gunnery radar was fitted to the director there. There was Type 273 lantern type radar on the main mast. Type 284 main gunnery radar was added to the director before the bridge. There was Type 285 radar on the director just aft of the main mast. *Revenge* did not require a tripod mast as the aft HACT position was carried low.

HMS REVENGE Pennant 06
Royal Sovereign class battleship early 1943

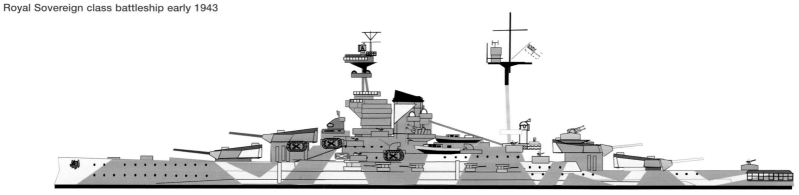

Revenge is depicted showing the port side camouflage pattern that was carried from early 1943. The layout was much the same as before but was simplified to only two shades of grey while serving with the Indian Ocean fleet. MS4a was now carried over a base of 507c. The Type 273 radar lantern had a Type 244 IFF aerial added to the top and Type 279M atop the forward fighting top. The 20mm Oerlikon guns on the quarterdeck were reduced from three to two. Two others near the main mast were also removed, leaving a total of eleven. The 15in gun mounts had larger blast bags. Note that, unlike other units of this class, *Revenge* did not receive a quad 2pdr mounting on 'B' turret. The lack of that mounting, the Admiral's walk aft, and the lack of a tripod main mast make her easy to distinguish from her sister ships in photographs.

Revenge displays her starboard side camouflage pattern of early 1943. This was worn until the end of active service. She had fought at Jutland in World War I, where she engaged the German battle-cruisers *Derfflinger* and *Von Der Tann*. In the early part of World War II, she took part in escort duty

guarding convoys from German raiders. In October 1940, she bombarded the German army near Cherbourg and in 1941 was part of the hunt for the battleship *Bismarck*. 1942 found her in the Indian Ocean, operating mostly from Colombo in support of troop convoys to and from Australia. By 1943, the ship was in serious need of a rebuild; her hull was showing stress and her electrical systems, which had been in need of attention since 1936, were in very poor shape. It was decided that, in view of her condition and huge crew requirement, it would be best to place the ship in reserve. So many new ships were entering service that the Royal Navy was suffering from a serious manpower shortage and the crew could be better used elsewhere. *Revenge* was in reserve at the Clyde in September 1943 then moved to Devonport as a stokers' training ship in January 1944. Her only return to active duty was when she was used to convey Prime Minister Winston Churchill to the Cairo and Tehran conferences at the end of 1944. On return to the reserve, the ship was deactivated and sold for scrap in March 1948.

HMS ROYAL SOVEREIGN Pennant 05
Royal Sovereign class battleship 1935

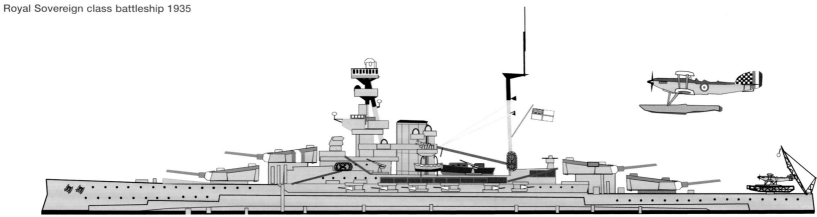

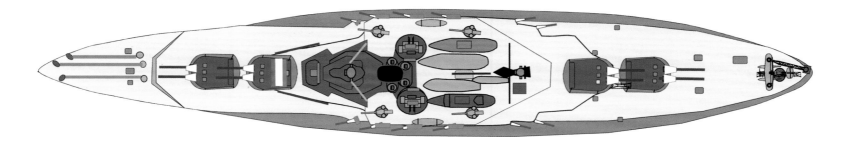

Royal Sovereign is shown during the Spanish Civil War painted in an overall shade of 507b for vertical surfaces; canvas areas were painted white. At this time, her wood decks would have been holystoned almost white as part of the daily routine of her crew. As part of the neutrality patrol, red, white and blue stripes have been painted on 'B' turret. During the 1932 refit, octuple 2pdr AA mounts were placed either side of the funnel and four single unshielded 4in AA guns were also carried. There were no other light AA weapons. There was a catapult on the quarterdeck with crane and a single spotter aircraft.

HMS ROYAL SOVEREIGN Pennant 05
Royal Sovereign class battleship 1940

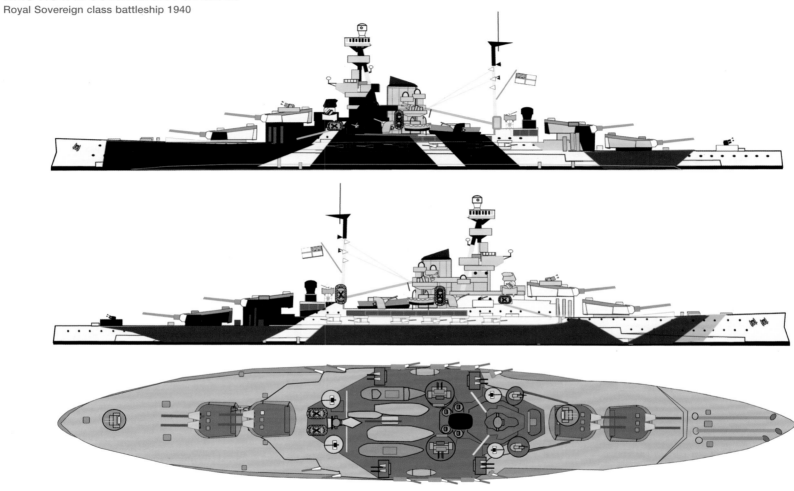

Royal Sovereign is shown at the time of her transfer to the Mediterranean fleet in 1940. The scheme was unofficial and comprised two shades of grey with black. The overall colour was 507c, also known as Mediterranean grey, to which areas of black and MS4a grey were applied. Like most major warships, she retained a black waterline. By this time, the aircraft facilities had been removed from the stern and there was no provision to carry aircraft at all. In view of the increased air threat expected; a quad 2pdr AA mount was placed on top of 'B' turret and another mounting well aft. Four single 20mm AA were added to supplement the pair of quad 0.5in MGs. The four single 4in

AA previously carried were replaced by twin mountings, but these had not yet been given splinter protection for the crew. There was no radar carried at all. The once daily-scrubbed decks were painted in plain grey. For service in the Mediterranean fleet, two quad 2pdr mounts were added along with four 20mm to increase the original AA power. It is probable that, when transferred, the wood decks were unpainted, as shown, but no longer holystoned to pale wood each day. However, some reports say the decks were grey when she left the UK.

HMS ROYAL SOVEREIGN Pennant 05
Royal Sovereign class battleship 1941-3

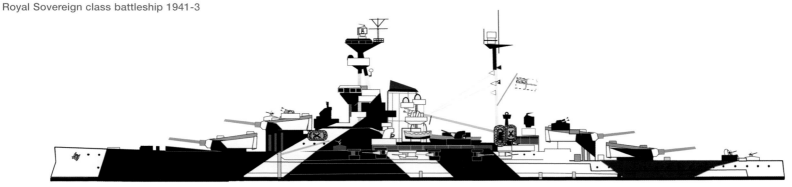

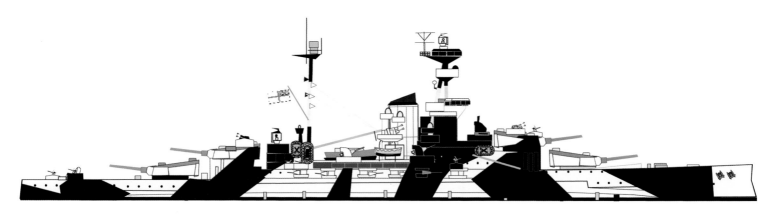

Royal Sovereign is shown after her transfer to the Mediterranean fleet and during her service back in the Atlantic and then the British Eastern Fleet. The scheme was simplified to black on 507c and produced a striking effect. It had the added benefit of being easier to maintain. Much of the original scheme layout was still in use, although the MS4a had been removed. The ship now had a Type 293 radar at the mainmast and there was a Type 284 main gunnery radar, in addition to the Type 285 radar for the 4in AA and secondary gun HACS. The armament now comprised her original eight 15in guns, ten 6in guns in single sponsons (the two forward 6in guns were removed to compensate for added weight), eight 4in AA guns in twin mounts, two octuple and two quad 2pdr mounts and thirteen 20mm guns.

HMS ROYAL SOVEREIGN Pennant 05
Royal Sovereign class battleship 1944-5

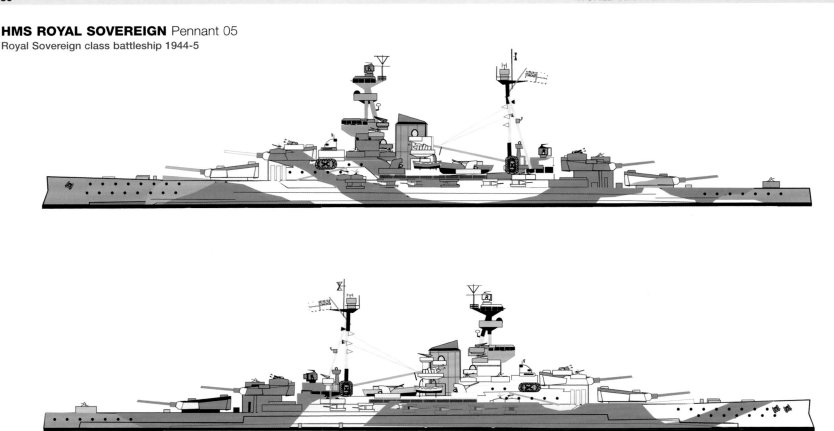

Royal Sovereign was refitted in the US before returning home at the end of 1943. The previous stark black and white was replaced by an Admiralty scheme that used G45, MS4, B5 and white. This Admiralty light scheme was probably designed for her and was the first official scheme applied since the outbreak of war. On her arrival in the UK, she went straight into reserve because the Royal Navy was suffering a serious manpower crisis with so many new ships coming online from shipyards both in the US and at home. Battleships required a lot of crew and, for the tasks then at hand, new escorts, carriers and cruisers received priority. Additionally, the Soviets had been complaining that the other Allies were dragging their feet in passing on warships Italy owed in

reparations. It was decided to meet the Soviet demands by transferring a battleship, a cruiser and some destroyers to the Russian Northern Fleet. The US provided a cruiser and the Royal Navy was to supply a battleship. Therefore, in May 1944 the British flag was hauled down and the ship transferred to the Soviet Union. Crews were sent to the UK to train on the ships and they then made their way to northern Russia. Note that the light AA armament was considerably strengthened during the US refit. The ship carried six twin 20mm and fourteen single 20mm. Type 244 and Type 253 interrogatory systems were carried for the identification of detected targets. Type 650 missile jammers were carried on the aft tripod legs.

ARCHANGELSK
Royal Sovereign class battleship 1944-5

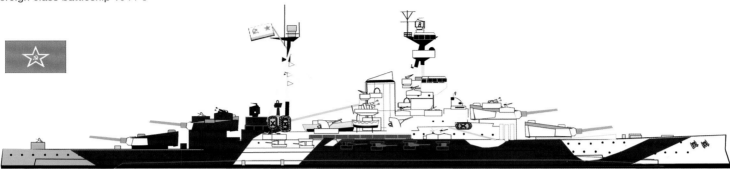

Although retaining the same general layout, sometime after transfer the colour scheme of the ex-*Royal Sovereign* was darkened by the Soviet Navy. This was in keeping with the Northern Fleet, where blue-black or black on white was a common part of Soviet warship camouflage. Note that the Type 244 and Type 253 interrogatory systems were removed prior to handing this ship over to the Soviet crew. While there had been considerable and open supply of secret equipment to the USSR, it seems this did not extend to the very latest electronics. Being a considerable status symbol, the Soviet Navy ensured the ship kept well away from danger during her service with them. She is shown here wearing the Soviet naval flag. Despite transfer, the ship retained her *Royal Sovereign* ship's bell and propaganda photographs exist showing this being rung by a young Soviet sailor.

ARCHANGELSK
Royal Sovereign class battleship 1945-9

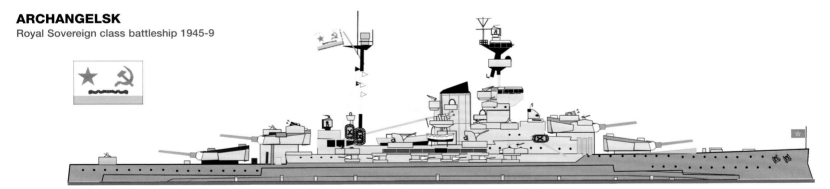

At the end of the war, it was presumed that the USSR would return the ship promptly. This, however, did not happen and it required considerable diplomatic exchanges before she was returned to the UK. Reportedly in a poor state of maintenance and a somewhat unhygienic condition, she did not even go to the reserve fleet; being sent straight to BISCO for scrapping. Note that there were no material changes during her Soviet service, but at some time during or after 1945 the ship was painted in typical Russian style. At the time of her return, the ship was wearing the flag of a 'Guard'-status ship of the Northern Fleet. *Archangelsk* was the largest and most heavily-armed battleship ever to sail under the Soviet flag. The old Soviet battleships still remaining carried 12in guns and were far less powerful than this ship. The 'Royal Rouble' finally returned home in 1949.

HMS RAMILLIES Pennant 07
Royal Sovereign class battleship 1917-8

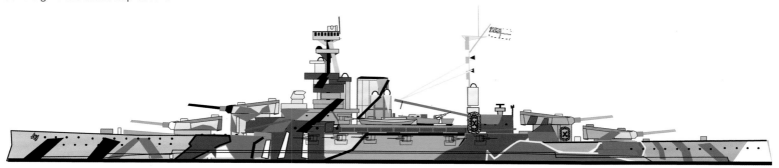

Ramillies is shown here in a dazzle paint scheme she wore until near the end of World War I. The Royal Navy had decided that no battleships of the Grand Fleet would be camouflaged but relented when growing reports of its effectiveness against submarine attack came in from ships involved in convoy service. Only two battleships were chosen to test schemes. *Ramillies* had an overall type, while *Revenge* had one that was mostly limited to the hull. The use of vivid and contrasting colours was intended to cause confusion for submarine commanders when trying to aim for torpedo attack. The ship was armed with eight 15in guns, twelve 6in guns and an AA armament of two 3in guns.

HMS RAMILLIES Pennant 07
Royal Sovereign class battleship 1936-9

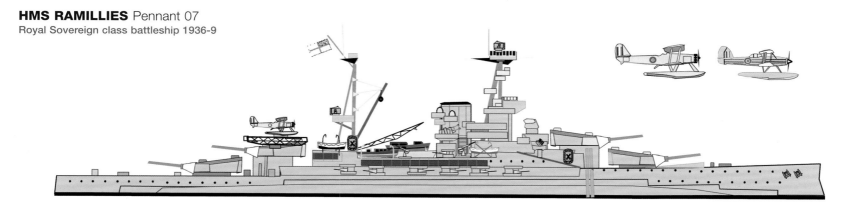

Ramillies is shown here in Home Fleet grey MS4a while acting as a fleet training ship from 1936-9. The decks were holystoned wood. The funnel was uncapped and single 4in AA guns were carried. The crane was of the same type as carried by *Royal Sovereign* and *Resolution* rather than the heavier type of *Royal Oak*. In the training role, her collection of boats was somewhat more extensive than her sisters. Despite the single 4in AA guns, the ship had been fitted with octuple 2pdr mounts opposite the funnel and quad 0.5 MGs on each side of the control tower. There were HACS directors on the fighting top and on a platform at the rear of the main tripod mast.

HMS RAMILLIES Pennant 07
Royal Sovereign class battleship November 1939

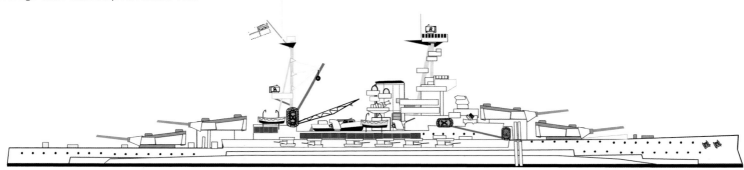

Ramillies was at Aden in November 1939 and was painted overall in 507c, which was also known as Mediterranean grey and Far Eastern grey. The decks were still wood but were allowed to fade instead of being holystoned each day. Her heavy AA was increased by replacing the single 4in guns with twin mounts. The light AA remained as it was immediately pre-war. The aircraft and catapult had been removed but the crane was still carried. Note that at this time the ship carried no radar of any kind.

HMS RAMILLIES Pennant 07
Royal Sovereign class battleship mid-1940

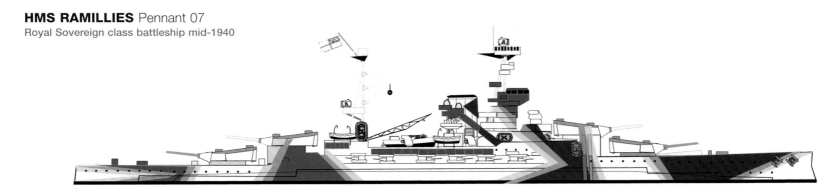

In mid-1940 it was decided to provide a camouflage scheme, which was almost certainly independent of Admiralty influence. The design utilised the light 507c the ship was already painted with and added two shades of grey that were probably mixed for the ship or were of local procurement. The intent was obviously to provide a graduated effect between the light and dark, but viewed from a distance could well produce an illusion of the viewer's vision being blurred. The port side pattern was the same. The decks were most probably over-painted with grey. There was still no change to armament, but the ship had so far not operated in areas with high chances of air attack.

HMS RAMILLIES Pennant 07
Royal Sovereign class battleship 1941

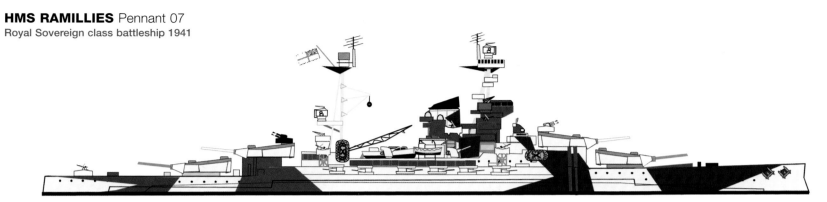

In 1941, the scheme carried by *Ramillies* was simplified. The graduations were removed but the pattern remained the same and was carried on both sides. The dark grey was possibly now G5/MS1, a shade of sooty black. This no doubt made maintenance much easier as only two colours were required. At this time, the deck was painted grey. A funnel cap similar to her sister ships was fitted and other upgrades had taken place. The ship now had a quad 2pdr mount on each of 'B' and 'X' turrets, the quad 0.5in MGs had been removed and ten single 20mm added. This ship was the only one of her class to carry 20mm AA on the funnel. Although some ships had landed the forward 6in casemate guns by this time, *Ramillies* retained hers. Type 79Y radar was on top of the forward fighting top and Type 285 radar was added to both Mk IV HACS. The main armament now had Type 284 radar for gunnery direction. A Type 273 radar lantern was placed at the top of the main mast for a good all-round sweep.

HMS RAMILLIES Pennant 07
Royal Sovereign class battleship 1941

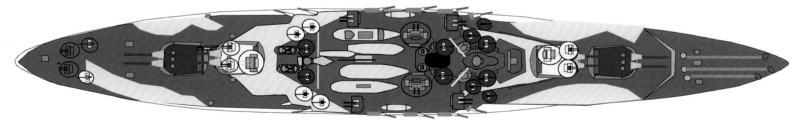

In 1941 the scheme carried by *Ramillies* was apparently carried up across the decks to confuse the aerial view of her. However, this illustration can only be taken as an approximation, based on some aerial views, which are far from distinct. It would appear that the light grey areas were intended to confuse her outline from above and probably also cause confusion about the speed at which she was steaming.

HMS RAMILLIES Pennant 07
Royal Sovereign class battleship 1944

After a major refit, *Ramillies* was given an Admiralty-designed camouflage scheme based on 507c, B5, MS3 and B15. The effect was intended to break the ship into two when seen from a distance and make it appear as two ships. This port side view was applied during her refit from December 1943 to January 1944, when she returned to British waters to have equipment for shore bombardment fitted ready for the Normandy landings. I have shown here the additional radar aerials and countermeasures fitted just before the Normandy operation. These were carried until January 1945 for the purpose of training new crews in their use; hence she had a somewhat more varied elec-

tronic fit than most ships. They included Type 281B on the fighting top; Type 279M on the top of the mainmast, with a Type 244 aerial atop the Type 273 lantern. A Type 253 sand-timer type interrogation aerial was just below the Type 279M. There was a Type 650 missile jamming set below the Type 281B. The main guns still had Type 284 radar on the director and there were Type 285 aerials on the HACS directors. The light AA was increased to a total of thirteen single 20mm and six twin, in addition to the two octuple 2pdr and two quad 2pdr. This camouflage scheme was carried for the rest of her active service.

HMS RAMILLIES Pennant 07
Royal Sovereign class battleship 1945

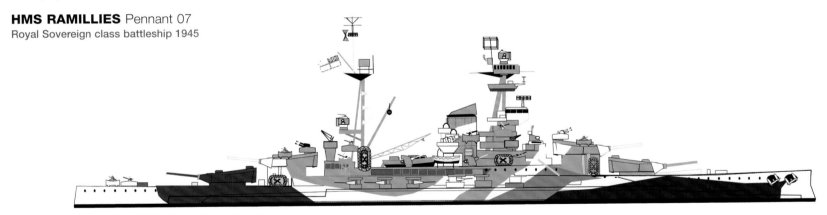

This shows the starboard side of *Ramillies* after coming out of refit in January of 1944, but with the radar aerials she carried up until just before D-Day, when the ship was part of the bombardment group. Radar carried was Type 279Y at the foretop, with a Type 273 lantern on the tripod mainmast. Type 284 and Type 285 radars were provided for gunnery. No IFF was carried. By March, her final radar fit included those already shown in the previous illustration, so the ship could also provide training for new operators and test new systems. Apart from that and a few more 20mm, the general appearance of the ship had not changed much since 1942. *Ramillies* retained the aircraft

crane until the end of her service. It was undoubtedly found to be useful or it would have been discarded to save weight, as was done on so many other ships. *Ramillies* lost the two forward 6in casemate guns on each side to compensate for the additional AA and radar. Although badly damaged by Japanese torpedoes at Diego Suarez, Madagascar in 1942, a survey of her at that time reported she was in very good shape for her age and, after repair, she continued in fleet service until January 1945.

HMS RESOLUTION Pennant 09
Royal Sovereign class battleship 1930

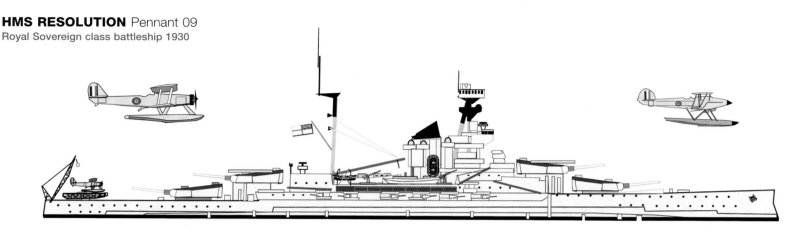

Resolution was with the 1st Battle Squadron in the Mediterranean during 1930 and was painted overall in a pale grey, similar to 507c, which was also known as Mediterranean grey and Far Eastern grey. The decks were wood and holystoned each day. The two 3in AA guns previously carried had been replaced by four single 4in AA guns, but she mounted no light AA at all. Turret tops were painted in Brunswick green. A funnel cap had been fitted but was higher than that carried by her sister ships. The upper deck single 6in gun carried on completion was removed in 1928, but the casemate remained for some time. At this time, the ship carried a catapult with crane right aft for a single Blackburn Ripon or Hawker Osprey seaplane. Despite the catapult, there were World War I-type flying-off platforms on the 'B' and 'X' turrets. These were removed in 1932. Note the very tall mainmast to which a blimp could be moored. The lower section search-light towers on the funnel had been removed in preparation for the fitting of octuple 2pdr mounts.

HMS RESOLUTION Pennant 09
Royal Sovereign class battleship 1939-40

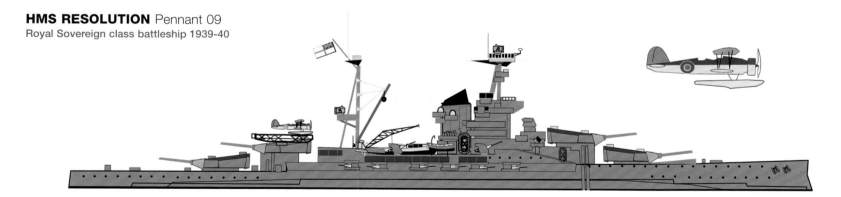

Resolution was in home waters at Portland as part of the Channel Force in 1939. However, within a short time the ship was transferred, first to the South Atlantic and then to the North Atlantic, for duties protecting merchant ships and early convoys. *Resolution* went home for the Norway campaign, where she was hit during an air attack. The ship appears to have been painted overall in 507b medium grey during this time; however, it is possible that this was a mix prepared on board by darkening Home Fleet grey MS4a. In the early part of World War II, there was considerable improvisation based on what paint was available. Turret tops appear to have been a few shades darker. Decks were still wood colour, but allowed to fade to grey as pre-war scrubbing was aban-doned. There was no radar of any kind fitted in this configuration. The single 4in AA guns had been replaced by twin shielded mounts. Multiple pom-poms were fitted either side of the funnel and quad 0.5in MGs by the conning tower. Type IV HACS directors were added. The catapult was now carried atop 'X' turret. During this period, the ship carried a Swordfish floatplane. This colour scheme was worn during the Dakar operation, where *Resolution* was badly damaged by four hits from shore batteries and a single torpedo hit from the French submarine *Bévéziers*. After repairs at Freetown, then Gibraltar, she returned to the UK for further repairs.

HMS RESOLUTION Pennant 09
Royal Sovereign class battleship 1941

Resolution was camouflaged immediately after the Dakar operation, possibly while at Freetown. The overall dark grey 507b was retained, but a dark area of 507a was added at the waterline in an irregular pattern. Additionally, a false bow wave and stern wash was added in WS white. The decks were over-painted in mid-grey, but the exact shade is not known. Note that, although there was no radar present, the ship was given four single 20mm Oerlikon guns and the quad 0.5in MG mounts were retained. Although the ship made it back to Portsmouth for major repairs after her serious torpedo damage off Dakar, her refit was continually interrupted by German air raids. *Resolution* went to the USA for completion of her repairs. The object at the head of the mainmast is not radar, but a homing beacon for her aircraft.

HMS RESOLUTION Pennant 09
Royal Sovereign class battleship Late 1941

This shows the port side of *Resolution* in late 1941. During the refit in the USA, Type 285 radar was added to the Mk IV HACS directors and Type 279 radar on the fighting top. 20mm AA guns were increased to ten. The catapult was retained, but the aircraft type was changed to a Walrus sometime during the year. Splinter-proof zarebas were around the 4in gun mounts. It takes a lot of paint to cover a battleship, but this particular camouflage scheme used shades that would have been relatively easy to find. The light AA would have been inadequate in many areas but during this time she spent most of her time in the Atlantic. The AA was much increased when she was sent out to the Indian Ocean in early 1942.

HMS RESOLUTION Pennant 09
Royal Sovereign class battleship 1942-3

Resolution was camouflaged with an Admiralty design prior to her departure to the Indian Ocean to become flagship of the British Eastern Fleet. This is the port side of the four-colour scheme. Type 285 radar was on the HACS directors and Type 279 radar on the top of both masts. This was because one was the transmitter and the other a receiver. Two quad 2pdr mounts were added, one on 'B' turret and one on the quarterdeck. This camouflage scheme was retained until the ship went out of service. The decks appear to have had some camouflage, but the exact pattern is not known and photographs are unclear. The number of light AA guns was now set at two octuple 2pdr, two quad 2pdr and ten single 20mm Oerlikons. The location of the aft quad 2pdr would change in late 1943, but the number of guns remained the same while the ship was in active service.

HMS RESOLUTION Pennant 09
Royal Sovereign class battleship 1943-4

The Admiralty-designed scheme applied prior to her departure to the Indian Ocean was retained on return to home waters. In her late-1943 appearance, the only changes were that the catapult was removed and the quarterdeck 2pdr moved to the top of 'X' turret. A total of ten 20mm Oerlikons were carried. The two forward 6in guns were removed by this time. Type 273 radar, with a 244 interrogator, was added to the tripod mainmast. Type 279M radar had replaced the earlier version of the same type and only required one aerial. Although ready for use if required for D-Day, *Resolution* was reduced to a stokers' training ship in May 1944 in order to release crew for newer ships. In June, she became part of the HMS *Impérieuse* training establishment. Her light AA guns were gradually removed for use on other ships and then the 15in main armament to provide spares. She was not sold for scrapping until 1948.

BATTLECRUISERS

HMS REPULSE Pennant 34
Renown class battlecruiser 1917

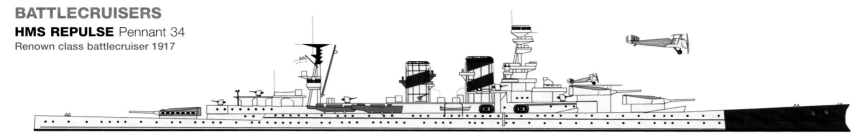

Repulse is shown above in her 1917 appearance. There were black stripes on the fore funnel and one on the aft. They sloped toward the stern on the starboard side and toward the bow on the port side. There was a panel of black at the starboard bow, but apparently not on the port side. The aft turret was painted dark grey and had deflection scales added. There was a flying-off platform on 'B' turret with a Sopwith fighter provided. The superstructure was quite light compared to later years. The ship was painted in an overall pale grey of unspecified type. These ships introduced a new triple 4in gun mounting, but the 15in guns were the same as carried by British battleships.

HMS REPULSE Pennant 34
Renown class battlecruiser 1918

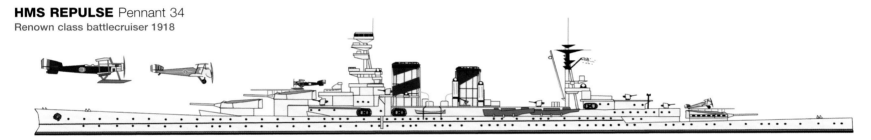

In the second illustration, *Repulse* is shown in 1918. The funnel camouflage in black remained, but was not carried on the hull. There were a few superstructure changes, including the relocation of searchlights. The flying-off platform on 'B' turret was increased in length to allow reconnaissance aircraft to be flown off and a flying-off platform for fighters added on 'Y' turret. Single 3in AA guns were carried each side of the aft funnel.

HMS REPLUSE Pennant 34
Renown class battlecruiser 1936-8

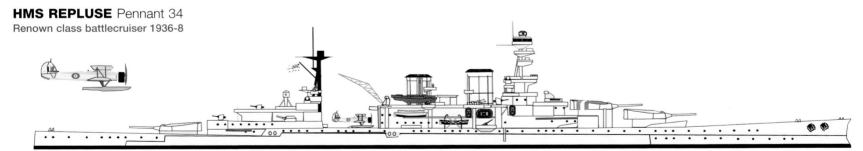

From 1933-6, the ship underwent a major rebuild. Hangars were added amidships around the funnels, an athwartships catapult was installed and Shark floatplanes provided. The AA armament was completely revised. Two experimental twin 4in AA mounts were added port and starboard of the mainmast as a trial of the mountings. Octuple 2pdr mounts were added abreast the fore funnel and quad 0.5in MG mounts on the sides of the same funnel. Many of the boats were moved to the top or the sides of the hangar. In 1938, the twin 4in mounts were removed to provide additional accommodation during a Royal visit. It was intended they would be replaced but events prevented this and single mounts replaced them. During the Spanish Civil War, the ship carried neutrality markings on 'B' turret. The decks were well-scrubbed wood.

HMS REPULSE Pennant 34
Renown class battlecruiser 1939

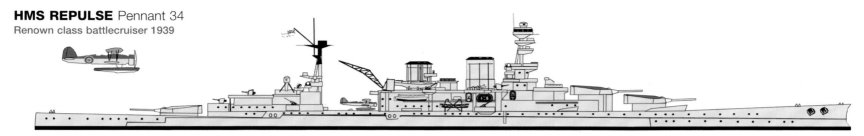

Repulse is shown above just after World War II commenced. The overall tone is 507b medium-grey. The decks remained unpainted wood but were no longer holystoned. There were still two triple 4in low-angle mounts carried aft. A pair of quad 0.5in MG mounts were installed near the HACS director aft. Her general appearance was much as she looked in 1936, except that the experimental twin 4in mounts had been removed and single 4in AA substituted. Swordfish floatplanes were carried at this time.

HMS REPULSE Pennant 34
Renown class battlecruiser late 1940

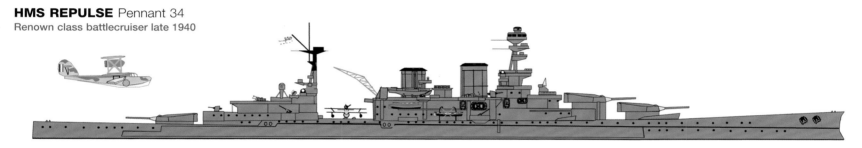

In 1940, *Repulse* had 507b applied overall. This shade of grey was worn while the ship remained with the Home Fleet, when she carried out operations in the Atlantic, the North Sea and up into the Arctic searching for German blockade runners. An additional octuple 2pdr mount was added aft in place of one of the triple 4in low-angle mounts. Type 284 radar for the main armament was also fitted. Walrus aircraft replaced the Swordfish.

HMS REPULSE Pennant 34
Renown class battlecruiser late 1941

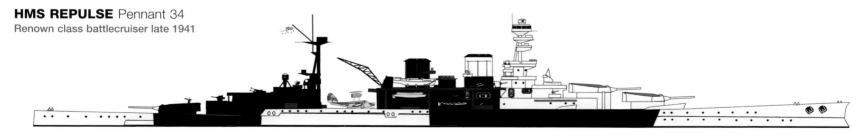

Repulse is shown in a rather dramatic camouflage in 1941. It comprised areas of black on a hull of 507c. The effect highlights the aft funnel and provides a shortening effect. It is believed the scheme was identical on each side. The deck remained plain unscrubbed wood. *Repulse* was wearing this camouflage at the time she joined *Prince of Wales* as part of the ill-fated Force Z. Force Z was sent to deter the Japanese from sending ships to attack Singapore and had only just arrived when the Japanese commenced their landings in Malaya. The ships sortied to intercept invasion craft but were caught at sea without air cover and overwhelmed by a large contingent of land-based Japanese naval aircraft. Despite some desperate evasive manoeuvres, *Repulse* was hit by five torpedoes, which completely overwhelmed her defences and she capsized. *Repulse* had been allocated a new ship's crest just prior to her loss. At least four, and possibly eight, single 20mm AA were added before the ship sailed for Singapore. Two were on 'Y' turret and two aft of the single 4in AA guns on the aft superstructure. The others were possibly on the shelter deck aft of 'B' turret and higher on the bridge. One photograph taken at Singapore the day before she was lost does seem to show brackets for Type 285 radar on the HACS, but no actual aerials fitted.

HMS RENOWN Pennant 72
Renown class battlecruiser 1918

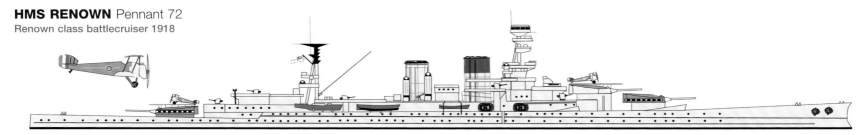

Renown is shown here in 1918 wearing a dark grey band on her fore funnel. Both 'A' and 'Y' turrets were dark grey to highlight the deflection scales painted on them. There were some structural differences between her and her sister ship, particularly aft of the funnels. The ship appears to have worn an unspecified shade of light grey during the latter part of World War I. Flying-off platforms were fitted on the turrets and Sopwith fighters carried. The 15in mounts were of the successful British type but the secondary armament was made up of triple 4in mountings, in keeping with the thinking of Admiral Fisher for heavily-armed ships to have only a light secondary armament. Two single 3in AA were fitted near the aft funnel. Torpedo tubes were submerged.

HMS RENOWN Pennant 72
Renown class battlecruiser 1933

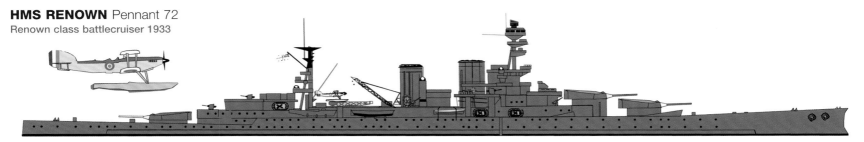

Renown was given a major refit from mid-1923 until late 1926. The armament remained much the same, but the 3in AA were replaced by two single 4in AA. A catapult was added before the main tripod mast and two Fairey III floatplanes were carried. However, no hangar was provided. The armour protection was improved. *Renown* served with the Home Fleet and is shown in an overall 507a. The decks were holystoned wood. A single Mk 1 HACS was mounted on the foretop. She had space for two octuple 2pdr AA mounts but, as an economy measure, only the starboard one was fitted, the port tub remaining empty.

HMS RENOWN Pennant 72
Renown class battlecruiser 1939

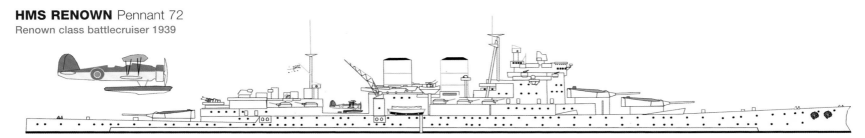

Renown underwent a major rebuild from 1936-9, reappearing as a much-modernised ship. As first recommissioned, she was painted 507c overall, with unpainted wooden decks. The ship remained in this scheme for a time but was darkened to overall 507b by early 1940. By then, the natural wood decks were no longer scrubbed and were allowed to fade to wood colour with a greyish tinge. The reconstructed ship was re-engined and had all the original triple and single 4in guns removed. In their place, she carried five twin 4.5in mounts per side. Octuple 2pdr mounts were carried on each side amidships and a third was positioned on the aft superstructure. Two quad 0.5in MG mounts were also carried. The 15in guns were the originals, but elevation was increased for extra range and each mount was completely refurbished. The armour protection was improved considerably over her original design. Hangars were fitted either side of the aft funnel and up to four aircraft could be carried. There were eight 21in torpedo tubes carried in pairs above water.

HMS RENOWN Pennant 72
Renown class battlecruiser 1942

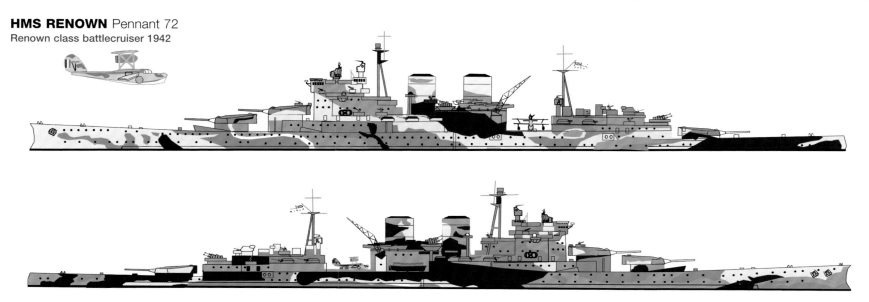

Renown is shown above in an Admiralty confusion scheme applied in mid-1942 and retained until July 1943. The confusion of colours in this disruptive pattern was intended to make the ship hard to identify, even if it did not conceal her. At a distance, the wide range of colours were expected to be very effective but, as with many of these type of schemes, they required a lot of crew time to maintain each colour and the pattern in general. By this time, her AA had been augmented with the addition of sixteen single 20mm mountings in various places and the quad MG mounts removed. Unlike other capital ships, it was not possible to mount any on the quarterdeck as, at high speed, this area was often awash or swept by waves. The radar systems were upgraded to include Type 271, Type 282, Type 284 and Type 285.

HMS RENOWN Pennant 72
Renown class battlecruiser 1944

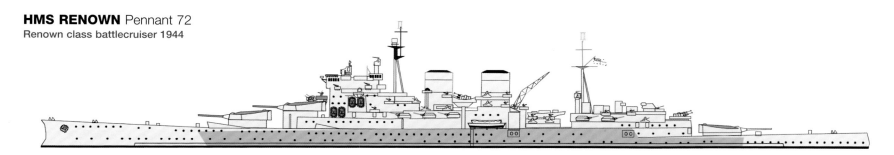

Renown was sent to the Indian Ocean where she was able to operate as a high speed escort for fleet carriers during operations against numerous Japanese targets. For a time, she was the largest British capital ship on that station and certainly the fastest. Like most ships there, she adopted a 507c overall scheme with a mid-blue hull panel. The wood decks were retained but most horizontal metal areas were painted in a very dark grey. The sixteen 20mm already carried were reinforced by another thirteen twin and three single 20mm and a quad 2pdr mount was added to the top of 'B' turret. An extensive radar suite was carried, along with the usual IFF and missile jammers. All aircraft facilities were removed and the area utilised for boats and other purposes.

HMS RENOWN Pennant 72
Renown class battlecruiser 1943

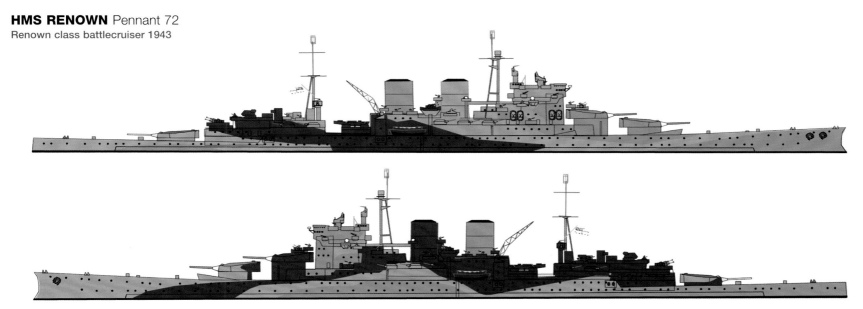

Renown is shown wearing an Admiralty design in 1943. The colours are G45, G15 and G5. When colours of similar hue were used, it was expected that, at a distance, they would blend together to create a certain level of invisibility. The dark areas would contrast with them, confusing the eye. When looking at the sea, we are really watching a whole range of colours that are also moving with the motion of distant waves. These combine together to give an impression of the colour of the sea. It is only in shallow areas where we can distinguish differences in shade, indicating depth. Therefore, the Admiralty designers often used colours which they hoped would blend to give the same effect as the sea from a distance. However, this was not entirely trusted and hence the occasional strong colour was used so that, if the eye of an observer started to distinguish the colours which were close, a darker shade would still confuse the outline.

HMS RENOWN Pennant 72
Renown class battlecruiser 1945

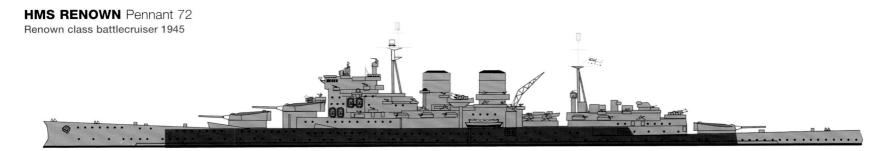

In February 1945, *Renown* was called back to the UK to provide a fast unit, which might be required to run down any remaining German ships trying a last ditch effort before the war ended. Events determined that she was not required for this purpose but, nonetheless, adopted the Admiralty Standard Home Fleet scheme of G45 with a B15 hull panel. The mast tops were white. She went into reserve in May 1945 and the six forward twin 4.5in mountings were removed. *Renown* was gradually disarmed before being sold to BISCO and was scrapped 1948-9.

HMS HOOD Pennant 51
Admiral class battlecruiser 1931-2

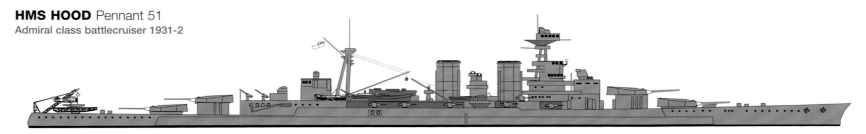

Hood was assigned to the Atlantic Fleet, later known as the Home Fleet, during most of her early service. Her grey was similar to 507b for the majority of that time. She was the pride of the Royal Navy and a favourite of the British public so her decks would have been scrubbed to fresh wood each day with holystones. The brass would have been shiny and the paintwork well-kept. Note the ship's boats were numerous, as she paid many flag-showing port calls and her crew were regularly

ashore as a public relations exercise. The public referred to her as 'The Mighty Hood' and, as the largest warship in the world, it was thought she was unsinkable. There were few external changes until 1931 when a catapult was installed at the stern. However, this area was always very wet when the ship was moving at high speed and the installation proved unsuccessful. Four single 4in AA were carried and octuple 2pdr mounts added.

HMS HOOD Pennant 51
Admiral class battlecruiser 1937

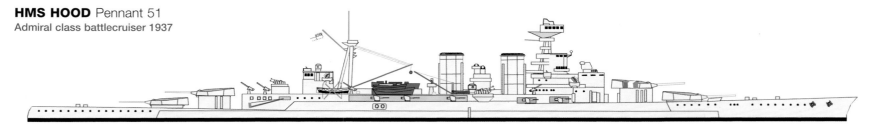

Hood was part of the Royal Navy force sent to the Mediterranean during the Spanish Civil War and various other political disturbances. She adopted the usual 507c pale grey usually worn in that region and wore red, white and blue stripes on 'B' turret as a recognition sign. Another octuple 2pdr was added aft while the ship was at Malta and, at some point, additional 4in single AA

replaced the 5.5in guns on the shelter deck. As usual, the decks would have been brightly scrubbed and the ship kept in immaculate condition as many dignitaries were entertained aboard and, when open for public inspection, *Hood* was always a popular ship for visitors.

HMS HOOD Pennant 51
Admiral class battlecruiser 1941

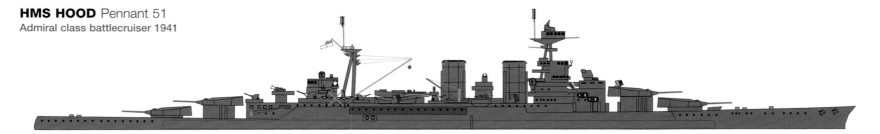

Hood was to have undergone a rebuild but the start of World War II caused this to be cancelled. Various modifications took place just before and after the start of the war, principally to strengthen her anti-aircraft armament, but there had been some attention given to her armour in various ways. This eventually proved inadequate when she blew up during an engagement with the *Bismarck*. Her scheme shown above uses 507a overall to present a very dull appearance, very different to most of her peacetime service. The decks were still unpainted wood but were no longer scrubbed daily.

There were a few leftovers from peacetime, with the Admiral's barge still having polished woodwork on the cabins and some wood derricks. The single 5.5in guns were all removed before her loss and fourteen 4in AA in seven twin mountings added. Five of the somewhat useless UP (Unrotated Projectile) rocket mountings were also added and the quad 0.5in MG mounts increased to four. At least two 20mm AA are said to have been added and possibly four. Type 284 radar was added for main gunnery control and Type 729 for air warning.

NELSON CLASS BATTLESHIPS

HMS NELSON Pennant 28
Nelson class battleship 1930-9

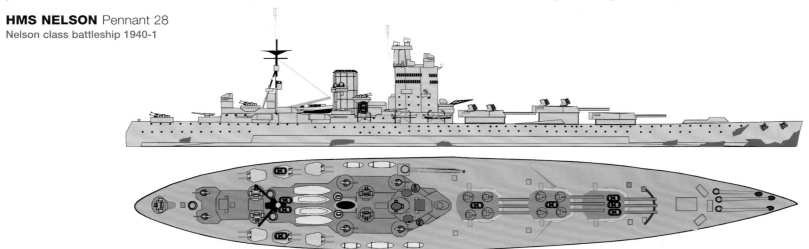

Nelson was the flagship of the Home Fleet from 1930-40. The ship is illustrated here in her 1930 appearance with metal surfaces painted in 507a battleship grey all over. Decks would have been scrubbed wood and, as flagship, would have been kept extremely neat. Horizontal metal areas were also in 507a. At this time, *Nelson* had eight, then ten, single 2pdr guns mounted as light AA as the octuple mounts were not available. The singles were carried two on each side abreast the bridge, between the bridge and funnel, at the base of the main mast and on the platform of the rear main gun director. There was no radar fitted, but she had more gunnery directors for her variety of arma-

ment than most battleships. At this time her 16in guns were still giving trouble and being worked on frequently to bring them up to a higher level of efficiency. Triple battleship turrets were new to the Royal Navy and there were many teething problems before they reached full efficiency. At this time, there was no foremast but a gaff protruded from the front of the bridge. The armour and bulges were never very prominent on this class, being mostly internal. Although this ship carried an aircraft crane on the starboard side, there was no catapult fitted and usually no aircraft carried. The HACS directors on the top of the bridge were older type Mk IV and were carried side by side.

HMS NELSON Pennant 28
Nelson class battleship 1940-1

When World War II broke out, *Nelson* was with the Home Fleet and all her metal surfaces were painted MS4a overall, with the tops of the main guns painted in 507a. However, at times she was described as painted with 507a in patches. The weathering effect on re-painted ships can result in areas of old paint showing through as seawater wore off the latest layer, so it is possible that the 507a was merely being exposed from time to time. I have illustrated the ship here as she might have looked if weathering was the cause of the mottled effect. I have deliberately concentrated the effect around the bow, as that was the area where the greatest effect of weathering was usually seen. Since 1930, there were several changes to the bridge. Octuple 2pdr mounts were added just in front of the funnel, on the aft deck house and right aft on the quarterdeck. There were no single 2pdrs on the after end of the deckhouse or elsewhere. Quad 0.5in MG mounts were carried on

platforms on either side of the bridge. There were four launchers each on 'B' and 'C' turrets for the weapon known as UP (Unrotated Projectile). These eight-barrelled weapons fired rockets that trailed wires behind them and were intended to snare dive bombers, or at least force them to turn away. As a weapon, it proved quite useless. There were two aerials for Type 281 radar, one on each mast. This set was good for detecting aircraft but had little to no capability against surface targets. The set required two aerials; one for transmitting and one for receiving impulses. The overhead view shows the ship with most horizontal surfaces painted 507a or a shipboard mix between that and MS4a. The decks were unpainted but the wood has been allowed to fade to its natural colour, rather than being holystoned almost white, as it would in peacetime. The 6in mounts had a form of grey Corticene on the roof.

HMS NELSON Pennant 28
Nelson class battleship mid-1942

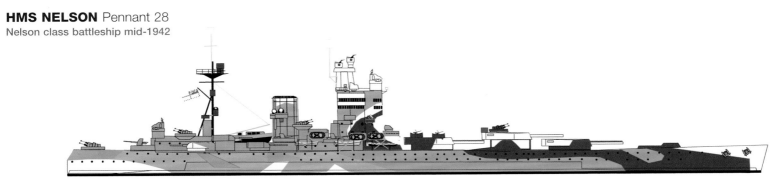

Nelson received a rather dramatic Admiralty-designed scheme in mid-1942 while under repair for torpedo damage received during the Malta convoy Operation Halberd. Pale grey 507c was applied to some extremities, but this was offset by areas of MS1 olive black, MS3 slate green and MS2 mid-olive. This confusion effect was intended to draw the eye toward the darker areas and confuse recognition. Note that the useless UP mountings on 'B' turret were removed and their place taken

by another octuple 2pdr mount, raising the total to six. Only a few 20mm could be spared, but four were mounted on 'C' turret and the quad 0.5in MG mounts on the side of the bridge were retained for now. Type 284 radar for the main guns was fitted to the directors and Type 285 radar was put on the AA directors. A Type 273 radar lantern was placed on the starfish level of the tripod mainmast.

HMS NELSON Pennant 28
Nelson class battleship

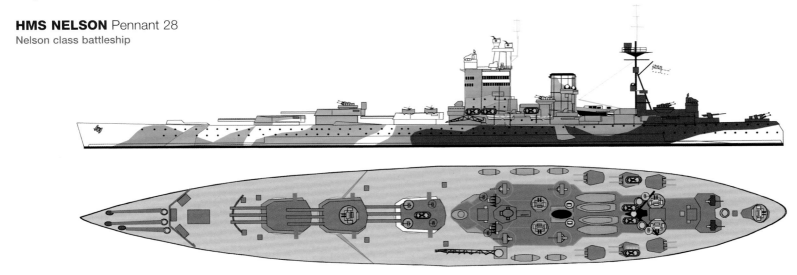

This illustration shows the port side of *Nelson* at the same time as above. The Admiralty plan had a different pattern on each side and the levels of colour use were not the same. As with the other illustration, the colours in use were 507c, MS1, MS3 and MS2. As some of these were very close together in shade, I have provided a faint edge so the reader can distinguish where they crossed or were side by side, but no such outline was applied in real life. The very dark tone of MS1 would tend to concentrate the eye of an observer and make it difficult to distinguish the actual length of the ship. Because the two ships of this class were so distinctive compared to most other battleships,

it was difficult to hide what there were and, but for the extensive time required to repair her torpedo damage, it is possible that there would not have been time to design and apply this rather complicated camouflage. The overhead view shows the previously wood decks painted with MS4a, while metal areas were 507a. The canvas over the boats appears lighter than the metal areas as was often the case. Wear on the decks often made them look patchy. The 4.7in AA guns were provided with shields, as experience had shown them too wet and exposed for efficient use.

HMS NELSON Pennant 28
Nelson class battleship 1943

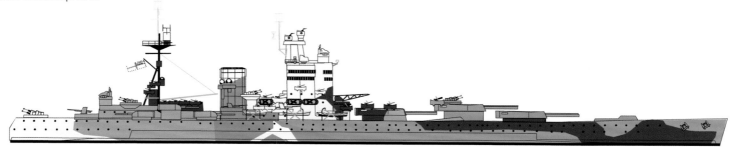

Nelson is shown here in a modification of the previous scheme, intended to be carried when ordered to the British Eastern Fleet. The heavy application of MS1 with G45 forward contrasts heavily with the use of B5 and 507b aft and with various areas of 507c. The ship was instead ordered to take part in Operation Pedestal in the Mediterranean before she could reach the Far East, then to return to the Home Fleet. But, within a month, she was sent to Gibraltar to join Force H and became involved in the Operation Torch landings. She remained with Force H and

took part in the landings on Sicily (Operation Husky), then various bombardments and followed by Operation Avalanche, the landings at Salerno. She took the Italian surrender at Malta and returned to the Home Fleet for the Normandy landings, having not yet reached the British Eastern Fleet as had been intended. During the period before departing the UK, her light AA was increased to twenty 20mm guns.

HMS NELSON Pennant 28
Nelson class battleship 1943

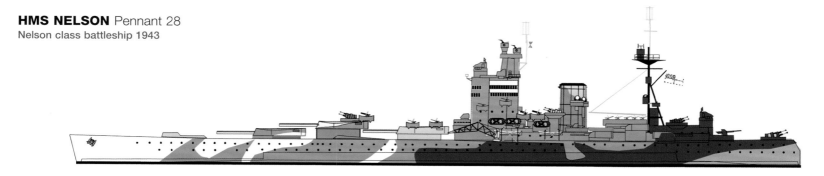

The 1943 scheme was an adaptation of that worn in 1942. MS3 was painted over and there were now some areas of B5 and 507b as well as 507c providing a light shade. Confidential Admiralty Fleet Orders (CAFO) had originally stated that it was too confusing within a squadron for a ship to have a different camouflage pattern on each side, but, from the appearance of *Nelson*, someone either forgot or decided to ignore the instruction. The effect of this scheme must have been very effective at a distance, especially in difficult visibility. Radar was now carried by all gun directors,

including Type 282 radar for light AA control of the octuple 2pdr mounts. Type 650 missile jamming gear was also carried as soon as available, plus Type 244 IFF on the Type 273 radar lantern, with a Type 253 IFF on the foremast. Although slow by World War II standards, *Nelson* was a very powerful ship and, after the pre-war teething troubles with her main guns had been resolved, she was a most effective and deadly bombardment unit.

HMS NELSON Pennant 28
Nelson class battleship 1945

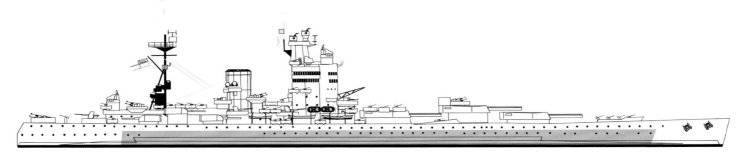

During D-Day, *Nelson* used her massive guns to support the landings but she was damaged by a mine on 22 June and was ordered to the USA for refit and repair. During this time, her light AA was substantially increased. Four USN-style quad 40mm guns were fitted, two before the bridge and two aft of the funnel. The 20mm guns were increased to sixty-five singles and, of course, she still had six octuple 2pdr pom-poms. Type 244 IFF and Type 253 IFF were upgraded along with Type 650 missile jammers. Although she initially returned to the UK to work up, the intent was that she would be sent to the Far East as soon as possible. The previous camouflage scheme was painted out and she now wore an overall 507c with a panel of washed out mid-blue. The tripod mainmast was painted with G5 grey black. *Nelson* was sent out to the Indian Ocean in April 1945

to join the British Eastern Fleet, where she relieved the battleship *Queen Elizabeth* as flagship. Her operations in the area were short-lived and limited to a few shore bombardments and covering minesweeping operations that were preparing for the invasion of Malaya. After the Japanese capitulation in August, she took the surrender of Penang and then went to Singapore to accept the surrender of all enemy forces in South East Asia. She was, in turn, relieved by the battleship *Howe* and returned to the UK where she became flagship of the Home Fleet during November 1945 and remained as such until 1946 when she was used for training. Reduced to the reserve fleet in 1947, she was used for target trials including live ammunition dive bombing tests. The ship was then sold for scrap in 1949.

HMS RODNEY Pennant 29
Nelson class battleship 1939-40

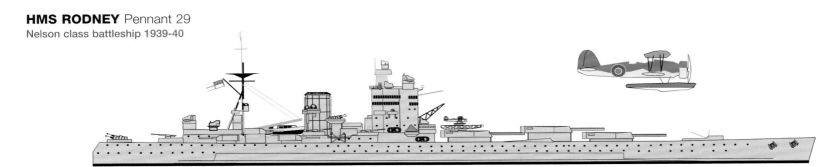

Rodney was dressed in overall MS507a at the commencement of World War II. The decks were wood but no longer scrubbed, which allowed them to fade to a pale grey. The ship was one of the few in the entire fleet with search radar and this illustration shows an aerial for Type 79Y radar on the mainmast. It was intended for air warning, and could pick up aircraft fifty to sixty nautical miles away, but had no capability against low-flying aircraft. It was able to pick up large ships at around ten to twelve nautical miles. It was only around 40% effective much of the time but, for the period, that was far superior to anything else in the fleet. Note that *Rodney* had a triangular-shaped recess in the bridge on the starboard side only. She was fitted with a catapult on 'X' turret and a large

crane for handling aircraft on the port side. There was no hangar, but the aircraft could be placed on deck in a relatively sheltered position abreast the bridge for maintenance. A Swordfish floatplane was provided. The ship had a powerful armament of nine 16in guns and twelve 6in secondary guns. Heavy AA was provided by six single 4.7in high angle guns. Light AA comprised an octuple 2pdr mount aft and one each side of the funnel. Quad 0.5in MG mounts were carried on each side of the bridge. Although the heavier weapons remained the same for the rest of the war, the light AA was vastly increased as time went on.

HMS RODNEY Pennant 29
Nelson class battleship 1940

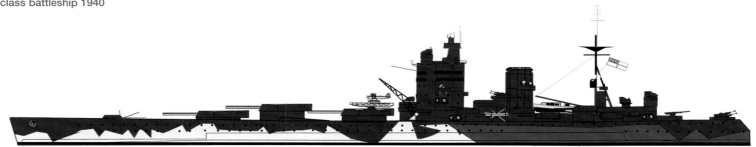

After air raids on Scapa Flow, some of the ships there were given a rather strange camouflage based on 1940 brown and 1940 green over 507c. This produced a considerable contrast but placing the brown high accentuated, rather than broke up, the silhouette of the ship. The life of this scheme within the fleet was quite short and was mainly intended for ships that spent time anchored in Scapa Flow. The decks were apparently painted 507a, as were all horizontal metal surfaces. The secondary turret roofs were covered with Corticene but of a grey type. The armament did not

change during this period but the radar was upgraded from Type 79Y to Type 279. This was a far more reliable set that could pick up aircraft between sixty-five and ninety-five miles away with reasonable accuracy and a low flying aircraft at six miles. It also had capability for surface search, being able to pick up a large ship at 16,000 yards and a smaller one at 10,000. Its disadvantage was that it required two aerials; one on each mast.

HMS RODNEY Pennant 29
Nelson class battleship 1940

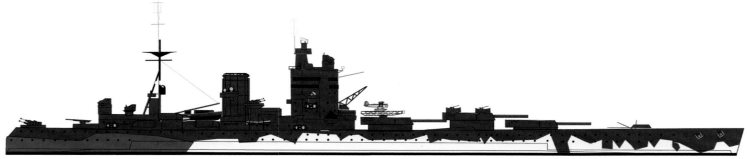

This illustrates the starboard side of *Rodney* in her brown and green scheme. As can be seen, this scheme may have been of help while at anchor in the Orkneys but at sea would have produced an easily recognisable silhouette. Only the pale 507c may have caused confusion as to speed through its location low and along the hull. The uppermost of the AA directors on top of the bridge was

painted white, apparently to make it harder to see when the ship was on the horizon, but one wonders why the same was not done to other parts of the upper works. At some point in the year, two 20mm AA were placed on top of B turret as shown here.

HMS RODNEY Pennant 29
Nelson class battleship 27 May 1941

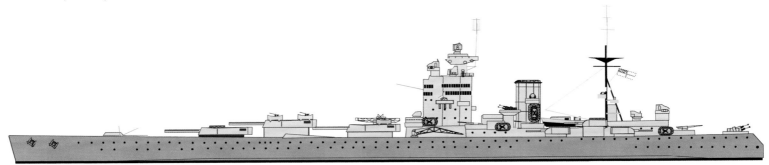

At the time of the sinking of the *Bismarck*, *Rodney* had reverted to an all-grey MS4a scheme with 507a on all decks and horizontal surfaces. However, examination of photographs seems to indicate the hull was darker, possibly 507a, or a mix of that with MS4a, which could fit with confusing reports of exactly what the shade of grey was at different times, it having been reported as both during 1941. There were two single 20mm on 'B' turret, but, again, photographic examination suggests there were also mounts either side of the catapult on 'C' turret. The quad 0.5in MG mounts were still carried on each side of the bridge. Note that the aircraft crane is stowed and there was no aircraft aboard during the *Bismarck* action. At the time of the *Bismarck* chase, *Rodney* was on her way to the USA for a major refit. Packing cases of extremely valuable equipment were stowed on deck for fitting in Boston and had to be thrown overboard to clear the ship for action. The secondary gun directors aft of the tripod mast were to be removed during the US refit but were in use during the battle when the 6in guns were recorded as having fired 716 rounds. The main guns fired 375 rounds, with a claimed 40 hits, having commenced firing at 25,000 yards after sighting the target at 28,000 yards. This compared favourably with HMS *King George V*, which did have gunnery radar. Note that, although Type 279 radar aerials can be seen fore and aft, the ship did not have gunnery radar fitted as some sources say. It may well have been aboard, for fitting in the USA, but it had certainly not been installed.

HMS RODNEY Pennant 29
Nelson class battleship 27 May 1941

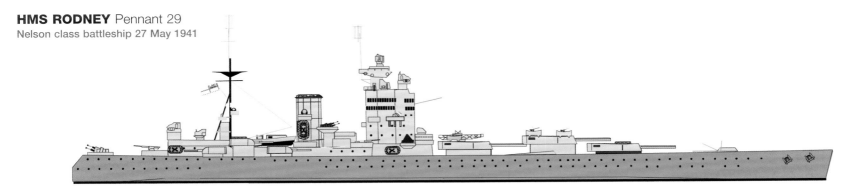

This illustration shows the starboard side of *Rodney* at the time of the *Bismarck* action. Note there had been changes to the bridge since 1940 and there were considerably more Carley floats carried. These included two or three on the rear of each main turret, one on each of the upper 6in turrets and three on top of 'A' turret. The foremast arrangement had been changed and it now also carried an aerial for Type 279 radar. Note that the ship's boats previously carried at the main deck level do not appear in photographs of *Rodney* at the time of the action. It is possible these were relocated to the boat deck or were jettisoned as a fire risk. Prior to the event, the top speed of the ship was considered to have dropped to 20 knots but, due to the work of her engine room crew, a speed of 22 knots was recorded. That was quite a feat for an ageing battleship with badly-worn machinery. It was not without repercussions and one of the boilers broke down and had to be repaired in extremely difficult conditions.

HMS RODNEY Pennant 29
Nelson class battleship 1942-3

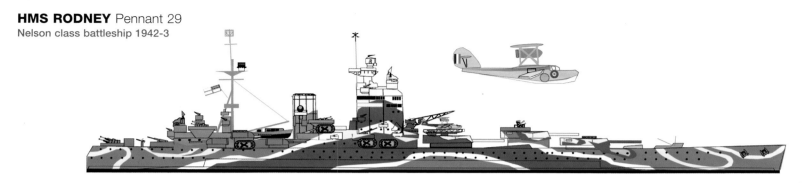

This illustration shows the starboard side of *Rodney* in an Admiralty disruptive scheme specifically designed for her. The colours were 507c, MS3, MS1, MS2 and B5. This pattern was to be retained until the end of her service. However, it varied a little in layout and the colours changed from time to time purely due to the paint available. It took around 15,000 litres to paint a battleship, so patching up was preferred to entirely new schemes being applied too often. In this illustration, a lantern for

Type 271 surface search radar has been added to the starfish of the rear tripod. This set was intended for use by escort vessels and the Type 273 for large warships. Presumably, the correct set was not available. At the head of the mainmast was an aerial for a Type 281 AW set. An aerial for a Type 291 general warning radar was at the head of the pole foremast. The main gun directors had Type 284 radar, the Mk IV HACS for the heavy AA had Type 285 and the 2pdr directors had Type 282.

HMS RODNEY Pennant 29
Nelson class battleship 1942-3

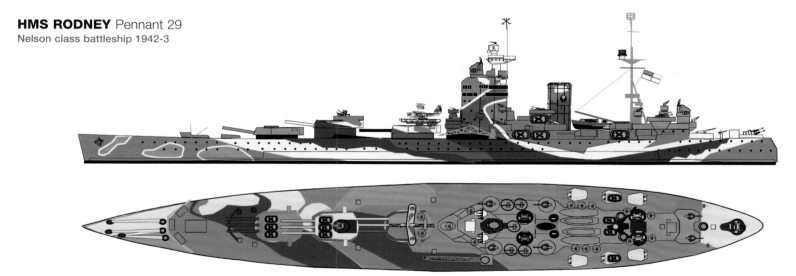

Port side and overhead views of the Admiralty disruptive scheme designed for this ship. The light areas are 507c pale grey, with MS3 and MS1 providing the darkest areas and B5 the blue grey effects. MS2 mid-olive is the darker shade around the bridge and amidships hull. This is the scheme as designed and first applied but, as time went by, there were patch ups by the crew and, in some cases, colours changed either slightly or dramatically. However, the same general pattern was followed. The Swordfish floatplane previously carried was replaced by a Walrus amphibian. The two single 20mm previously on 'B' turret were relocated on the side of the bridge and others

added. The tubs aft with projections were not light AA; they were directors for the 2pdr mounts with Type 282 radar. There was another mid-way up the side of the bridge. The most prominent one was at the rear of the aft gun director, just above the aft 4.7in mounts. By 1943, this ship was badly in need of a major overhaul and, despite breaks for refits, was in an increasingly poor condition. But she was considered an essential asset for the support of amphibious landings and forced to keep on serving. Since her burst of speed during the *Bismarck* action, her service speed was now below 20 knots.

HMS RODNEY Pennant 29
Nelson class battleship 1944-5

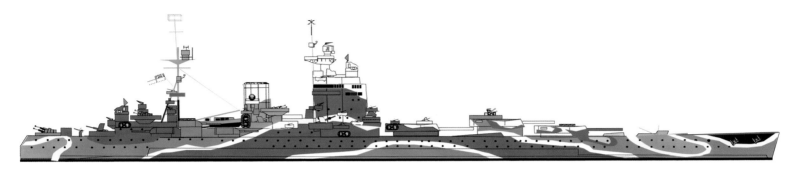

Although retaining the same basic camouflage scheme as planned for her, over a period of time it was changed according to available paint and who was available to carry out the work. During a quick refit, this would be the dockyard but at other times it was the duty of the crew to tend to her paint. The two patches forward that were originally B5 were painted with MS1 for the foremost one and MS3 for the other. They still retained the same general shape. Similarly, the patch at the stern, outlined in 507c, also became MS3. Most of the aft superstructure was changed to MS1. However, one must not presume these were the only variations from the Admiralty Disruptive

Scheme. It was carried for three years and photographic evidence suggests the above were far from the only changes. Although quite worn out, the ship was kept in service for the D-Day landings and other operations. However, without the time to spare for a major rebuild of her engines and other equipment, it was obvious any future service would be as a bombardment vessel. For this reason, there does not seem to have been the same effort put into her maintenance as her sister ship HMS *Nelson*, which was in a far better state of repair

HMS RODNEY Pennant 29
Nelson class battleship 1944-5

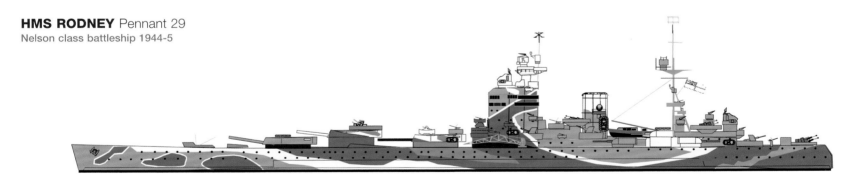

Rodney wore her Admiralty Disruptive Scheme until she was scrapped. In 1944, she took part in numerous operations supporting land forces during the liberation of Europe. Tired and limping on faltering engines, she continued to give heavy fire support to the ground forces until the fighting had reached a point where she was no longer needed. The ship was then in such a poor state, due to lack of repairs and essential maintenance, that she was reduced to an almost static flagship at Scapa Flow from the end of 1944. She would not sail from there again until she went into reserve and then to the scrap yard. As can be seen on the port side, various changes were made to colours and some boundaries. This could fool the reader into thinking it is a completely new camouflage but it

was merely the result of hasty maintenance and the use of whatever paints were available. Even a battleship could not be expected to carry huge amounts of paint, and they would have been a fire hazard even if it had. By the end of 1943, the Type 271 radar lantern had been replaced by the originally-intended Type 273 lantern, with a Type 244 IFF on top. The small boxes at the join of the tripod and on the light foremast were for Type 650 missile jammers, to counter the German guided bombs increasingly being encountered. There were now five twin and fifty-six single 20mm guns carried and the 4.7in AA guns were provided with shields.

KING GEORGE V CLASS BATTLESHIPS

HMS KING GEORGE V Pennant 41
King George V class battleship 1940

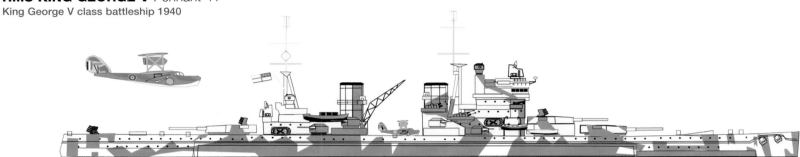

King George V was painted in camouflage by her builders while still in the yard. War had broken out and it was feared the Luftwaffe may attack her before she could even be handed over to the Royal Navy. The scheme was intended to hide the ship in a dockyard, hence the high contrast of dark and light grey. The peaks were probably intended to match the roofs of local industrial buildings. However, it was retained during her trials and for the first few months of her active naval service. The ship entered service with multiple UP (Unrotated Projectile) rocket launchers; one on 'B' turret, two on 'Y' turret and another on the quarterdeck. She was supposed to have four quad 0.5in MG mounts but reports from the fleet on their limitations were already coming in and they were never fitted. Instead, the ship waited many months until 20mm Oerlikon weapons became available.

HMS KING GEORGE V Pennant 41
King George V class battleship 1940

King George V was the only one of her class that had an external degaussing cable for protection against magnetic mines; all her sister ships carried it internally. As on the starboard side, the camouflage scheme included many peaks which would have been suitable camouflage against a dockyard background. At sea, the lines would have broken up the appearance of the ship and could have been of some value. The decks are believed to have been wood on delivery, but no doubt they were not holystoned. The triangular aerial on the aft tripod was an early HF/DF. The main gunnery directors carried Type 284 radar, which was quite advanced for its day. No radar was fitted for the HA directors and the 2pdr mounts had no directors at all, although positions for them had been allocated. At the head of the masts were aerials for an early Type 291 radar: one for the transmitter and the other for the receiver. Compared to her appearance at the end of the war, the ship was very bare of aerials for radar sets, light flak directors and light AA weapons.

HMS KING GEORGE V Pennant 41
King George V class battleship December 1940

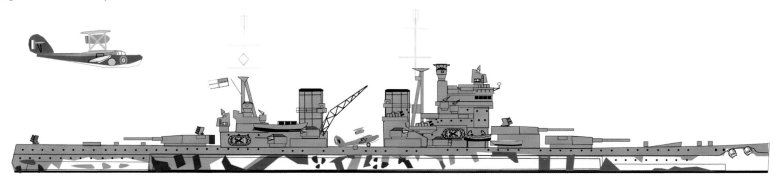

An unofficial camouflage with some resemblance to World War I dazzle was applied to the ship some months after completing her trials and work up. With colour paints in short supply, the paints used were 507a, 507b and 507c, all of which were probably available in quantity. The design for each side was quite different, as can be seen. Some of the small patches of the darker shade may have been of limited use since they were applied to such a tiny area. Nonetheless, the pale 507c may have given the impression of a ship at high speed. A base for Type 271 radar was fitted between the two HA directors on the back of the bridge top. It was not unusual for capital ships to carry this set when there were no Type 273 radar sets available and it would take a few months for an actual set to be installed. Note that the armament has not changed since completion, but directors for the 2pdr mounts had been added, although they still lacked their Type 282 radar.

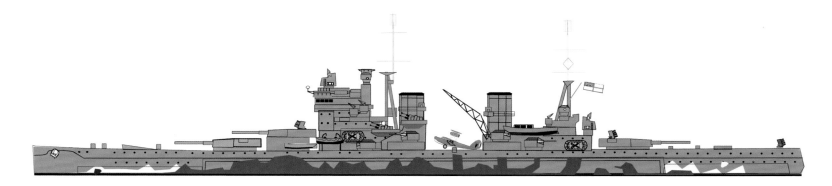

The port side view of the camouflage worn from the end of trials and work up. Unlike the starboard side, the port side had very little 507c showing. Perhaps they ran out of paint! But apparently there was a lot of 507a and 507b still available. Nonetheless, the amount of 507c at the bow and stern was still sufficient to give the impression that the ship was underway at speed. This scheme was painted out prior to the action that sank *Bismarck*. The decks were wood, not painted, but allowed to fade to grey. *King George V* spent all her early service as part of the Home Fleet, much of that time as flagship.

HMS KING GEORGE V Pennant 41
King George V class battleship 1941

At the time of the *Bismarck* sinking, *King George V* was in overall MS4a Home Fleet grey. The decks and horizontal metal surfaces were painted in the same shade but the turret tops were 507a dark grey. This illustration shows her some months later, still in the same scheme, but with changes to radar and armament. The main gun directors had Type 284 radar fitted for the main guns but the HA directors still lack Type 285 radar. Directors for the 2pdr mountings were added and these were fitted with Type 282 radar. Type 291 remained at the mastheads as the air search radar but it also had a surface detection capability similar to that of Type 271, although not as reliable or clear.

HMS KING GEORGE V Pennant 41
King George V class battleship 1941

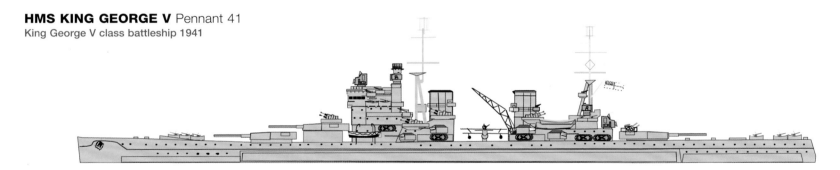

The alterations and additions by late 1941 included the removal of the useless UP mountings, adding another octuple 2pdr mount to the top of 'B' turret and a quad 2pdr mount on top of 'X' turret. There were five single 20mm on the forecastle, five more on the quarterdeck, four on the aft superstructure and two on each side of the bridge for a total of eighteen. Two Walrus amphibians made up the air complement, although four could be carried if necessary. Placing the Type 271 radar lantern on the top of the bridge between the HA directors was unusual and her sister ships had it on the foremast tripod or the tripod mainmast. The lack of Type 285 radar on the HA directors made the 5.25in secondary guns less effective against aircraft but radar would be fitted in 1942.

HMS KING GEORGE V Pennant 41
King George V class battleship June 1942

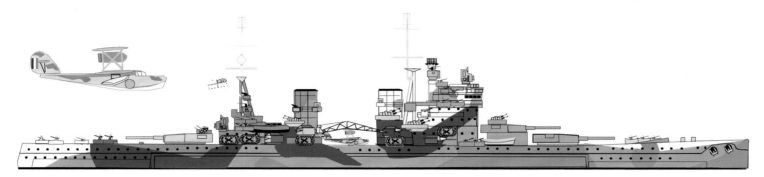

An Admiralty-designed camouflage was provided in mid-1942 and was worn in similar fashion by the three remaining ships of the class. The shades were 507c pale grey, B6 mid-grey, B5 blue grey and 507a battleship grey. The decks were a dark grey, possibly also 507a. This scheme provided for colours that were quite close in shade, allowing them to blend together to help make the ship's details harder to define. The dark areas were specifically intended to concentrate the viewer's vision and make the recognition details harder to determine. Extra AA directors for the 2pdr mounts were added and these were fitted with Type 282 radar. The HA directors were finally fitted with Type 285 radar, making the 5.25in guns far more useful in the AA role. The 20mm AA was increased to thirty-six singles and one twin mount. One of the problems with this class was the low bow and lack of sheer made them very wet forward and, as a result, they were often unable to use some of the 20mm guns in a strong sea. Although the main guns had given considerable trouble when the ship entered service, the problems were eventually solved but the 14in turrets were never as reliable as the twin 15in mounts of the older classes.

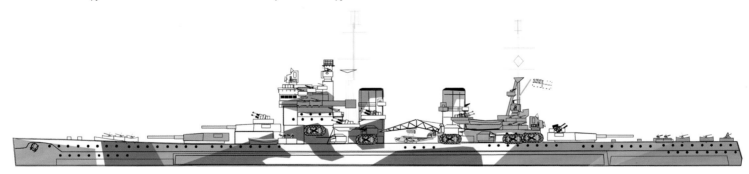

Port side view of the camouflage worn from mid-1942 until early 1944. The pattern was different on both sides, as can be seen. During the period it was worn, there were minor variations when paintwork was touched up and rust chipped. As with other ships, this could mean that a different shade was used in some areas or that the actual shape of the patterns could alter slightly; but, in general, the scheme remained much the same. The 2pdr mount on the aft turret remained a quad mount through this period, as a replacement octuplet mount was not available. After protection duty for convoys to Russia and various other operations, she was moved to Gibraltar as part of Force H for the various amphibious landings conducted in the Mediterranean. She was present for the surrender of the Italian fleet and escorted it to Malta, before returning to the Home Fleet.

HMS KING GEORGE V Pennant 41
King George V class battleship July 1944

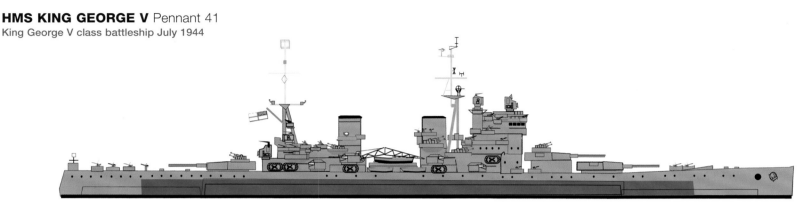

King George V is shown here in the Admiralty standard scheme for ships in UK waters. B55 formed the overall shade, with a panel of B30. The ship was given an AA upgrade and general refit at Liverpool from February to July 1944 during which many changes took place. American quad 40mm Bofors mounts were placed on the deck house on each side of the aft tripod. The quad 2pdr on 'X' turret was replaced by an octuple version. A bank of six twin 20mm guns in a raised platform was added between the aft funnel and the aft tripod, displacing the boats previously stored there. She also carried another twenty-six single 20mm Oerlikon guns. All aircraft facilities were removed. One

hangar was converted to a cinema for the crew and the other into offices and extra berths. A large number of scuttles were plated over, although many of those around the officers' quarters aft remained unchanged. The external degaussing cable was removed and another fitted internally. The direction finder hut and its aerial was banished to the very stern, to keep it away from interference from the other electronics. One starboard anchor was landed to save weight. These ships proved rather short-ranged for Pacific operations and the Royal Navy lacked a strong fleet train; thus, they had to call on the USN for assistance, somewhat straining relations between the two navies.

HMS KING GEORGE V Pennant 41
King George V class battleship 1945

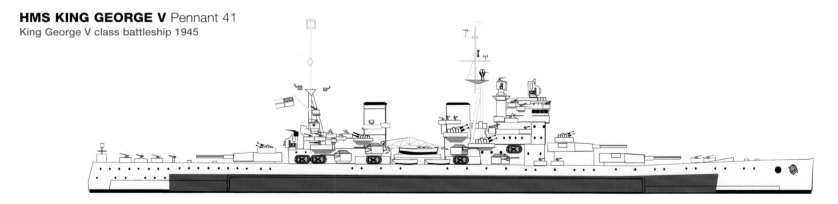

On transfer to the Pacific theatre, a scheme of overall 507c with a panel of B20 was applied. For recognition purposes, this fitted in with many of the US ships the British Pacific Fleet operated with. The intent behind a pale grey ship with a dark blue panel was to confuse the viewer as to how far away it was by making the ship look shorter. Since the early war period, the ship had gained lots of electronics, many of which had not even been thought of prior to the war. It is a tribute to British manufacturing that they were able to design, build and continually improve radar sets. At the top of the mainmast, there was a Type 281B AW set and below that was the HF/DF set. The boxes at the

end of the crosstree were for the Type 650 missile jammer. The 2pdr directors now carried Type 282 radar. At the foremast was a Type 293 radar with 'Headache' missile jammers, Type 242 and Type 253 IFF. At the head of the tripod was a Type 277 general warning set. The HA directors had Type 285 radar and the main gunnery director had an upgraded Type 274. In addition, there were various aerials for TBS (Talk Between Ships) and other radios. Her light AA armament at this time totalled eight 40mm Bofors, sixty-four 2pdr, and thirty-eight 20mm. Other modifications were made to the armament and electronics when the ship returned home immediately after the end of the war.

HMS PRINCE OF WALES Pennant 53
King George V class battleship early 1941

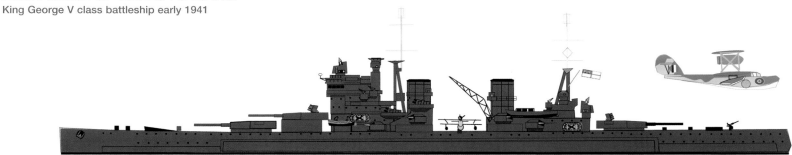

While still under completion, this ship's hull was badly damaged during a Luftwaffe bombing raid and her entry into service delayed. That sort of damage is always considered very unlucky and, for the typical sailor, a bad omen with some considering her ill-fated from the start. *Prince of Wales* is shown here in 507a battleship grey, which was also worn by *Hood* during the *Bismarck* action. The decks were natural wood. As completed, she carried three UP (Unrotated Projectile) mountings with two on 'A' and one on 'B' turret. There was a single 40mm Bofors fitted on the quarterdeck. Type 279 AW radar was carried at the mast tops, one being the transmitter and the other the receiver. She was to be fitted with a platform for a Type 271 radar between the two HA directors on the bridge top, but this was not immediately available and only the platform was initially installed. However, Type 284 gunnery radar was supplied for the main gun directors. The planned four quad 0.5in MG mounts were never fitted. An octuple 2pdr AA mount was positioned on each side of the bridge rear and each side of the fore funnel. Shortly after completion she was given Type 285 radar on the HACS directors and the 2pdr directors were fitted with Type 282 radar. Why a single 40mm Bofors gun was fitted aft is unclear but it appears to have been considered a substitute for another UP launcher intended to be fitted there. No doubt it was a far better weapon when needed.

HMS PRINCE OF WALES Pennant 53
King George V class battleship July 1941

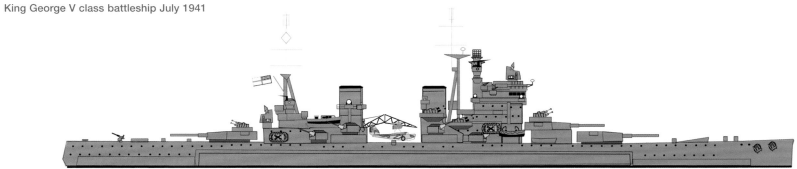

During the Denmark Straits battle with *Bismarck*, the *Prince of Wales* was not fully worked up. There were still civilian dockyard workers on board trying to fix the numerous teething problems the new ship had and her turrets suffered many defects. 'A' turret flooded and then jammed completely just before the end of the action; 'Y' turret jammed after twenty salvoes and only 'B' turret functioned well. In addition, the Type 284 gunnery radar was not functioning and the Type 281 set was used to obtain ranges, although not intended for that purpose. Nonetheless, she was able to score some hits, one of which contributed to the final loss of *Bismarck*. In return, *Prince of Wales* suffered four 15in shell hits. One passed through the bridge without detonating, but caused casualties, the second, which also did not explode, went overboard, another only partially deto- nated and the last one was located, unexploded, and defused after the ship had returned to port. Hits from the 8in guns of the German cruiser *Prinz Eugen* comprised one that did not explode and was thrown overboard and two that only partially detonated. Had German ordnance not been so defective, there would certainly have been more damage. During repairs, she appears to have been repainted in 507b overall, which was carried until August 1941. The UP mountings were removed and she received octuple 2pdr mounts instead, one each on 'B' and 'Y' turrets. It was intended to also fit similar mounts each side of the aft funnel but these were unavailable. Type 271 radar was installed on the platform between the two forward HA directors. In July, she rejoined the Home Fleet.

HMS PRINCE OF WALES Pennant 53
King George V class battleship August 1941

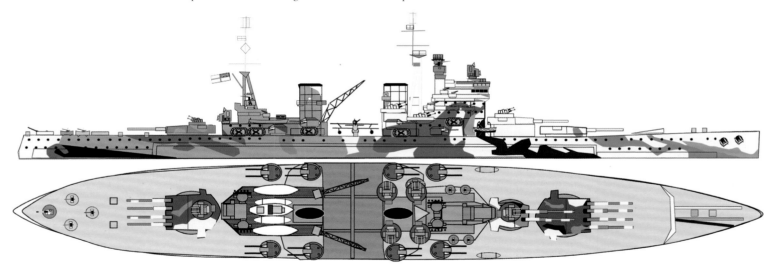

In August 1941, *Prince of Wales* was repainted to an Admiralty Disruptive scheme comprising six colours. These were MS1, B5, B6, 507c, MS3 and dark stone. The intent was obviously to break up the outline of the ship to make it hard to identify or determine speed and course. Once at sea, however, the theory of this combination of colours was not as effective as expected and adjustments were made. Schemes such as this would be found to be difficult to maintain as the ship had to carry sufficient amounts of all six colours in order to repair rust and wear damage. It was also found to be a time-consuming task to continually touch up so many different shades. The armament was increased by seven single 20mm AA, three on the quarterdeck and two each side of the bridge. There is conflicting information regard the 40mm aft but I have left it in for this illustration. For all intents and purposes, the ship was in excellent state after her battle repairs and set about working up to her full extent. Most of the turret defects were corrected and she was considered a fully operational unit of the Fleet.

This illustrates the starboard side and provides an overhead view of *Prince of Wales* in her Admiralty Disruptive scheme. It is much darker than the port side and used less MS3. The deck remained natural wood. The patterns on the hull are quite different on both sides. This had been frowned upon in Confidential Admiralty Fleet Orders, which stated it was confusing for ships in the same squadron if individual units looked different on each side. However, that seems to have been frequently ignored by the Design Department, with this scheme as a classic example. For ships that spent a lot of time at sea, elaborate patterns were subject to continual wear and tear from heavy seas, which could peel paint off whole areas and streak the ship with rust, completely changing the focus of the designed camouflage. For this reason, the scheme as shown here was altered before the ship sailed for Singapore on 25 October 1941. Some camouflage was initially applied to the turret tops but it is unclear if this was retained or painted out later. There are also reports that some of the camouflage may have been carried up over the wood decks, but evidence of this is not conclusive.

HMS PRINCE OF WALES Pennant 53
King George V class battleship 8 December 1941

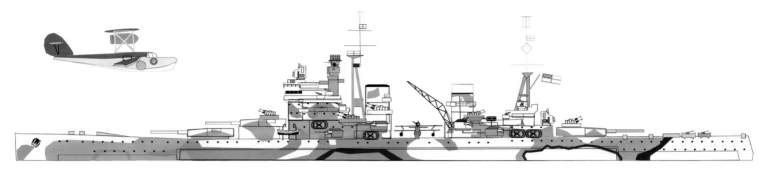

Prince of Wales had her Admiralty Disruptive Scheme simplified by the time she was ordered to Singapore as the flagship of Force Z. The general pattern remained the same but some colours were deleted. The basic colours were now 507c overall, with areas of B5, B6 and MS1. Interestingly, the top of the aft funnel was painted out in white. This could have been to confuse the enemy as to which ship she was. Prince of Wales and Repulse, the other capital ship assigned to Force Z, both had three turrets, but Repulse's aft funnel was lower than the fore. The provision of a heavy black line under the white area on the funnel is further evidence of making the top of the funnel appear lower.

HMS PRINCE OF WALES Pennant 53
King George V class battleship 8 December 1941

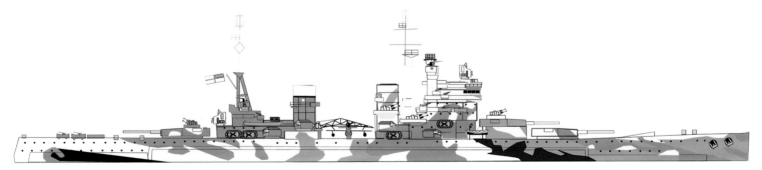

Starboard side of Prince of Wales after the camouflage had been simplified. The colours are 507c, B5, B6 and MS1. Some MS3 was present when the ship left the UK but was probably painted out when she stopped to rendezvous with Repulse at Colombo. The aft funnel top was painted out on this side as well. The upper decks may have been camouflaged; no record of this exists but, where it was done, it was usual to carry colours over the deck from each side. There was no air support available for Force Z when it sailed to intercept the Japanese landings in Malaya, even though it was known how important this was from battles in the Mediterranean. But the Japanese were an unknown quantity and pre-war intelligence had downplayed the efficiency and the quality of Japanese aircraft. The devastating accuracy the attackers showed shocked the world, in that two first-line capital ships in fully worked up condition, able to manoeuvre at speed and heavily armed with anti-aircraft guns could be so quickly overwhelmed. At the time, Prince of Wales was the most modern battleship to be sunk at sea by aircraft of any nation. The battleship theorists were shocked and the air power enthusiasts could say they had told them so.

HMS DUKE OF YORK Pennant 17
King George V class battleship 1941

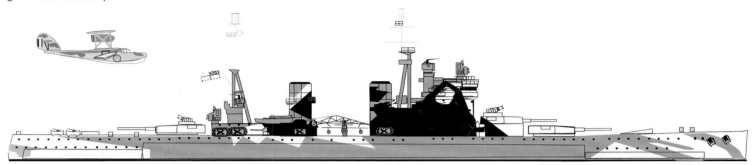

Duke of York on completion. This was an experimental camouflage scheme produced by the Admiralty Design Department and was worn by the ship from September to November 1941 only. It was the same on both sides and comprised B15, MS2 and 507c. The intent appears to have been to hide the dimensions of the hull while creating an impression of speed. The very dark blue could have been a special mix, although it is similar to B15. This colour was obviously intended to create a false impression of the size of the upper works as well as helping with a general distortion of the outline. When viewed at sea, it was considered insufficiently confusing to be worth the maintenance it required. The ship was completed with Type 284 radar for the main guns, Type 285 for the 5.25in HA directors, Type 282 for the 2pdr directors and Type 281 air warning radar. An air observation platform was installed between the two HA directors on the bridge but not a base for a radar lantern. That was installed on the mast later.

HMS DUKE OF YORK Pennant 17
King George V class battleship 1942

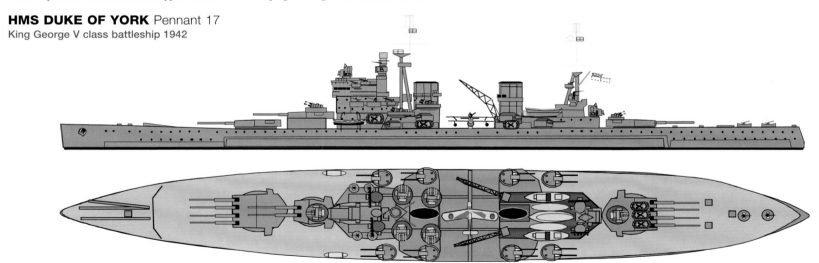

This view of *Duke of York* illustrates her appearance in mid-1942, when her initial camouflage was painted out in 507b medium grey. The overhead view shows the wood decks remained unpainted. However, all other horizontal surfaces were painted in 507b. Six 20mm single Oerlikon were added, two on the quarterdeck and two each side of the bridge, and octuple 2pdr mounts were placed on 'B' and 'X' turrets. A Type 273 radar lantern was placed on the tripod foremast.

HMS **DUKE OF YORK** Pennant 17
King George V class battleship March 1943 – September 1944

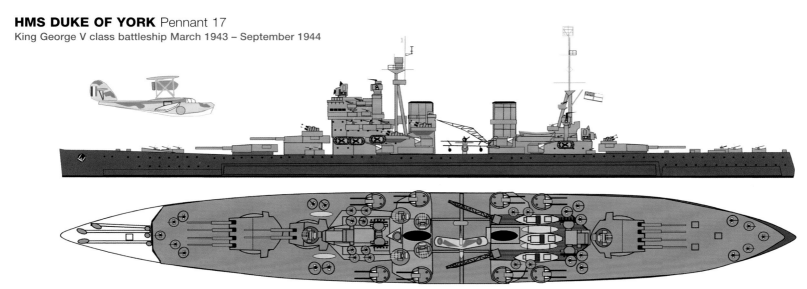

Duke of York from March 1943. The hull is painted in 507a/G10 and the superstructure in MS2. This style of camouflage was widely used by the Home Fleet, where *Duke of York* was stationed from her commissioning until late in the war. In dull northern areas, this proved a satisfactory camouflage and was easy to maintain. The wood decks have been painted grey, possibly 507b, but the area at the bow appears to have been painted pale grey. The ship was fitted with additional 20mm AA and carried a total of thirty-two at this time. Type 273 radar was added to the top of the fore tripod and Type 281 AW radar replaced the earlier Type 279. There were also aerials for IFF, HF/DF and TBS.

HMS **DUKE OF YORK** Pennant 17
King George V class battleship late 1944

Before sailing for the British Pacific Fleet, *Duke of York* had further modifications. She is illustrated here in 507c as the overall shade, with a panel of B20 on the hull. The decks apparently remained grey. The searchlight platform on the aft funnel of this ship had an emergency bridge added on the forward end, which was larger than that carried by any other ships of this class and is a recognition point when distinguishing this ship from her sisters. The light AA was considerably increased. There were quad 2pdr mounts either side of 'A' turret, on each side of the bridge, and two side by side on the quarterdeck. There was a single 20mm on either side of the bridge, above and forward of the 2pdr mount, with a twin 20mm lower down. Behind the aft funnel, the former boat deck carried a set of twin 20mm and below that another octuple 2pdr mount was fitted. Aft of that, near the legs of the tripod mainmast, a USN-style quad 40mm mount was fitted on each side of the ship. There were two single 20mm on the aft deckhouse on each side of the director and two more on each side at deck level. She has Type 277 radar set in place of the Type 273 previously carried on the forward tripod. She also had the usual IFF, TBS and 'Headache' fittings. Aircraft facilities were removed and the boats moved amidships.

HMS ANSON Pennant 79
King George V class battleship 1941-3

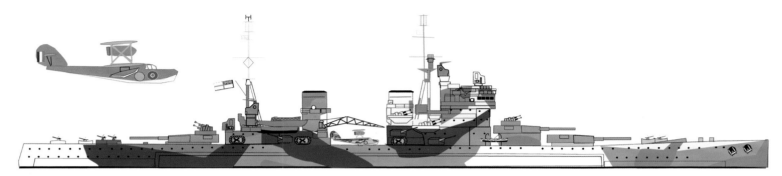

Anson is shown here while with the Home Fleet during 1941-3. The dark paint of this Admiralty scheme tends to shorten the ship while the light shades help to make the other areas less prominent and thus accentuate the effect of the dark. The camouflage was designed for this class and *Anson* was completed this way. The areas that appear white are 501c, the dark shade is MS1, the mid-grey is B6 and the blue grey is B5. The decks remained plain wood but the turret tops were MS1. All other horizontal surfaces were B6 mid-grey. Although the pattern was used on three ships of the class, there were individual variations in the shapes of the panels. Later, when the paint was being touched up, these variations could be further changed slightly. She was completed with octuple

2pdr mounts on 'A' and 'X' turrets as well as the four other mounts carried by the rest of the class. There were eighteen single 20mm Oerlikon guns fitted. Type 279 aerials dominated the mast tops along with a Type 244 IFF on the mainmast. A Type 271 radar lantern can be seen on the forward tripod and was later replaced by the similar Type 273, which was specifically designed for large ships. Type 285 radar was also carried, along with Type 282 for the 2pdr mounts, but, surprisingly, there was no Type 284 radar fitted to the main gun directors until the end of 1942. This camouflage was retained until early 1944.

HMS ANSON Pennant 79
King George V class battleship 1941-3

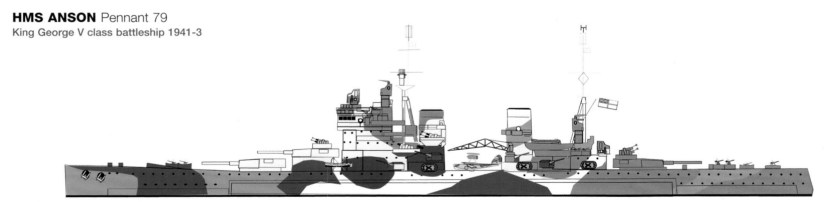

Anson's port side in the Admiralty-designed Disruptive Scheme. Here, the dark and light colours are arranged with most of the centre painted out to suggest the viewer is seeing two ships. Again, the light colour on the hull was 501c but the masts were mostly white, as was most equipment carried above the bridge level. The other shades were again MS1, B6 and B5. This scheme was worn by all ships of the class, except *Prince of Wales*, but there were variations from one ship to another. The armament and electronics were the same as in the illustration of her starboard side above. This ship carried Mk V HA secondary gun directors in place of the older Mk IV on the earlier ships of the class.

HMS ANSON Pennant 79
King George V class battleship 1944

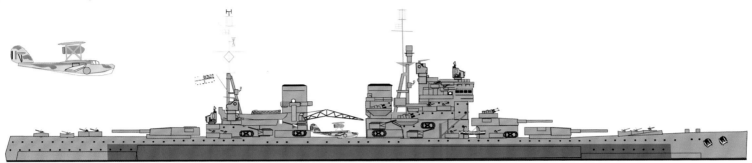

Anson is shown here in the Admiralty Standard Scheme B for Home Fleet units introduced in 1944. The combination of a B30 panel on an overall B55 ship was thought to be the best colour for ships in the North Atlantic and, as it only required two colours, was easy to maintain. The decks remained unpainted but all metal horizontal surfaces were painted in B6. The mast tops are shown here in pale grey, so they can be seen by the reader, but the scheme called for them to be white. Changes to the light AA included an additional eighteen 20mm Oerlikon guns. The forward radar lantern was changed to a Type 273. The forward tripod was given a reinforcing strut. The box aerials on the tripod masts were for Type 650 missile jammers to counter the Luftwaffe's increasing use of air-launched missiles. This ship had Mk V secondary HA directors on completion.

HMS ANSON Pennant 79
King George V class battleship March 1945

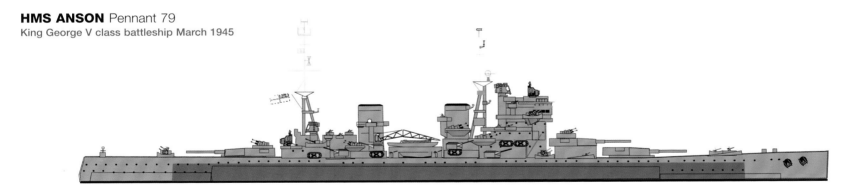

Admiralty Standard Scheme A is illustrated here on *Anson* in 1945. The hull was to be G10 and the superstructure G45. All steel decks were 507a/G10 but wood decks were unpainted. The entire hull could have been in G10 or just the central panel. The masts were painted white. The ship underwent a major refit from July 1944 until March 1945. The period was extended due to repairs and refits on other ships being prepared for service in the Pacific region, plus the slow delivery of the new Mk VI secondary gun directors, of which four replaced her earlier Mk V type. She was the only ship of this class to carry that type of secondary director. AA armament was substantially increased with the addition of two quad 2pdr mounts on the quarterdeck, two more on the side of the bridge structure, as well as two on deck abreast the bridge. Two US-type quad 40mm were added on the aft deckhouse and her 20mm guns altered to twenty-five in total in six twin and thirteen single mountings. Type 262, Type 275, Type 277 and Type 291 radars were added. The replacement of the previously-mounted Type 279 radar by Type 281 meant she only required one aerial but the masts were still crowded with all kinds of aerials for TBS, IFF and Type 650 missile jammers.

HMS ANSON Pennant 79
King George V class battleship July-August 1945

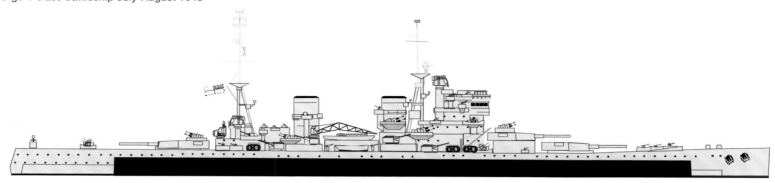

Anson left the Home Fleet on 25 April 1945 under orders to join the British Pacific Fleet and proceeded to Colombo via Malta. By the time she reached Sydney, she was wearing a typical British Pacific Fleet scheme of MS4a with a hull panel in B15. It is possible that some ships used 507c for an even lighter look. All horizontal metal surfaces were painted 507a/G10 but the wood area of her decks remained unpainted. Masts were white. The only change to her armament was the fitting of another quad 2pdr on each side of the bridge and some 20mm were removed. The war with Japan ended while she was still in Sydney but she joined Task Force 111.4, which sailed for Hong Kong with naval personnel to restore the naval base there, as well as carrying medical stores for ex-prisoners of war. Anson then went to Singapore and was part of the Far East Fleet until mid-1946.

HMS ANSON Pennant 79
King George V class battleship late 1945

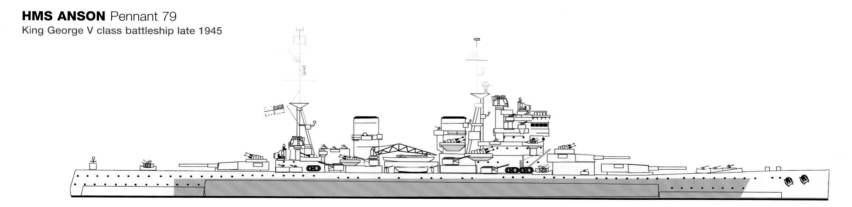

The British Eastern Fleet adopted a scheme usually only worn in the Indian Ocean region. The ship was painted in overall 507c with a hull panel in 1941 washed-out blue. Anson is shown here in that scheme just after the war and prior to returning to the UK. On her arrival at Portsmouth in 1946, she had been painted in overall 507c, some of the 20mm singles were removed almost at once, and more removed later, when she carried out peacetime cruises.

HMS HOWE Pennant 32
King George V class battleship 1942-4

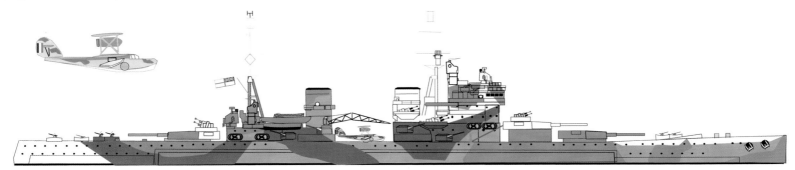

Howe 1942-4. This ship is shown wearing the scheme designed for this class but, as with the others, there are variations that make her distinctive. Considering that many operations of the Home Fleet took place in northern waters, this scheme was very appropriate. At a distance, the combination of dark, medium and light shades would make her blend in to a dark and stormy Arctic background,

especially as most cover for convoys to Russia was provided in winter. The ship entered service in this pattern, but there were some minor changes to its layout during a refit in 1943. The paints used were B5, B6, 507a and 507c. Note there is more 507c aft than forward to shorten her appearance. A much-increased light AA armament was fitted soon after joining the Home Fleet.

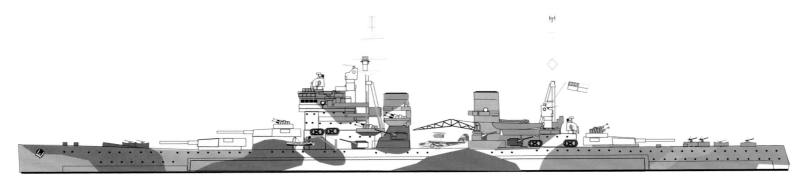

Port side view of *Howe* in the Admiralty-designed disruptive scheme. There was more 507c showing amidships, with B6 and 507a concentrated near the bow. Most of the B6 was toward the stern of the vessel and on the bridge. This pattern was retained until 1944, with only some minor variations in 1943. The decks remained natural wood but all horizontal metal surfaces were painted 507a/G10. Although unpainted, the decks were not scrubbed and holystoned in the pre-war fashion, instead the wood was allowed to fade to a greyish shade due to contact with salt water. This could lead to a patchy look that may appear to be camouflage but that was not the case. The ship carried Type 279 radar with a transmitting aerial on one mast and a receiving aerial on the other. HF/DF was also fitted, along with Type 273 radar, and Mk V directors for the 5.25in secondary guns were fitted at completion.

HMS HOWE Pennant 32
King George V class battleship May 1944

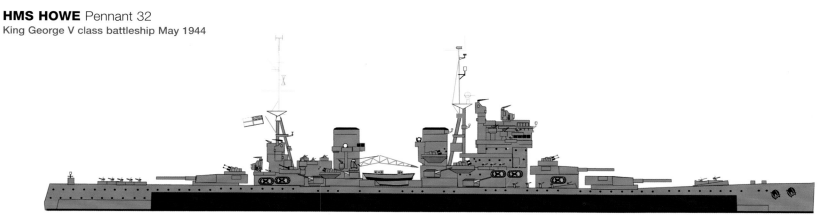

Howe as she appeared in early 1945 after her May 1944 major refit with a B20 hull and a G45 superstructure. She had a major radar update, adding Type 274, Type 278 and Type 285 radar, while the earlier radars were removed. 'Headache' equipment was added along with various IFF aerials, TBS etc. Although US-type quad 40 mm mounts had been added, as well as octuple 2pdr pom-

pom on either side of the aft funnel, there were no quad 2pdrs as in the other ships. Several power-operated twin 20mm were added and the single 20mm guns numbered thirty-four. Naturally, both sides of the ship were painted the same.

HMS HOWE Pennant 32
King George V class battleship September 1945

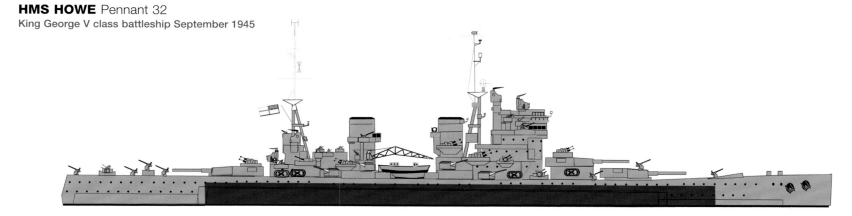

After extensive operations with the British Eastern Fleet and then the British Pacific Fleet, *Howe* was ordered to Durban for a refit. She adopted a version of the Admiralty Standard Scheme A. The bulk of the ship was painted in B55 with a panel of B20. Some sources say G45 with a panel of B20. The upper masts remained white. Of particular note is that all single 20mm AA guns were removed in this refit. The twin power-operated 20mm mounts were retained. Six quad 2pdr

mounts were fitted, two on the quarterdeck, two on each side of the bridge structure and two just aft of 'B' turret at upper-deck level. Eighteen single 40mm Bofors guns were also added. With the two USN-type quads already carried, that gave her a light AA armament of thirty-six 40mm and eighty-eight 2pdrs. Her electronics remained unchanged. She returned to the British Eastern Fleet as flagship but the war with Japan was over before she left Durban.

HMS TERROR Pennant I 03
Erebus class monitor 1936

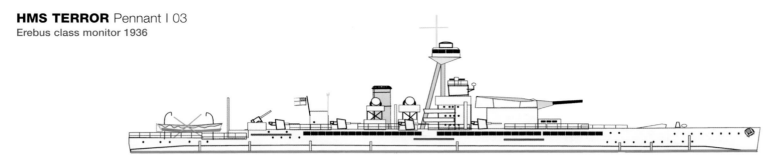

Terror was laid down in 1916 to fill the need for ships that could carry out bombardments of German positions. A spare 15in turret was used and eight 4in guns were provided as protection against enemy destroyers and torpedo boats. Two 3in AA guns were also provided. Initially, one was mounted aft and one on a small superstructure in front of the 15in gun turret. The 3in guns were later moved to port and starboard aft. The ship is shown here in the peacetime colours she wore for her usual deployment in the Mediterranean or the Far East. The funnel and tripod legs were primrose; the bulk of the ship was white. The canvas covers of the 15in guns were buff.

HMS TERROR Pennant I 03
Erebus class monitor January 1941

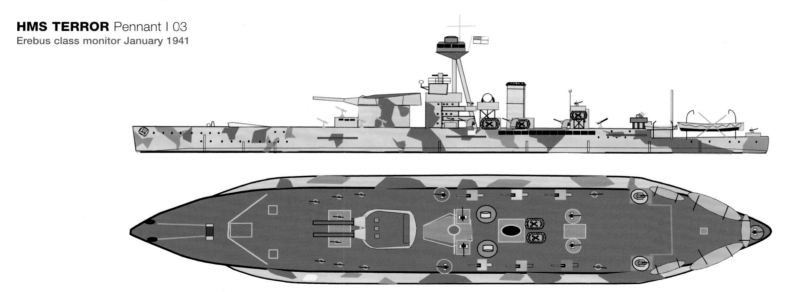

Terror became a valuable asset during the operations of British and Commonwealth troops in North Africa. However, her extremely slow speed meant that she often had to hide from enemy air attack, which posed a deadly threat. The ship was painted in the shades available but exact details have not survived. The camouflage scheme would have been quite unofficial and photographs are rare. This illustration is therefore only an estimation based on what little information is available. Due to the difficulties of getting supplies into the eastern Mediterranean, it is quite possible that some paints were actually British Army colours. After examination of what photographic evidence there is, under different conditions of dark and light, I have illustrated the ship as shown. I have used a base grey, sand stone (pale), dark sand, light stone, mid-stone and khaki, the closest to which is MS4. My maternal uncle served in the area from 1940 until 1942 and his recollections were invaluable. He stated that it was common for army paint in stores that were about to be blown up in the various see-saw advances and withdrawals to be used as impromptu camouflage – officially or unofficially! It was also very common for ships to utilise captured Italian light AA guns to supplement inadequate RN and RAN armament. *Terror* had seven 20mm Oerlikon added before her loss. In addition, there were seven or more Italian 20mm Breda AA guns, or a mix of those and 12.3mm heavy machine guns, which can be confirmed in photographs. The ship was very active and was damaged several times before being severely damaged by air attack on 23 February 1941 after which she tried to make port only to sink the next day.

HMS EREBUS Pennant I 02
Erebus class monitor 1941

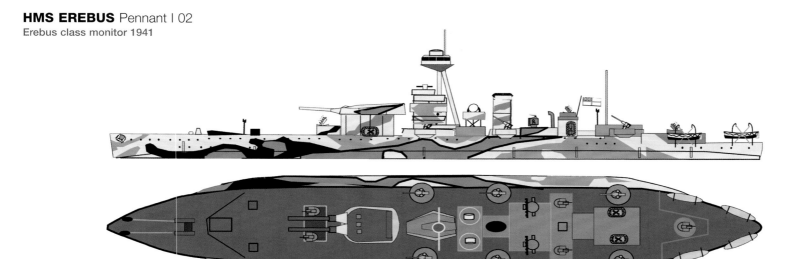

HMS EREBUS Pennant I 02
Erebus class monitor 1943

Erebus is shown at top and centre in an early Admiralty disruptive scheme. It displays the usual area of colour with a heavy black edging, as was common to many of these designs. The colours used were B30, B15 and 507c. The deck was dark grey but the exact shade is not known. The ship had her original 4in low-angle guns replaced by 4in AA. Five quad 0.5in MG mounts were also added. In the lower illustration, the ship wears a later Admiralty scheme using B55, B30 and B15. The

deck probably remained dark grey. The AA armament was increased to include three quad 2pdr mounts and one single 2pdr. A single 40mm Bofors was also carried, along with a final total of fifteen 20mm AA. This ship saw wide service in World War II, taking part in bombardments during many operations. She was sold in 1946, but not scrapped until 1947.

HMS ABERCROMBIE Pennant F 109
Roberts class monitor 1943

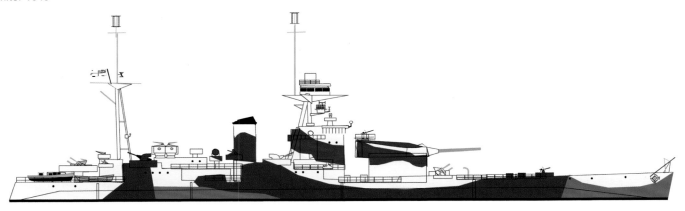

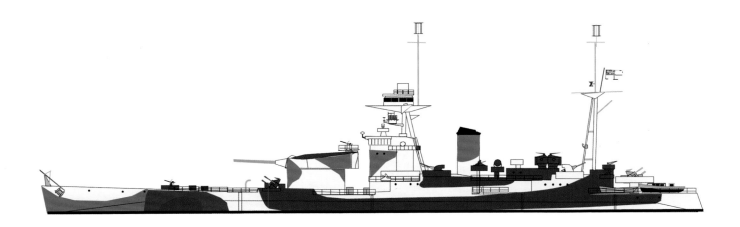

Abercrombie is shown mid-war in an Admiralty scheme. The colours were white, G5, B20 and B30. The deck was dark grey, possibly G5. Both ships of the class were seriously damaged in WWII but their protective scheme held up well. This ship was somewhat unluckier than her sister, *Roberts*, and was badly damaged several times. As a result, she spent a lot of time under repair, therefore seeing less combat service. She carried her 4in AA mounts a deck higher than *Roberts* and had only a

single 20mm on the main turret. There were two quad 2pdr mounts forward and another aft. The 20mm were carried in a mix of twin and single mountings. Because monitors so often operated in shallow waters, both were fitted with acoustic hammers at the bow to deal with influence mines. As result of damage received during the war, *Abercrombie* was broken up in 1954 – a full thirteen years before her sister ship.

HMS ROBERTS Pennant F40
Roberts class monitor 1944

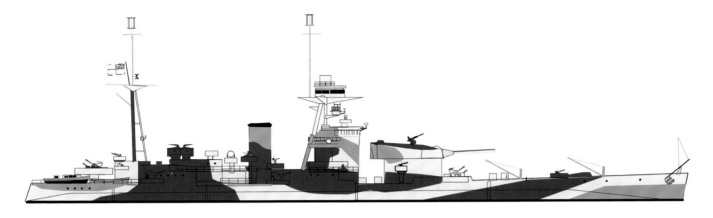

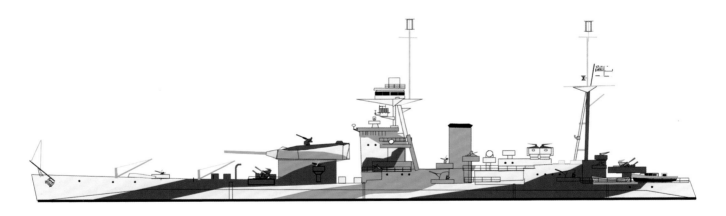

Roberts is shown here in G5, B5 and 507c in a mid- to late-war Admiralty scheme. The deck was dark grey, probably G5. The turret had originally been carried by the World War I monitor *Marshal Soult*, but was removed when that ship was disarmed. *Roberts* was completed in October 1941, by which time the lessons of air power had been learnt, and, as a result, her AA armament was quite strong. There were four twin 4in AA, three quad 2pdr mounts, sixteen 20mm and a single Bofors on top of the main turret. There were a total of twenty 20mm by the end of the war, through replacing single mounts with twins. Her combat service was rather more extensive than her sister and the ship was retained after the war until being broke up for scrap in 1965.

HMS ARGUS Pennant I 49
Argus class aircraft carrier 1918

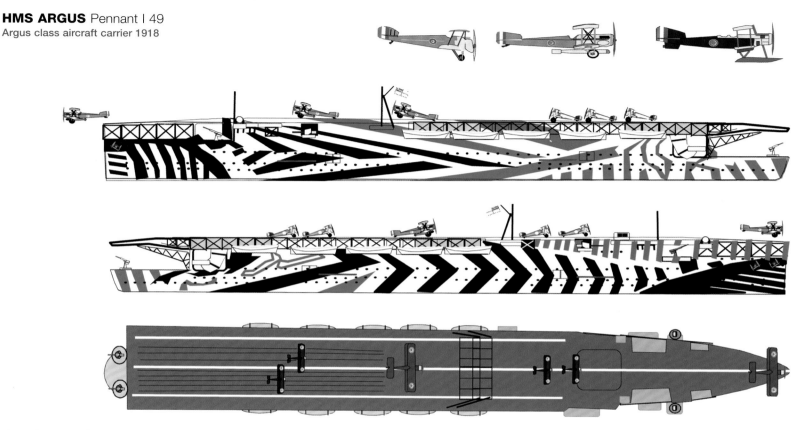

This striking camouflage was a typical World War I 'Dazzle Scheme'. Colours and lines ran in confusing directions to deny an attacking U-boat commander an easy time plotting course, range and speed. The shape of an aircraft carrier would always prove difficult to hide in later times but, in World War I, it was still an unknown type. In the mid-1960s, I had the honour to interview a veteran who had been a signaller on the staff of Admiral Beatty when this ship first arrived at Scapa Flow. He told me that he was so confused by it that, when he reported 'ship sighted', the Admiral had turned to him and said 'Well? Which ship is it man?' The Admiral had been used to him being so familiar with every ship in the fleet that his reports were usually detailed and included identification. The veteran told me that he responded 'I'm afraid I dunno Sir! 'aint never seen nothing like that before Sir.' Admiral Beatty walked to the rail and raised his own binoculars to look but, as he did so, he said to the veteran 'Well what does it look like man?' – to which the veteran gave the reply 'It looks like a floating Ditty Box to me Sir.' The Admiral looked, laughed, concurred and the *Argus* had picked up her first nickname. The second often used was 'The Flatiron'.

The ship had been constructed to Beardmore-inspired plans as an aircraft carrier, using the partly completed liner the *Conte Rosso*, which was being built at the Beardmore Yard, as the base design. Construction had halted at an early stage due to World War I breaking out. As only some of the lower part had been completed, it gave full scope for conversion to a flush-deck aircraft carrier that could steam at the same speed as the Grand Fleet. Floatplanes had great disadvantages when compared to land planes in payload, range and manoeuvrability. So the Fleet requested the Admiralty come up with a solution and *Argus* was the response. She joined the Grand Fleet only two months before the war ended and had no opportunity to carry out combat operations. The problem of funnels getting in the way had been solved by running smoke ducts aft, an idea taken up by the Japanese as well. However, since they were inside the hull, this caused restrictions on the width of the hangar and problems with heat. Nonetheless, for her day, she was the ultimate in aircraft-carrying vessels. The deck was mostly supported by a lattice work of steel beams and inclined down at the bow to assist with aircraft take off. She carried two low-angle 4in guns and four single AA guns for defence but was intended to be protected by the fleet. On entering service, she carried Sopwith Cuckoo torpedo bombers and Sopwith Camel fighters, with a capacity of twenty aircraft in total. She could also operate seaplanes via the open stern area using the cranes provided. At 20-25 knots, *Argus* was as fast as most battleships of the Grand Fleet. Although converted from a merchant vessel, she was never considered, or intended, to be an escort carrier in the later World War II style. She was a fleet carrier from start to finish and was originally referred to as a 'strike carrier'.

HMS ARGUS Pennant D49

Argus class aircraft carrier 1935-8

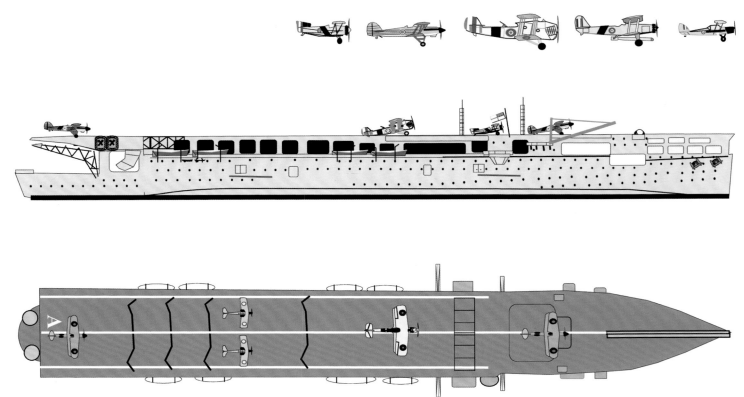

This shows the ship in an overall scheme of MS4a grey with deck in 507b. *Argus* underwent several refits and modifications and this view shows her in the mid-1930s, when she was operating as a mother ship for radio-controlled aircraft used for gunnery practice. The target planes were modified Tiger Moth trainers with, for the time, quite sophisticated remote controls. However, she also took on the role of a deck training carrier for new pilots learning how to operate from a carrier. During rebuilding, anti-torpedo bulges were added, the previous lattice work supports for the flight deck were greatly strengthened and the gaps near the bow closed in to provide more space during take-off. All the 4in guns had been removed by this time, leaving the ship unarmed. The flight deck down slope to the bow was removed, giving an entirely flat flight deck. After experimentation with other means, arrester wires had been settled on during

the late 1920s. An accelerator was added at the bow to allow the target drones to be launched. This was not the same as a full catapult and had less power. There were discussions in the Admiralty with regard to providing a wider bow area for the deck, rather than the ship bow shape, but nothing came of it and *Argus* always had a pointed front to her flight deck. Note that the bow still shows its original hull lines. In the training role, *Argus* operated various types of aircraft, including the Hawker Nimrod fighter and later the Gloster Gladiator. These were the last of the aircraft types that were reasonably within the size limits of her design for a full complement to be carried. From this time on, her air complement had to be reduced in number. It is interesting that this ship was capable of operating an air complement similar to that of the purpose-designed *Hermes* and the battleship conversion *Eagle*.

HMS ARGUS Pennant D49
Argus class aircraft carrier 1941

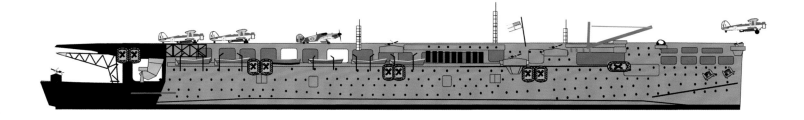

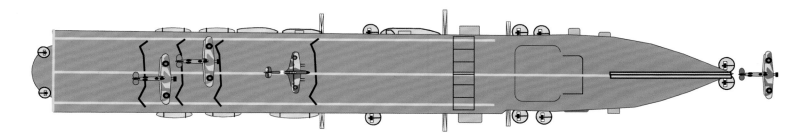

Argus was painted in overall 507b medium grey while operating with the Home Fleet. Note that, due to the funnel discharge gases, the aft part of the ship was painted black. Deck markings were previously white but were changed to a dull yellow in 1940. They were painted white again in mid-1943. She went to the Mediterranean just before the war and was based in Toulon, during which time she was painted overall in 507c, except for vertical surfaces which were 507b. *Argus* returned to the Clyde in June 1940, when she was painted in the scheme shown. Although it had been envisaged that she would operate in the training role, the loss of *Glorious* and *Courageous* early in the war meant she had to be called on for operational duties in support of convoys and providing air cover for the fleet. These duties included escorting troop convoys as far south as Freetown and, during one such operation, the convoy was attacked by the German heavy cruiser *Admiral Hipper.* Poor visibility prevented *Argus* from flying off a strike and a great opportunity was lost, but only one transport was damaged. Other duties included ferrying aircraft to Africa's Gold Coast, from where they flew to Egypt. As all previous armament had been removed, it was necessary to provide some defensive armament. This was initially provided by fitting quad 0.5in MGs on the sponsons previously used for the low-angle 4in guns and some other machine guns. As soon as possible, she

was fitted with 20mm single AA guns and, by 1941, the total had risen to ten such weapons. Due to the increased size of aircraft being operated by the Royal Navy, *Argus* was limited to carrying around ten or twelve planes. She was invaluable in the role of ferrying aircraft and took part in many such missions, including heavily-contested operations to relieve Malta and the less well-known Operation Benedict, when RAF Hawker Hurricanes were flown off to operate from North Russia. As if not busy enough, any spare time was used to assist with the training of new pilots. *Argus* was in the thick of things again in 1942, supporting the landings in North Africa, and was damaged during an air attack off Algiers, when she took one direct hit and damage from several near misses. Early 1943 saw the ship back in action escorting troops to North Africa but she was badly in need of a refit and repairs. A repair enabled her to return to service in April 1943 and from May on the ship was finally able to take on her intended role as a deck-landing training carrier. By 1944, the ship was thoroughly worn out from long service and frantic war activity, which had strained her machinery and equipment. With new carriers now in service, *Argus* was relegated to an accommodation ship in December 1944 and was finally scrapped in 1947. It could be said that this first through-deck carrier provided value far beyond what had been originally expected of her.

HMS FURIOUS Pennant 47
Furious class aircraft carrier 1917-8

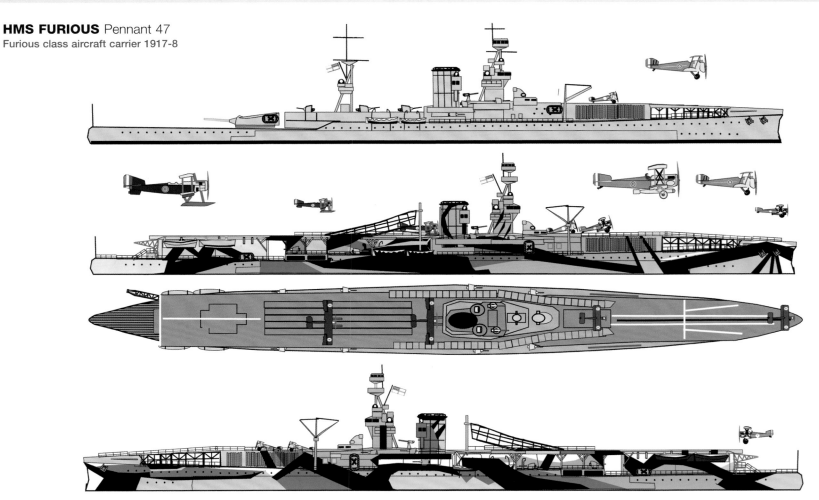

Furious was originally intended to be a light battle cruiser armed with two single 18in guns. The heaviest weapon ever carried by a Royal Navy ship, it was too powerful for the lightly-built hull and caused damage whenever it was fired. Before entering service, the forward turret was removed and *Furious* was converted to carry a flying-off deck for fighters and scout aircraft. The idea was not considered a success as the aircraft could not return, having instead to ditch or try to reach land. The ship was painted in plain MS4a or similar.

After initial trials with a single turret aft, *Furious* was further modified. The turret was removed and a hangar built over the stern. Her gun armament was ten single 5.5in and two single 3in AA between the funnel and bridge. The air complement comprised Sopwith Camels, Pups and Cuckoo torpedo bombers. Seaplanes could be operated as well and *Furious* could also act as a mother ship for dirigibles. Ramps each side of the bridge allowed aircraft to pass from the landing-on deck aft to the

flying-off deck forward. There was an aircraft lift aft and a hatch forward to enable aircraft to be moved to and from the hangars. A cramped and awkward arrangement, it worked with smaller aircraft. The arrester system comprised longitudinal cables and cross-cables weighted with sandbags, plus a very large crash barrier. Beams each side of the forward deck could be raised as a wind break.

In 1918, some ships of the Royal Navy adopted a camouflage scheme known as 'Dazzle'. The idea was to paint the ship in a range of contrasting colours that would break up its silhouette and confuse an enemy observer. It was mainly intended for use against attacking submarines, where the enemy commander would only be able to take a brief glimpse through his periscope. He relied on estimating the length, speed, bearing and course of the target in order to aim his torpedoes. If he could not ascertain these with accuracy, the torpedo attack would miss. *Furious* is shown here in green, blue, black, pink and grey in a series of erratic patterns.

HMS FURIOUS Pennant 47
Furious class aircraft carrier 1926-32

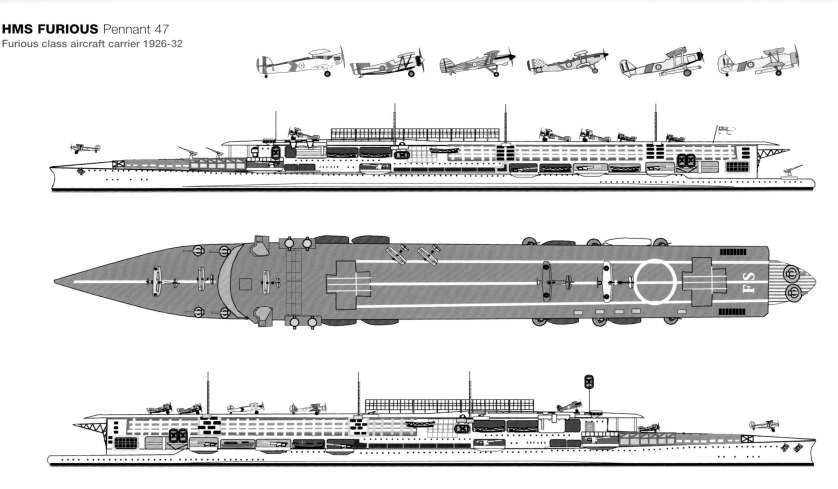

These illustrations show the ship in Mediterranean fleet colours of 507c overall, except for the flight deck, which was 507b. At this time, some ships of the Mediterranean fleet showed a line of red at the waterline with black boot topping above it. No doubt there were many other areas made to look fancy, considering she was seen as a very special ship visited by many curious foreign dignitaries. The previous conversion had proved very limiting and she was again modified during a rebuild from 1922-5. The mid-deck superstructure, tripod mast and funnel were removed to create a large flush upper flight deck and a smaller one at the bow, where fighters could be launched direct from the hangar. There was still a slight hump on the flight deck but the round down was designed by the National Physics Laboratory for maximum air flow to assist aircraft take-off. Anti-torpedo bulges were provided and these also helped with stability as the ship was long and narrow. As completed, her armament was ten 5.5in guns and six single 4in AA. The port side illustration

shows the ship as originally armed. The quarterdeck was as per the original hull and proved very wet at speed. The starboard side illustration shows the ship after the 4in AA had been removed. The two 4in AA guns aft had to be removed, as they were almost unworkable at speed. The other 4in at the edges of the forward flying-off deck were also removed, as they hindered air operations from that deck. For a time, Furious carried no AA weapons at all – although files indicate she had four single 2pdr guns added as per the starboard side drawing. The deck plan shows the two lifts installed and, while they proved to be quite adequate for most aircraft, she was only able to operate thirty to thirty-six aircraft. This was because the ducts provided for the removal of funnel gases were internal and reduced the hangar's width. The deck plan also shows the six 4in AA guns that were eventually removed and note that the small quarter deck was still wood. Furious proved invaluable to the Royal Navy in learning how to operate fast carriers working with the main fleet.

HMS FURIOUS Pennant 47
Furious class aircraft carrier 1932-5

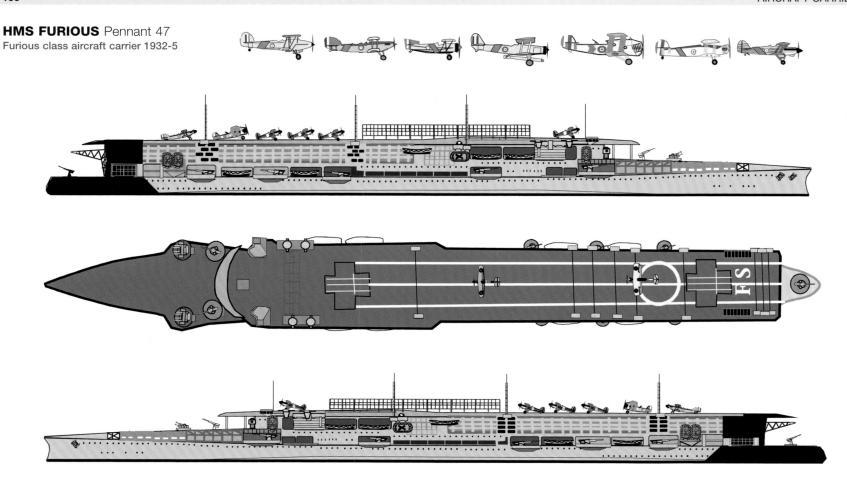

In 1932, *Furious* returned home for modifications based on her experience of service with the fleet. The flashy waterline was removed and the ship wore a typical scheme for the Home Fleet utilising the darker 507b instead of MS4a Home Fleet grey. The quarterdeck was raised to main deck level, a single 4in AA placed there and the wood deck was removed. At this time, there seems to have been quite a variation in which grey colour was used in the Home Fleet. Some ships appear in 507a battleship grey, while others are MS4a. This could have been a matter of which shipyard a vessel was in when refitted, or it could have been a matter of the whim of individual admirals or the availability of paint during the Great Depression. In discussion with an old dockyard hand years ago, he said that, in the period concerned, they found it hard to order stocks of almost anything and had to explain why it was required. It is therefore quite possible that Royal Dockyards were instructed to use up available stocks rather than order new. The 4in AA guns on the flying-off deck had been removed, but two were now returned and an octuple 2pdr

mount placed in front of each of them. HACS directors were placed port and starboard at the head of the lower flying-off deck. By now, the forward flying off deck was rarely used and considered far less useful than had been expected when designed, due to the increasing size and power of naval aircraft. The 5.5in guns remained and improvements were made to smoke discharge. Nonetheless, they were still not enough and the rear end of the ship was usually painted black. The actual area of black seems to have varied from time to time, including times when the forward slope was not used. The flight deck was made somewhat darker to ensure the white lines were more visible. The deck was widened just aft of the bridge area due to crowding experienced as aircraft became larger. Cross-deck arrester wires were also fitted. The former forward flying-off deck was no longer used; therefore, the white line was removed. The deck was also sponsoned out to give the 2pdr mounts a wider range of fire. The four single 2pdr were landed.

HMS FURIOUS Pennant 47
Furious class aircraft carrier 1939

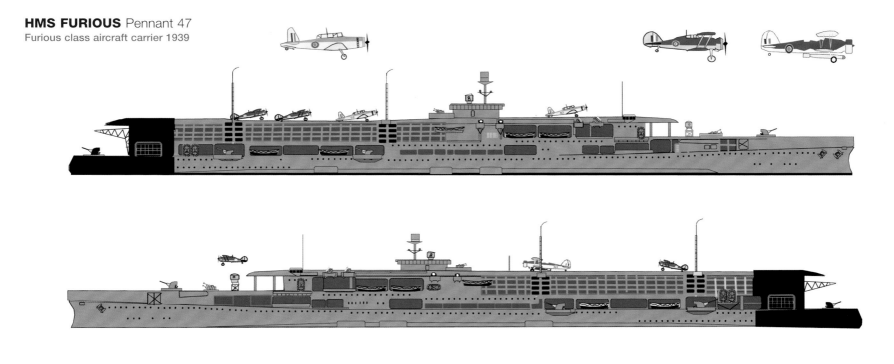

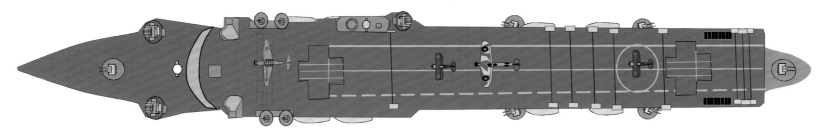

Like many other units of the Home Fleet, this ship wore 507b at the outbreak of war and into 1940. This shade was possibly considered more suited to the dull conditions of the winter of 1939-40, which was one of the coldest and worst on record for many years in Europe. The flight deck lines were changed to dark yellow and the port side became a broken line. The recognition letters were painted out when war was declared. *Furious* underwent some radical changes in her 1938-9 reconstruction. All the 5.5in guns were removed and replaced with six twin 4in AA. HACS direc-tors were added, one on the foredeck and one on the new island that was added to improve avia-tion and gunnery control. For some unexplained reason, the top of the forward HACS was painted white. The canvas covering the ship's boats was painted grey. The directors for the 5.5in guns were removed and replaced with quad 0.5in MG mounts. The bow was raised to improve seaworthiness and the deck was slightly changed again. Aircraft capacity was now rated at thirty or less comfort-ably, with a maximum of thirty-three.

HMS FURIOUS Pennant 47
Furious class aircraft carrier 1941-2

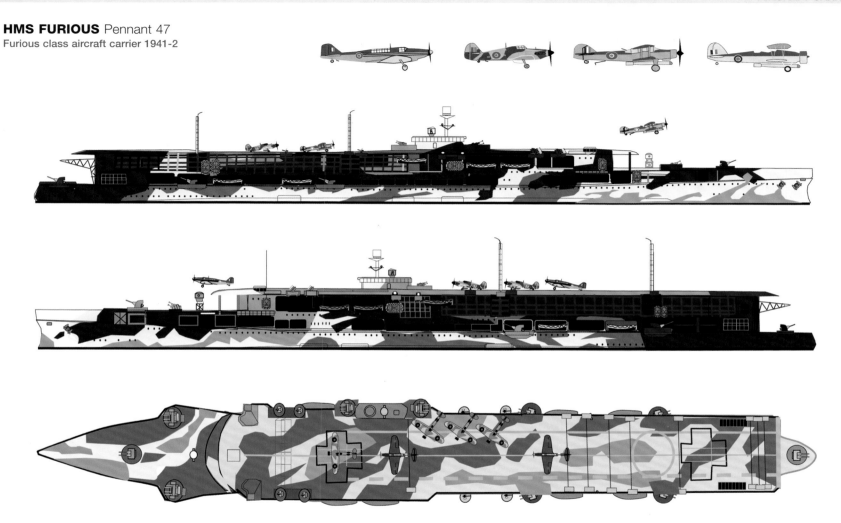

Furious was provided with an Admiralty early disruptive camouflage in late 1940. It was of a style similar to other large ships and may, or may not, have been of Admiralty design. The MS3 areas on the starboard hull forward were much like the first scheme worn by *Duke of York*. Further aft, MS3 seems to have given way to MS2. It is not surprising that quite an amount of dark blue, PB10 or B20, was used as, like all carriers, she had many recesses that were dark areas in almost any light. The stern had been painted black previously, so that dark blue would be applicable as a substitute. For the first time, the deck was camouflaged in three shades, the overall being 507c grey with irregular areas of MS3 and MS2. The flight deck lines were dark yellow, as previously worn. During the period this scheme was carried, an additional octuple 2pdr mounting was added before the bridge, as is shown on the starboard side illustration. Four single 20mm Oerlikon guns were also added and the quad 0.5in MG mounts were retained until late 1941, when they were replaced by four single 20mm. The object at the head of the mast was a homing beacon for the ship's aircraft, not a radar set. Type 285 radar had not yet been fitted to the directors and she carried no other radar at this time.

HMS FURIOUS Pennant 47
Furious class aircraft carrier 1943

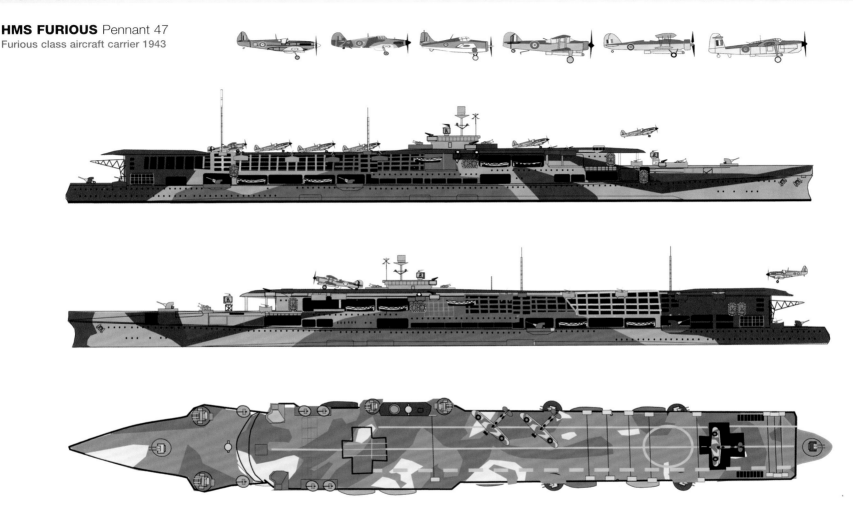

Furious had the more complicated early camouflage over-painted in mid-1943. It was replaced by an Admiralty disruptive type that used fewer colours and with blocks of colour that were easier to maintain. The shades used were G5 grey black, B15 blue black, B30 dark olive and B55 grey for the hull. The flight deck was also camouflaged as before, with the pattern merely altered somewhat. The colours used were G45 light olive, B30 dark olive and MS4a Home Fleet grey. The deck markings remained dark yellow. In 1944, the deck was painted 507a dark grey and the deck markings were white from then on. The ship retained this general camouflage until she was reduced to reserve in September 1944. Type 285 radar was fitted to the Mk IV HACS for the 4in guns and Type 282 for the 2pdr directors. Type 291 general warning radar was carried on a pole mast at the front of the bridge. The ship carried eighteen single 20mm AA by late 1942 and

another four were added late in 1943 for a total of twenty-two. The ship saw wide-ranging service during World War II from Norway, through a short period in the Mediterranean to Operation Torch. However, most of her service was with the Home Fleet, which included air strikes against the German battleship *Tirpitz* hidden away in various Norwegian fjords. The speed of this ship was greatly valued, although, as larger, more powerful aircraft came into service, she was seriously restricted by the number of aircraft she could operate. She was reduced to reserve in 1944 because her machinery was becoming worn and, with a capacity of only thirty-three aircraft, sometimes fewer, she was far more expensive to run than the other carriers then entering service. The new escort carriers could carry just as many aircraft and required far less crew, even though they were much slower.

HMS HERMES Pennant I95
Hermes class aircraft carrier 1923-30

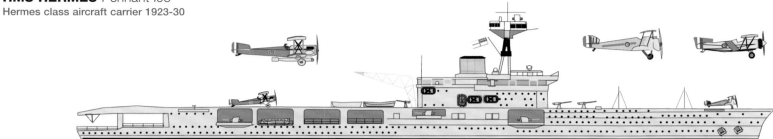

Hermes is shown in MS4a as completed. The deck was a dark grey, possibly 507b. The ship had a heavy black waterline. Her design and small size came from a 1917 requirement for a fast carrier along cruiser lines which could accompany scout cruiser groups to provide them with longer-range reconnaissance. The general hull form was along light cruiser lines with a very large flare at the bow to give width for the flight deck. Speed was 25 knots, which was well in keeping with cruisers of the period. She was laid down in January 1918 but, with construction slowed down after the

Armistice, did not commission until 1923. Her air group size was planned to be twenty aircraft but, of course, the dimensions considered were those of World War I aircraft. Her only AA armament was provided by three 4in guns, but there were six 5.5in in case she became involved in a surface action while operating with the scout cruisers. No catapult was provided and she had longitudinal wire arresters initially, but they were soon replaced by a transverse type.

HMS HERMES Pennant I95
Hermes class aircraft carrier 1937

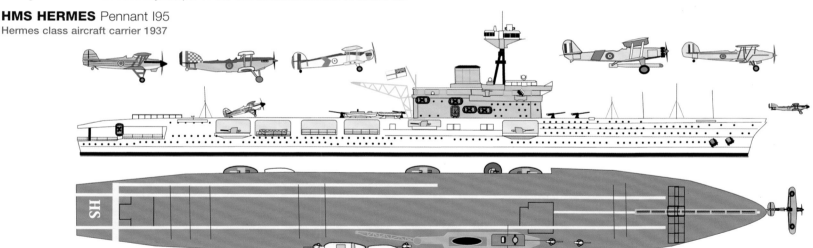

Hermes spent the majority of her service on the China station, where smart livery was more likely to impress than actual fighting power. The ship was painted with a white hull, and upper fighting top, whilst the bridge structure, 5.5in guns and lower fighting top were in primrose. Even the very large crane she carried was repainted in primrose. At the waterline, the boot topping was black but with a line of red showing below it. The deck was still grey, possibly 507b. The flight deck markings were white. Her air complement was small, usually eight Fairey IIIF, four Ripons and seven Flycatchers (the latter were usually carried unassembled) and, at a pinch, she could carry fifteen assembled

aircraft. The large fighting top was part of her design to operate with cruisers and provided gunnery control along World War I standards. The bridge structure was unusually large for a ship of her size. A fourth single 4in AA gun was placed on the deck aft of the island. Quad 0.5in MG mounts were also added, with one set on the starboard side of the bridge and the other just below flight deck level, on the port side. By this time, the speed of most cruisers was higher than those she had been intended to operate with in World War I, and her small air complement made her of little value in the fleet carrier attack role, but she did ASW and raider-hunting work in the Indian Ocean.

HMS HERMES Pennant D95
Hermes class aircraft carrier 1942

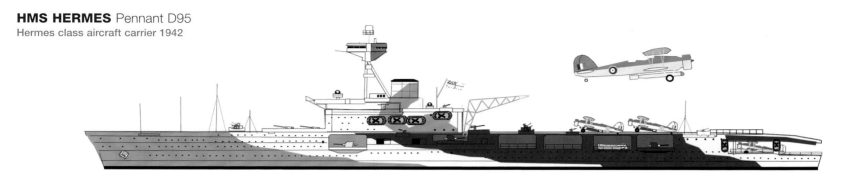

Port side camouflage scheme of *Hermes* at the time of her sinking. It was not an official design and was typical of schemes that used paint already available in quantity at naval dockyards. The three shades are 507a, 507b and 507c, all of which were probably in stock in South Africa where the ship is believed to have been repainted. The same paint was used for the starboard side and the pattern was similar. The quarterdeck area, under the stern round down, was able to be used during mainte-nance. Aircraft could be rolled into that area so engines could be run up and tested outside the confines of the closed hangar. The Royal Navy changed the flag superior of this ship from the letter I to the letter D in 1940. This was part of a general reshuffle across most ships in service. However, *Hermes* retained the same number despite the change of letter.

HMS HERMES Pennant D95
Hermes class aircraft carrier 1942

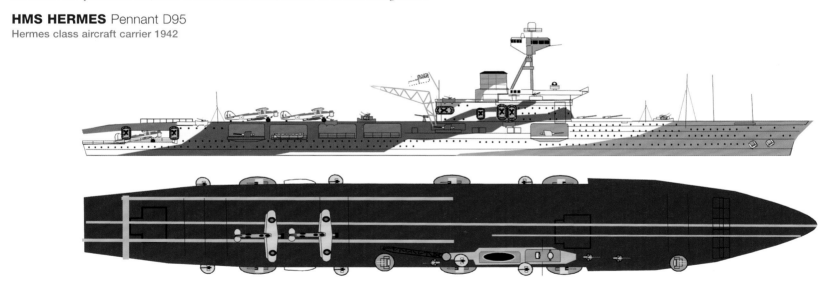

Hermes was painted in camouflage around five months before her loss to Japanese aircraft in 1942. The deck was dark green of unknown type, most likely a local procurement. The deck markings were probably dark yellow, which was Royal Navy standard at that time, but may have been white. Note that an aircraft homing beacon was placed at the head of the mast, but no radar fitted. The light AA was increased with the addition of two quad 2pdr mounts and seven single 20mm Oerlikon guns. Light AA was in high demand in the European theatre and ships of the Far East were on low priority until the war with Japan commenced. By the time of her sinking, the aircraft complement was only twelve Swordfish. However, none were aboard when she was lost. Even if the ship had been carrying fighters, they would have been such a small number that it is unlikely they could have driven off the Japanese carrier aircraft that overwhelmed her.

HMS EAGLE Pennant 94
Eagle class aircraft carrier 1924-6

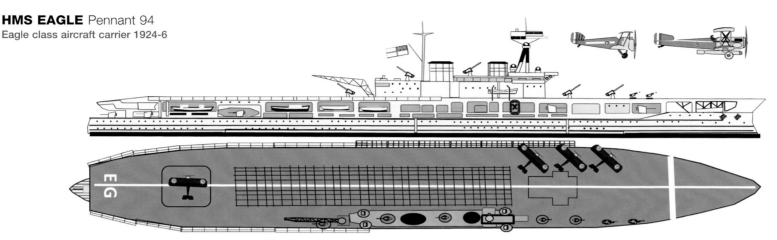

Eagle spent the early years of her service in the Mediterranean fleet. She is illustrated here in 507c light grey with a black waterline. The quarterdeck was scrubbed natural wood. The flight deck was mid-grey, probably 507b. The deck markings were white, with a single line running fore and aft, and a cross line just before the bow. During periods of service with the Home Fleet, she was painted in MS4a. Whereas *Hermes* had been deliberately designed to operate with the scouting forces of the fleet, this ship was converted from the hull of the incomplete Chilean battleship *Almirante Cochrane*. With similar speed and armour distributed on battleship lines, although thinner, she was intended to operate with the battle squadrons. Her air complement was intended to be twenty-four, which

seemed adequate for World War I, when she was under construction, but was small by later standards. Her initial landing aids were fore and aft wires. As completed, she had ten 6in guns and five 4in AA. There were two single 2pdr AA ahead of the forward 4in guns. Her landing system comprised longitudinal wires with a system of catch lines. The longitudinal wires guided the wheels of an aircraft in a straight line until it hooked on a catch-line. This system was considered inadequate but also seemed unnecessary because, when the ship was steaming into the wind, most aircraft of the era could cut their engines and brake to a halt within the length of the deck. The longitudinal system was removed in 1926 and the ship operated without an arrester system until 1936.

HMS EAGLE Pennant 94
Eagle class aircraft carrier 1926-32

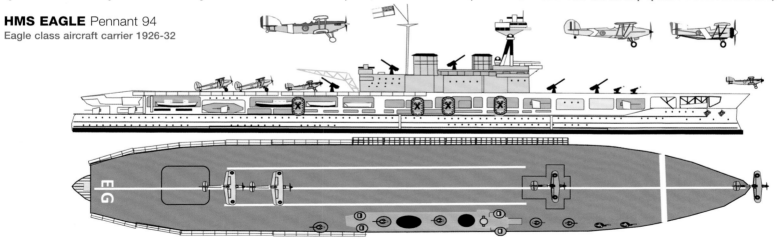

After the Mediterranean, *Eagle* spent most of her service on the China station. For this, she was painted in the white and primrose scheme used there. Note that the 4in guns were painted black and the Carley rafts yellow. Because of her flight deck length and speed, *Eagle* could operate Fairey IIIF and Osprey aircraft without the need for a catapult or accelerator. The aircraft could also land

without any arrester gear. The Flycatcher was also able to operate from this ship. The deck markings were again white, after the removal of the old-style arrester gear, but included two other lines to assist the pilot with assessing where he was if the central line was not visible over the engine of his aircraft. There was also a heavy white line at the bow as an aiming point for landing.

HMS EAGLE Pennant 94
Eagle class aircraft carrier 1941

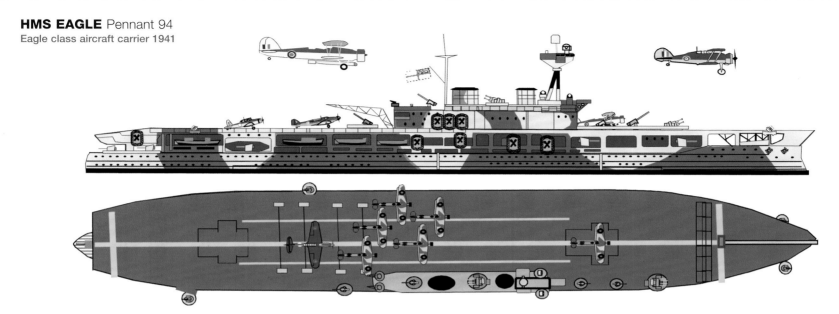

With this paint scheme it is possible that, with the layout of the dark areas, the ship could be mistaken for a distant freighter, with bow, bridge, funnel and breaks in superstructure. But I am not aware if this was actually the intention. The scheme was quite unofficial and no doubt made up of paint that was available. The base colour was MS4a with 507a for the dark areas. The flight deck was also 507a and the deck markings were painted dark yellow, as was usual from around 1940.

Light AA was increased with the addition of twelve single 20mm Oerlikon guns before the ship was lost on 11 August 1942. A Mk IV HACS director was provided on the fighting top. Directors for the two octuple 2pdr mounts were fitted with Type 282 radar. All 6in guns were retained, but consideration had been given to removing them to save weight and crew in order to fit more light AA weapons.

HMS EAGLE Pennant 94
Eagle class aircraft carrier 1941

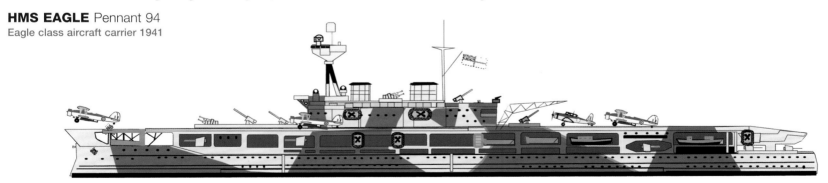

Eagle had a very small complement of aircraft at the time of her loss. However, for such an early carrier, she had given good service to the Royal Navy, being instrumental in the development of aircraft carriers in general and their operation with the fleet in particular. During World War II, she performed valuable service in the attack and patrol roles, and took part in various operations to fly-

off RAF aircraft to reinforce the besieged island of Malta. No doubt, with newer ships, with larger air complements, coming into service, she would have ended up in a secondary role, but she was designed and introduced as a fleet carrier and died as one.

HMS EAGLE Pennant 94
Eagle class aircraft carrier 1942

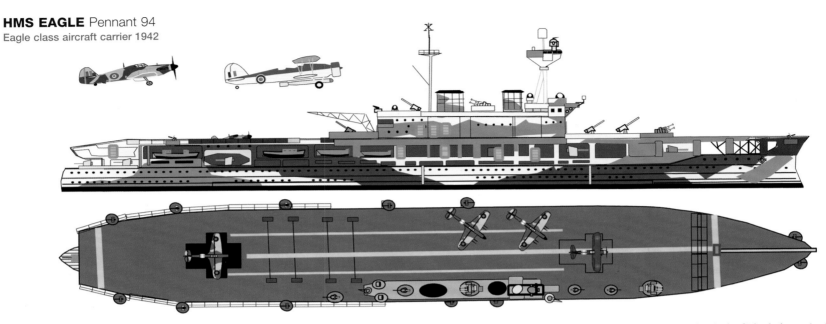

After her UK refit, *Eagle* appeared in a new Admiralty-designed disruptive camouflage scheme. The shades used were 507a and 507b on a base of 507c. The ship now carried Type 285 radar on the HACS director, which had been fitted to the fighting top. Type 291 radar was carried on the pole mast. Two directors for the multiple 2pdrs were provided and fitted with Type 282 radar. The quad 0.5in MG mounts were removed and twelve single 20mm fitted. The flight deck remained 507a. There have been some claims that the deck may have been camouflaged, but I cannot find any evidence to support that.

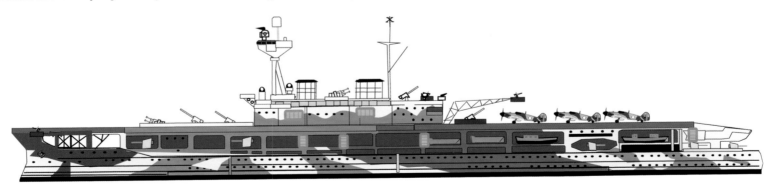

Eagle went to the South Atlantic on anti-raider patrol after her Simonstown refit. During this time, she sank the German blockade runner *Elbe* and helped capture the steamer *Lothringen*. The ship was ordered to report for a refit in the UK [is this the same UK refit referred to above? If so, these paragraphs are out of chronological order], after which, she returned to the Mediterranean and took part in several convoys and fleet operations flying off aircraft for the RAF at Malta. On 11 August 1942, while taking part in Operation Pedestal, the ship was hit by four torpedoes fired by U-boat *U-73*, capsized and sank completely within five minutes. Remarkably, 927 members of the ship's company were picked up but 160 were lost. Some of her aircraft were in the air at the time and landed on other carriers, thus survived the sinking of their ship.

HMS GLORIOUS Pennant 77
Courageous class aircraft carrier 1930

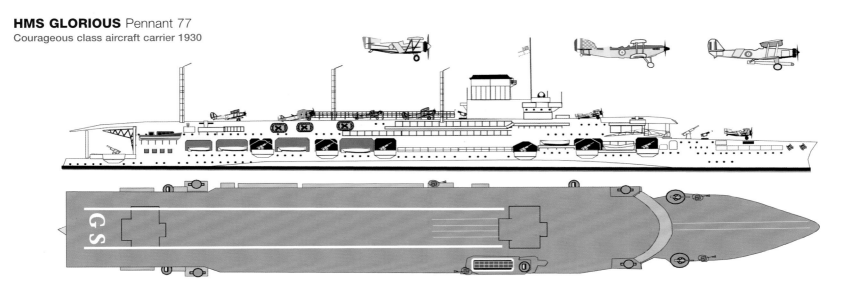

Glorious and *Courageous* were originally built as a light form of battlecruiser for a World War I special project in the Baltic. The project did not see fruition and, although fitted with 15in guns, their thin armour and large size made them white elephants for fleet use. As they were new, large and expensive, it was decided they should be converted to aircraft carriers when post-World War I treaties enabled this to take place. All superstructure and guns were removed, the ships being stripped to the main deck, with some work below that as well. As completed, they were very satisfactory vessels and provided excellent service before World War II. At the time, the newly-formed RAF insisted on taking control of carrier aircraft and, in an era of post-war financial shortages, it was decided that the Royal Naval Air Service should be disbanded and its duties take over by the RAF. While seemingly a good idea, it proved to be a bad one in the long run as the RAF preferred to develop aircraft that were suited for its own requirements and neglected carrier types. As a result, the carriers were forced to use land aircraft adapted for naval use. *Glorious* initially carried sixteen Flycatcher fighters, sixteen Fairey III reconnaissance aircraft and sixteen Ripon torpedo bombers. The original layout enabled the fighters to take off over the bow from the hangar deck, leaving other aircraft free to be spotted on the flight deck ready for launch. *Glorious* is shown here in 507c light grey as used in the Mediterranean, which was her main operating area. The flight deck was 507b with white lines. Boot topping was black and, for a time, some red from the hull was allowed to show. Aircraft carriers were somewhat unique and she was a show boat during most port visits. The AA armament was very heavy for its day, comprising sixteen single 4.7in guns, but the light AA was limited to four single 2pdr.

HMS GLORIOUS Pennant 77
Courageous class
aircraft carrier 1937

Glorious was refitted in the UK during 1935 before returning to her usual position with the Mediterranean fleet. She is once again shown in 507c overall but the deck was apparently given a darker shade of grey. The aft round-down was improved and the bridge modified. The old quarter-deck was removed and the deck raised a level to keep the stern drier. Octuple 2pdr mountings were placed on the foredeck, which was no longer to be used for aircraft take-offs, and the original singles removed. An aircraft beacon was placed at the top of the mast, which was moved a little further aft. Mk IV HACS directors replaced the earlier type for the control of the 4.7in AA. Tub directors were provided for the 2pdr mounts but, of course, had no radar fitted. A more austere Admiral's barge replaced the earlier one. Two catapults were provided on the flight deck so that heavier aircraft could be launched.

HMS GLORIOUS Pennant 77
Courageous class fleet aircraft carrier 1940

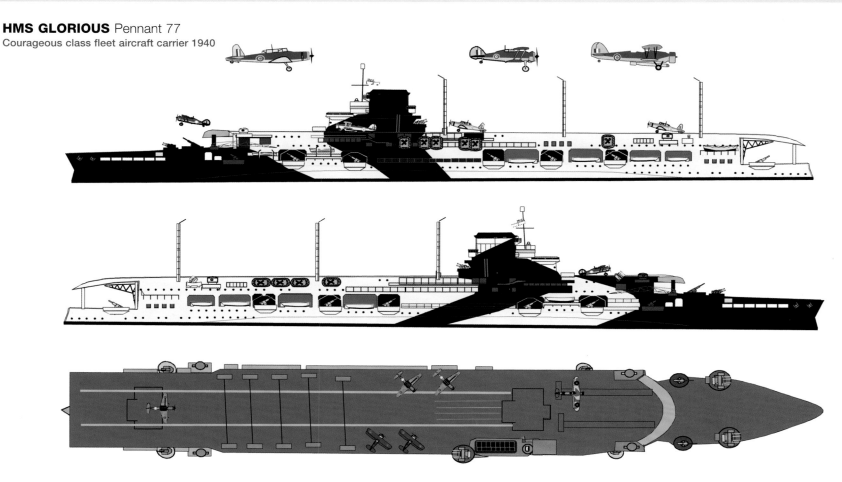

Glorious was stationed in the Mediterranean when World War II broke out but did not participate in any offensive operations there. Instead, she was sent to the Indian Ocean to hunt for German raiders and merchant ships running for home. However, with the loss of her sister ship *Courageous* in the second week of the war; she was called back to the UK urgently. By early 1940, the ship was painted in an unofficial camouflage scheme. Her previous 507c was retained but areas of black were added to confuse her outline. Additionally, the deck markings were changed to dull yellow, as with most other carriers during 1940. On 10 April 1940, her air group was made up of twelve Sea Gladiators flown by 802 Squadron, 6 Blackburn Skuas of 803 Squadron, 6 Sea Gladiators of 804 Squadron and 12 Swordfish of 823 Squadron. However, the aircraft of 803 and 804 Squadrons were detached on the 18 April. On 24 April, she conveyed 18 Gladiators of 263 Squadron RAF to Norway, where they flew off to operate from the frozen Lake Lesjaskou. Along with *Ark Royal*, she continued to carry RAF aircraft to Norway, where they flew off to take part in that campaign from Bardufoss. Her own

Skua and Sea Gladiator aircraft also flew a number of missions harassing German lines of supply and assisting allied land forces. On 17 June, when Norway was evacuated, the ship received all the surviving Gladiators and Hurricanes from Bardufoss. These aircraft all landed on safely, despite having no deck landing equipment. But, on the following day, with her flight deck crammed with aircraft, the ship was intercepted by the German battleships *Scharnhorst* and *Gneisenau* and sunk by gunfire within 40 minutes, despite a heroic defence put up by her escorting destroyers. There was considerable controversy as to the failure of her captain to allow the RAF aircraft to be jettisoned and a strike launched to delay or drive off her attackers. Less than forty men survived the sinking. A complement of forty-eight aircraft was better than most other British carriers of the time, but small by the standard of Pacific navies. No doubt the number carried would have decreased as larger aircraft entered service, but this ship and her sister had more room for aircraft than most other Royal Navy carriers of the era. Two catapults were installed during her last major pre-war refit.

HMS COURAGEOUS Pennant 50
Courageous class aircraft carrier 1930

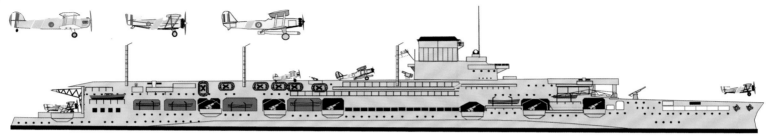

HMS COURAGEOUS Pennant 50
Courageous class aircraft carrier 1939

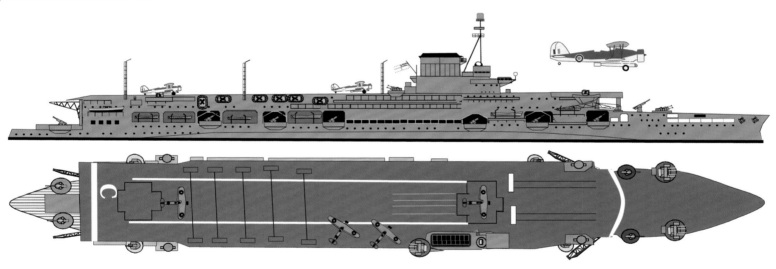

Courageous was the first of the two sister ships of her class to undergo conversion to an aircraft carrier under the terms of post-World War I treaties. The ship was stripped down to the main deck and an entirely new structure built on top. The flight deck was shorter and flatter at the round downs than that of her sister *Glorious*. She could always be distinguished by the flight deck not being carried all the way to the stern and the generally flatter look to the forward edge of the flight deck. When first completed, there were only a few machine guns as light AA but, eventually, four single 2pdr were added. The ship was attached to the Atlantic Fleet, which later became the Home Fleet, for most of her career, but made a cruise to the Mediterranean annually for exercises with that fleet. As a 'show ship' of the fleet, there were many port visits and each year there were cruises to various places to show the flag. Of all the early carriers, this ship and her sister *Glorious* were probably the most successful and gave the most value for the money spent on them. The first

illustration shows the ship around 1930, during which she was painted in MS4a with the flight deck 507b. At this time, *Courageous* was involved with night fighter experiments using the Fairey Dart, which was nicknamed the 'bent nose bastard' by its crews. Sky blue was a recognition colour for her aircraft.

Just prior to World War II, the ship was refitted. A light tripod mast with an aircraft homing beacon was fitted. The single 2pdr guns were removed and octuple 2pdr mounts fitted as shown. There were apparently four quad 0.5in MG mounts fitted as well. The deck colour was changed to 507a and the hull to 507b. A mere 14 days into the start of the war, she was torpedoed by the German U-boat *U-20* and sank with the loss of 514 of her crew. At the time, she was only carrying Swordfish aircraft and was engaged in an anti-submarine hunt. The U-boat avoided counterattacking destroyers and returned safely to Germany.

HMS ARK ROYAL Pennant 91
Ark Royal class aircraft carrier 1937-40

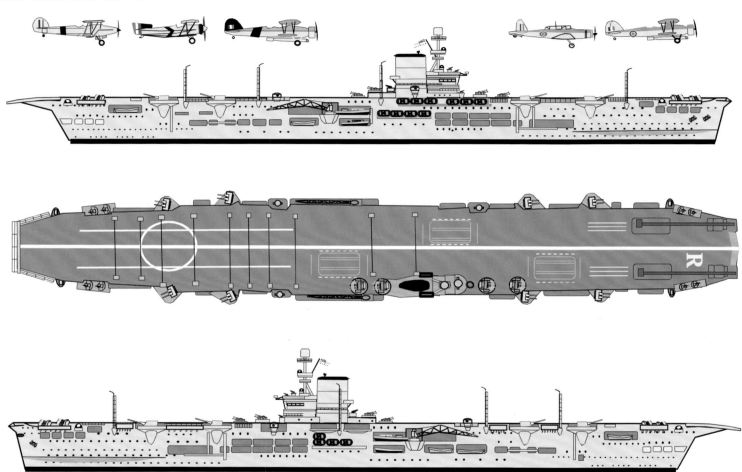

Ark Royal was completed just prior to World War II and had only just received all her correct aircraft and worked up to full efficiency when the war commenced. Due to a shortage of aircraft, the ship initially carried Ospreys, instead of Skuas, and Flycatcher fighters because they were available and good for training. Only her Swordfish were ready when she commissioned but, over the next two years, more Skua and Swordfish were received, enabling the older aircraft to be put

ashore. The ship is shown here wearing MS4a Home Fleet grey, which remained her scheme for most of the early part of the war as she was a very busy ship. Her Skuas scored one of the first successes of the war when they shot down a German flying boat on 26 September 1939. The Norway campaign was a severe trial and she was attacked many times, although not hit, with Nazi radio broadcasts claiming her sunk on several occasions.

HMS ARK ROYAL Pennant 91
Ark Royal class aircraft carrier 1940

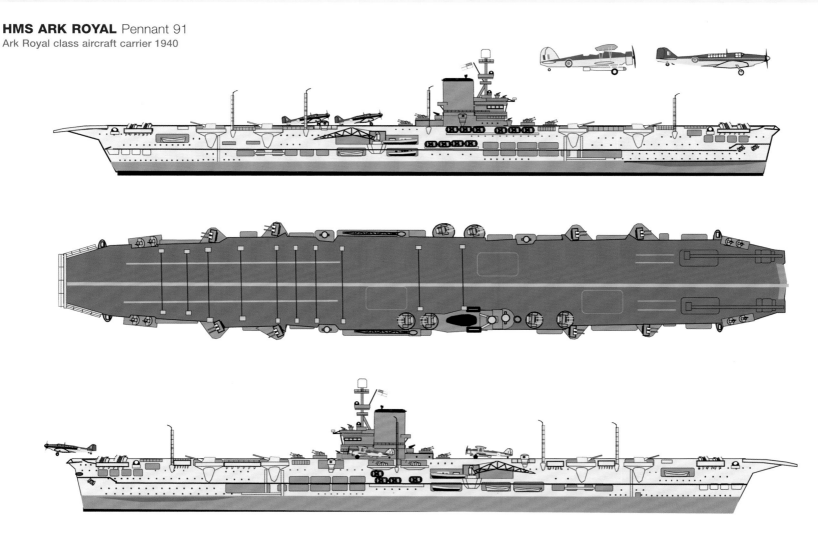

Ark Royal adopted a two-tone scheme of MS4a Home Fleet grey with 507b medium grey for a time in 1940. The deck was darkened with 507a and all deck markings changed to dull yellow. Two more octuple 2pdr pom-pom mounts were added on the port side, but there was no time to replace the multiple machine gun mounts with 20mm or carry out other modifications. As part of Force H, she took part in the hunt for the *Bismarck* and it was a Swordfish from *Ark Royal* that scored the telling torpedo hit that jammed *Bismarck*'s rudder. This enabled Royal Navy battleships and cruisers to bring *Bismarck* to action and sink her. At that time, she was one of the few major ships in the Royal Navy not to have radar. The ship was slated to receive it in 1942 but, on 13 November 1941, she was hit by a torpedo fired by U-boat *U-81*, rupturing a starboard boiler room. Extensive flooding followed and it was found that the watertight integrity of her compartments was not as good as it should have been. Eventually, all power was lost, and therefore the pumps, and she sank almost within sight of Gibraltar.

ILLUSTRIOUS CLASS AIRCRAFT CARRIERS

HMS ILLUSTRIOUS Pennant 87

Illustrious class aircraft carrier August 1940

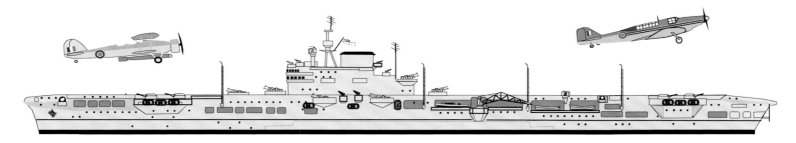

HMS ILLUSTRIOUS Pennant 87

Illustrious class aircraft carrier October 1940

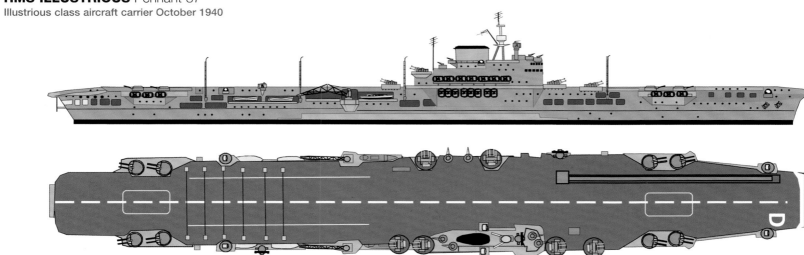

Illustrious entered service in overall MS4a Home Fleet grey but this was changed to 507b medium grey by October 1940 and was worn until December, when it had a pattern painted on it as per the second profile illustration. The deck was 507a and, initially, the deck markings were white. The letter D was carried at the starboard bow of the flight deck but was soon painted out. Within a few months, the deck lines were changed to dull yellow. On entering service, the ship was well-equipped with AA defence for the period. There were eight twin 4.5in guns, grouped in pairs, and six octuple 2pdr mounts. Thought had been given to installing quad machine gun mounts as well, but that was decided against. The cruiser *Belfast* was undergoing major repairs after being mined and, due to shortages, two of the pom-pom mounts were taken from that ship for *Illustrious*. The large aircraft beacon on the mast was lowered compared to that of *Ark Royal*, but was still a distinctive feature of Royal Navy carriers. The initial air group comprised fifteen Fairey Fulmars and eighteen Swordfish.

HMS ILLUSTRIOUS Pennant 87
Illustrious class aircraft carrier December 1940-Late 1941

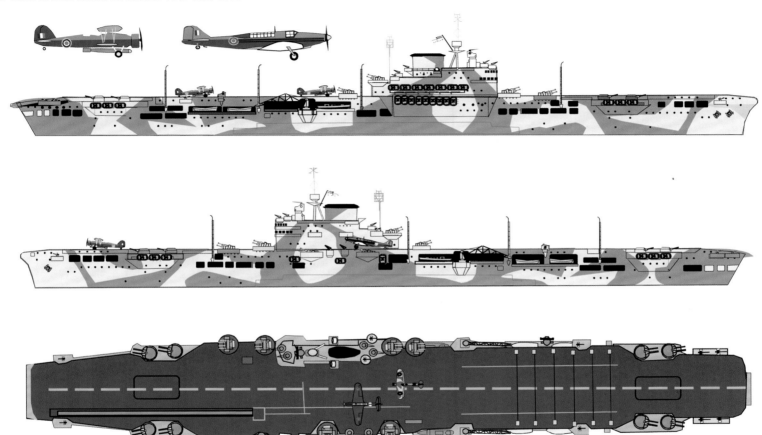

Illustrious had a pattern in MS4a applied over the existing B6 to provide her first camouflage scheme. It was probably an unofficial pattern, and was extremely similar on both sides, but the port side seems to have had some more curves. The deck was 507a and the markings were dull yellow. At some point, the broken line on the deck was changed to a solid one. The deck identification letter was removed, but when this was done is unclear. Later in the war, the identification letter was changed to Y. The majority of aircraft operated were Swordfish and Fulmars. The lifts of this class were narrow, which meant that only aircraft with folding wings could be moved to the hangar. While the aircraft complement was small compared to carriers of other nations, the great advantage of this class was its armour protection, especially of the flight deck. Most other carriers had an armoured deck as the base of the hangar, which meant bombs that pierced the flight deck could explode there. The *Illustrious* class had a flight deck intended to defeat bomb hits before they could penetrate, thus limiting damage to the ship, reducing fire risk and, of course, the loss of aircraft. Instead of the accelerator fitted to earlier carriers, this class carried a hydro–pneumatic catapult that could launch up to three aircraft per minute. The light AA armament was increased by the addition of ten 20mm Oerlikon guns. The electronics suite was updated with improved radar. A Mk V HACS was fitted to the bridge but, at that time, it was the only director fitted with Type 285 radar.

HMS ILLUSTRIOUS Pennant 87
Illustrious class aircraft carrier first half 1942

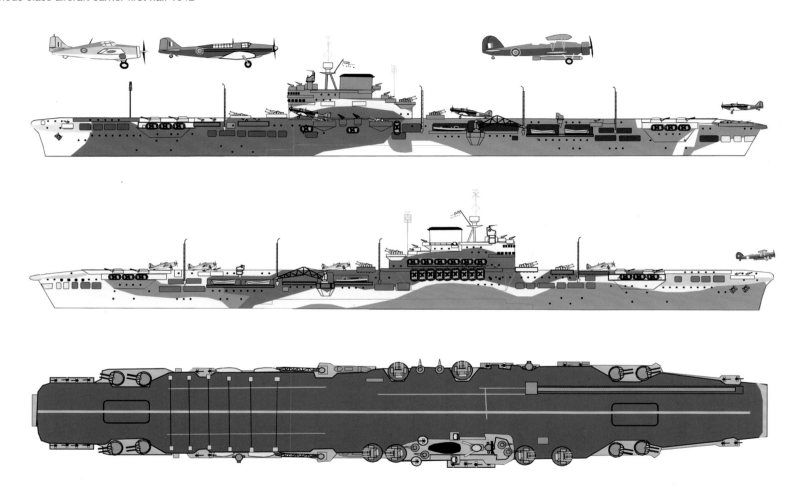

During the first half of 1942, this ship had an Admiralty-designed disruptive camouflage scheme applied that was similar to the general pattern on other carriers. On a base of 507c, patterns of 507a and B6 were used to present a wavy appearance. By their very shape, aircraft carriers were difficult to disguise. The distinctive island and a flat deck were a design feature; therefore, the dark colour was carried up from the hull onto the island to confuse this shape. Additionally, the areas of B6 and 507a were concentrated to give an appearance of being two separate ships. Flight deck markings were in dull yellow with the central line now solid. All 2pdr directors were fitted with Type 282 radar, but Type 285 radar could only be fitted to director A on the bridge. The other HACS had to wait until an aerial that did not project over the flight deck could be provided. The number of 20mm AA was increased to twenty-six.

HMS ILLUSTRIOUS Pennant 87
Illustrious class aircraft carrier second half 1942-March 1943

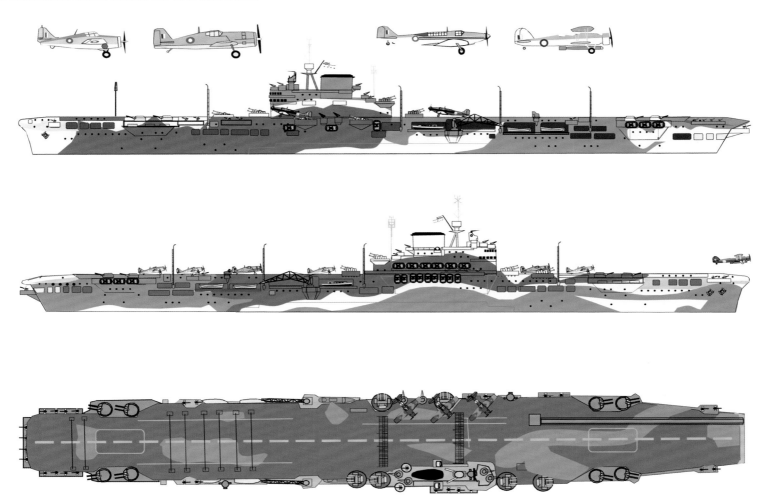

The scheme of *Illustrious* was altered in mid-1942 with MS2 replacing 507a in addition to the layout undergoing some changes. The deck camouflage is estimated from photographs. The number of 20mm AA was further increased with a battery of four across the stern. The ship was stationed in the Indian Ocean at this time and operated Fulmars, Martlet I and Martlet II fighters as well as around twenty Swordfish ('Martlet' was the Royal Navy's name for the US Grumman Wildcat). Note that the flight deck at the stern had been extended to provide more deck space.

HMS ILLUSTRIOUS Pennant 87
Illustrious class aircraft carrier second half 1943-mid-1944

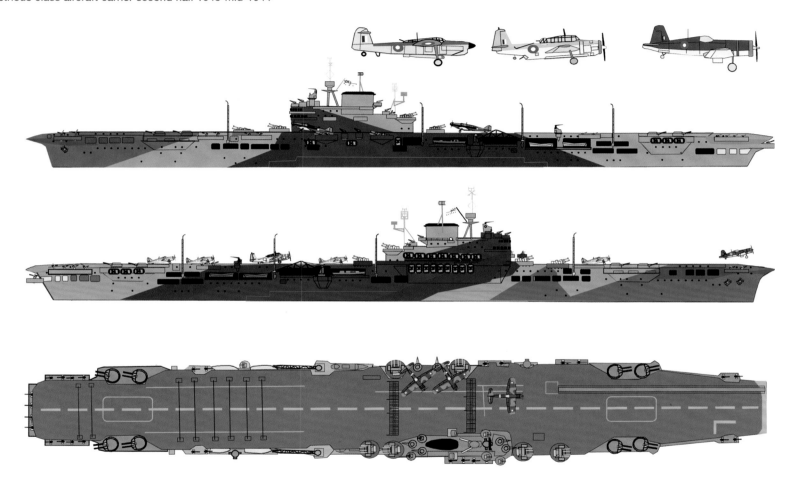

Illustrious is shown here in the last of the Admiralty disruptive schemes she wore. The colours were G5, B30, B55 and G10. The deck reverted to dark grey and the recognition letter L was adopted in early 1944. At first, the air complement comprised Fairey Barracudas and Vought Corsairs but the Barracudas were replaced by Grumman Avengers to allow compatibility with the rest of the fleet while serving in the Indian Ocean. Note that the useable length of the flight deck was lengthened and the round down made flatter as part of the process. All HACS directors now had Type 285 radar fitted. The 20mm AA were increased to forty. Much of 1943 was spent with the Home Fleet and then in the Mediterranean. On transfer to the Far East in early 1944, it was necessary to remove the red spot from the British roundels to prevent the aircraft being mistaken for Japanese ones and fired on.

HMS **ILLUSTRIOUS** Pennant 87 (BPF Pennant R2)
Illustrious class aircraft carrier 1945

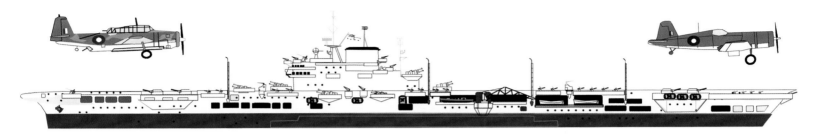

Illustrious served with the British Pacific Fleet (BPF) in 1945 and was heavily engaged in operations against Japan. For this service, the ship was given a paint scheme of 507c light grey with a dark lower hull in B15. The heavy AA armament remained the same, but all HACS directors had Type 285 radar. A single 40mm Bofors gun was placed on top of the bridge and two more each side of the bow. The number of 20mm was raised to a total of fifty-two. In March 1945, the air complement comprised sixteen Avengers and thirty-six Corsairs. The original very distinctive type 72DM radar beacon was removed. The ship had many new electronics fitted and the early, almost bare, masts were now very cluttered with aerials of all kinds.

HMS **ILLUSTRIOUS** Pennant 87 (BPF Pennant R2)
Illustrious class aircraft carrier 1945

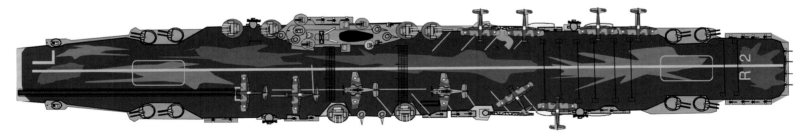

The flight deck remained dark grey but, due to the continual wear of aircraft landing and other factors, it was heavily worn. This makes it hard to distinguish exactly which shade it was. I do not believe it was camouflaged while with the BPF. It could thus be quite correctly described as a dark patchy grey. Note the large number of light AA visible around the deck edges. In order to allow more aircraft to be carried, there were outriggers projecting out from the deck. An aircraft's tail wheel was run out and the front wheels lashed to the deck. This kept more of the flight deck free for flying operations.

HMS VICTORIOUS Pennant 38
Illustrious class aircraft carrier May 1941

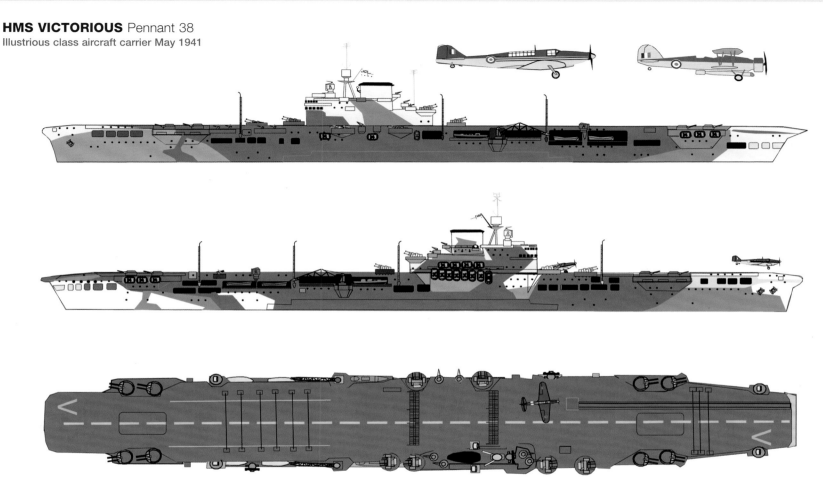

Victorious entered service in a four colour pattern comprising 507a, 507c, B5 and B55. Like all of the early schemes, this was designed in an Admiralty office and went for the maximum effect, with the arduous task of maintenance not really being considered. This particular scheme seems to have concentrated on making the ship appear shorter and, with the panels used on the bridge, perhaps further away than the observer might have thought. It seems that the designer decided that, as the lines of an aircraft carrier were rather hard to conceal, then the next best thing was to confuse the viewer as to length and distance. To that extent, the effect is reasonable.

The deck colour was 507a and MS2 or MS3. Information varies as to which of the two shades was used. All lines were in dull yellow, consistent with practice since 1940. The lifts were not outlined and indeed markings were kept to a minimum. A large letter V was carried as deck identification.

Victorious was a brand new aircraft carrier at the time of the *Bismarck* chase and, as part of her working up, had been allocated to run RAF Hurricanes to Malta. Her air complement comprised only nine Swordfish, flown by 825 Squadron, and six Fulmar fighters of 800Z Squadron, which were to have operated only in defence of the ship. The aircraft of 825 Squadron had not been able to undertake torpedo attack training for some time. *Victorious* was also supposed to be carrying Fairey Albacores of 828 Squadron, which had been working up in the Orkneys. However, they were under the control of the AOC Coastal Command, which would not release them even though the squadron had completed their training and were operationally ready. Thus, the ship sailed with only a small air group. Nonetheless, the nine Swordfish carried out a midnight attack on *Bismarck* in very bad weather. A single torpedo hit was scored but, unfortunately, on the armoured belt and did little damage. All the Swordfish returned safely but two Fulmars were lost while shadowing the enemy ship.

HMS VICTORIOUS Pennant 38
Illustrious class aircraft carrier late 1941-late 1942

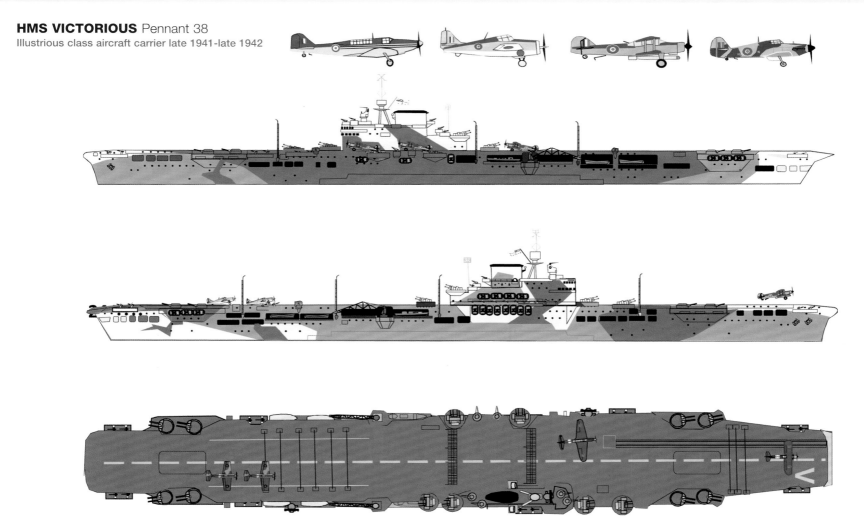

During the year after the *Bismarck* sinking, there were gradual changes. The former four-colour camouflage scheme was simplified to three colours. 507a and 507c were retained, along with the general layout, but MS3 has replaced B5 and B55. During September 1941, 802 Squadron, B Flight operated Martlet fighter aircraft from the ship. However, the majority of aircraft operated were Fulmars and Albacores. For the operations against Petsamo, Finland, and Kirkenes, Norway in July 1941, 809 Squadron was equipped with twelve Fulmars, 827 had twelve Albacores and 828 had nine Albacores. The ship operated as a Home Fleet carrier from August 1941 to December 1942. During this period, 809 Squadron still had twelve Fulmars, 817 flew nine Albacores and 832 flew

twelve Albacores. However, 832 was replaced by 820 Squadron from November 1941 to February 1942, operating twelve Albacores. Eight 20mm were added and then progressively increased; by late 1942, there were sixteen single 20mm Oerlikon guns.

Victorious took part in Operation Pedestal escorting a convoy to Malta during August 1942. The air complement was 809 Squadron with twelve Fulmars, 884 with six Fulmars, 885 with six Sea Hurricanes, 831 with twelve Albacores and a detachment of two Albacores from 817 Squadron. Note there were only six arrester wires on the flight deck at this time.

HMS VICTORIOUS ('USS ROBIN') Pennant 38
Illustrious class aircraft carrier 1943, operating with US Fleet

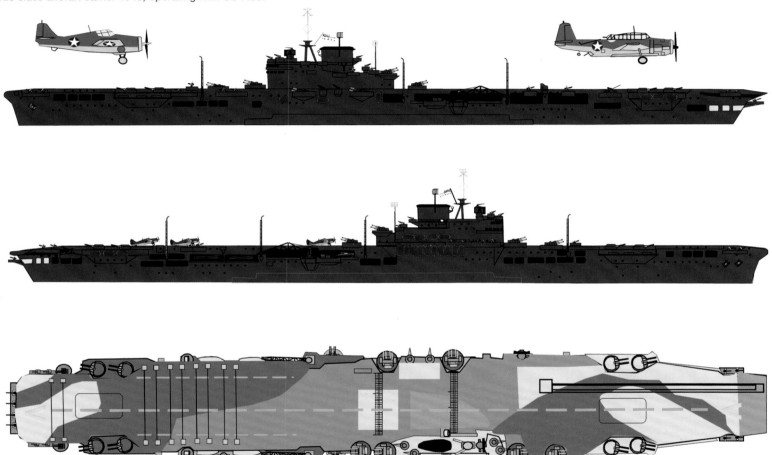

After crippling aircraft carrier losses, the US asked the British to lend them a carrier until new construction carriers came online. In the spirit of allied cooperation, the Royal Navy sent this ship. After a refit on the US East Coast, *Victorious* arrived at Ford Island, Pearl Harbor wearing the previous Royal Navy camouflage. However, it was decided to paint the ship in USN fashion, so that she would not be mistaken for a Japanese vessel. The paint scheme was retained until her return to the UK. The deck was given a disruptive pattern, which included an attempt to hide where the aircraft lifts were by creating a false one. Aircraft were all painted to US Navy style, but the Royal Navy Martlets were a different model to the Wildcats flown by the USN, which did

cause some spare parts problems. In some cases, US aircraft were issued to replace losses and break-downs. Changes included the addition of a US YE homing beacon and the removal of the Royal Navy Type 72. During the period *Victorious* was with the US fleet, there were no major carrier battles but she did take part in several smaller operations. To confuse the Japanese, the ship was referred to in radio signal traffic as USS *Robin*, a take-off on Robin Hood, but the name was never actually changed, it was merely a ruse. Over thirty 20mm AA guns were carried at this time. Two extra arrester wires were added behind the aft lift.

HMS VICTORIOUS Pennant 38
Illustrious class aircraft carrier 1944

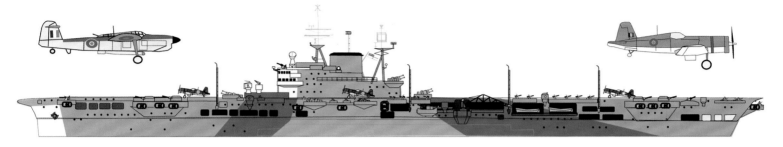

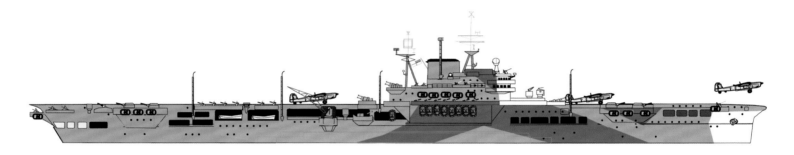

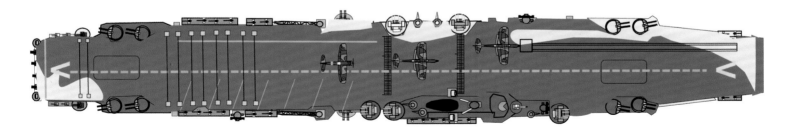

On return from service with the US fleet, *Victorious* underwent a major repair, refit and alterations period that lasted from September 1943 to March 1944. Her USN blue was painted out and replaced with an Admiralty scheme similar to others of her class. Colours used were 507a, G45, B55 and 507c. The deck was given a camouflage of three colours that were the same as those used on the sides of the ship, except for B55. Deck markings remained dull yellow but were somewhat different, including the addition of parking areas on deck. On re-entering service, she carried twenty-eight Corsair fighters of 1834 and 1836 Squadrons. Her strike power was provided by

twenty-one Barracudas from 827 and 829 Squadrons. On 3 April 1944, accompanied by the carriers *Furious*, *Emperor*, *Pursuer*, *Searcher* and *Fencer*, a major strike was launched against the German battleship *Tirpitz*. This attack, known as Operation Tungsten, inflicted severe damage on the German ship, putting her out of action for three months. *Victorious* took part in two further shipping strike operations against German-held ports in Norway, in April and June 1944, with the same air complement each time. On return from these operations, the ship was sent to join the British Eastern Fleet.

HMS VICTORIOUS Pennant 38
Illustrious class aircraft carrier 1945

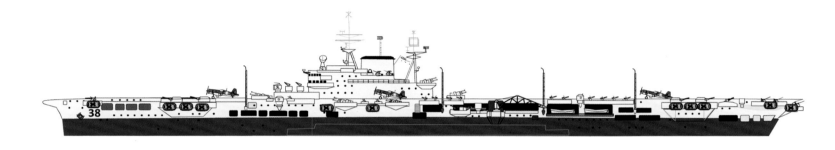

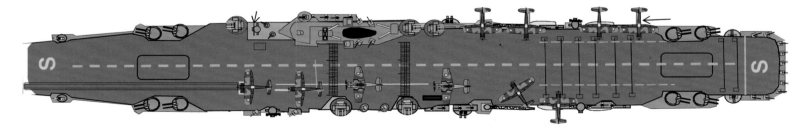

On completion of her duty with the Home Fleet, *Victorious* was sent to join the British Eastern Fleet. There, she adopted the scheme typical of that theatre. A washed-out blue panel amidships on an overall 507c light grey was intended to provide low visibility in that very hot region where shimmering heat reduced visibility. After several raids against Japanese forces in the Dutch East Indies and Burma, the ship was transferred to the British Pacific Fleet. Here, the scheme adopted was 507c overall with a lower hull in B15. This style was worn by many ships of the BPF but at some point near the end of the war, the dark blue was reduced to just a central panel. On 9 May

1945 the ship was hit by two Japanese Kamikaze suicide aircraft. Thanks to her armoured flight deck, operations were resumed within an hour, which greatly impressed US commanders. The damage was repaired in Sydney and the carrier was able to return to the fleet within a month. In late 1945, yellow was abandoned for deck markings and white used instead. The end of the war saw the ship engaged in trooping duties, which included carrying war brides, until 1947. Post-war she underwent a radical rebuild, re-entering service with a fully angled deck and operating jet aircraft. An engine fire resulted in a decision to scrap her and she was sold out of service in 1969.

HMS FORMIDABLE Pennant 67
Illustrious class aircraft carrier 1940

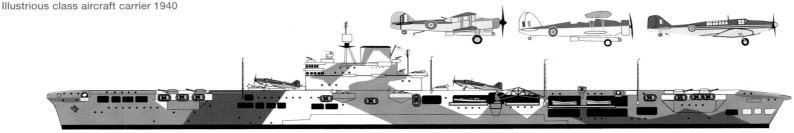

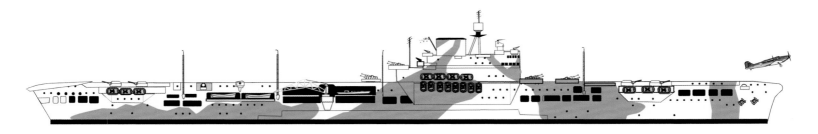

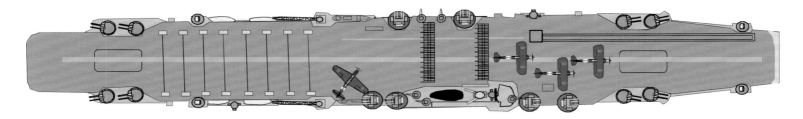

Formidable was completed by Harland and Wolff on 24 November 1940, under hurried war-time conditions, and, after a brief three-month work up that included hunting German surface raiders in the South Atlantic, was sent to the Mediterranean to replace her damaged sister ship *Illustrious*. Her camouflage scheme was also hastily applied to an unofficial scheme that used 507a, 507b and 507c, all of which were readily available Royal Navy paints. The flight deck was painted 507b with dark yellow markings. Her air group comprised eighteen Fulmar fighters of 803 and 806 Squadrons, with a strike group of twenty-one Albacores of 826 and 829 Squadrons. These squadrons were experienced, having previously operated from land bases and some from *Eagle*. There had been no time to add to her designed armament. After some initial convoy support operations, she took part in the Battle of Matapan, during which her Fulmars denied the enemy vital reconnaissance about the presence of the British fleet. The Albacores launched torpedo attacks on the Italian fleet, damaging the

battleship *Vittorio Veneto*, which barely escaped the pursuing British fleet. As dusk fell, the Albacores torpedoed the cruiser *Pola*, which was left without power but, as the Italian admiral did not know the British were present, he left two destroyers as well as the cruisers *Zara* and *Fiume* to assist. As a result, all three cruisers were intercepted during the night and sunk by the Royal Navy. Further operations in the Mediterranean saw many aircraft losses and Swordfish were supplied to replace Albacores, but the Fulmars were harder to replace and she was eventually reduced to only twelve patched-up Fulmars. On 25 May 1941, the ship was attacked by thirty Ju-87 Stukas of II/KG 30 and suffered two serious bomb hits, as well as damage from near misses. Although the armoured deck design showed itself to be sound, the ship was forced to retire from the region for repairs. She was the last Royal Navy carrier to be stationed with the Mediterranean fleet for thirty-eight months. Six Swordfish accompanied the ship for ASW protection during her voyage to the USA for repairs.

HMS FORMIDABLE Pennant 67
Illustrious class aircraft carrier 1942-3

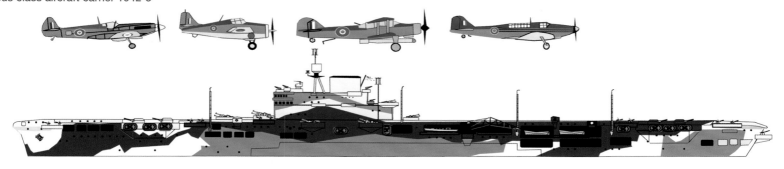

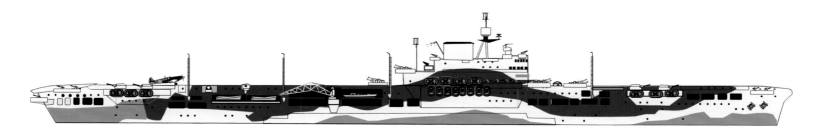

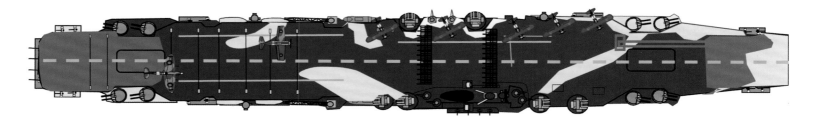

Formidable completed six months of repairs in the USA and then joined Force H for Operation Torch, the invasion of North Africa. By this time, she was wearing an Admiralty scheme similar to that designed for her sister ships. There were areas of B5, G5 and 507c to produce a disruptive pattern. The flight deck was also camouflaged using B5, MS4a and MS2. As before, the deck markings were dark yellow. Her air group was made up of whatever was available. 885 Squadron provided six Supermarine Seafires, 888 provided six Martlets and 893 had a mix of eighteen Martlets and Fulmars. A strike element was provided by 820 Squadron with twelve Albacores.

This meant that ten aircraft had to be parked on deck, since the ship was only designed to carry thirty-six aircraft in the hangar. The main role of this ship was to provide air cover for other units engaged in providing support for the landing forces. An Albacore of 820 Squadron sank U-boat *U-33*. During the US refit, an additional twenty-four 20mm AA had been added. The Type 79 radar was removed and replaced by Type 279. Type 291 radar was added and the 2pdr directors received Type 282 radar. Only the MkV HACS director on the bridge had Type 285 radar fitted.

HMS FORMIDABLE Pennant 67
Illustrious class aircraft carrier 1943-4

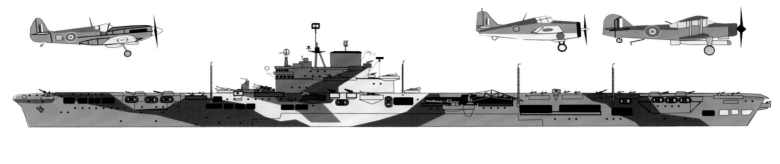

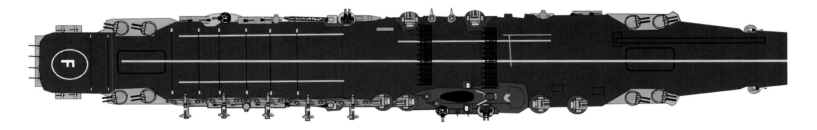

An Admiralty disruptive scheme was adopted utilising B30, B15, G5 and MS4a. The deck was painted a non-standard dark green with yellow markings, later changed to white. *Formidable* remained with Force H to support operations in North Africa working mostly out of Oran. For a time, she was the only Royal Navy fleet carrier operating in the region after the withdrawal of *Furious* in January 1943. There was a return to Gibraltar for a short time when it was feared the German battleships *Tirpitz* and *Scharnhorst* would make a combined breakout into the Atlantic and some of her aircraft were left behind to operate from land bases. In July 1943, with the *Indomitable*, she took part in Operation Husky where her fighters provided cover for the Sicily invasion forces. *Indomitable* had only recently been repaired after being damaged during Operation Pedestal and,

after she suffered torpedo damage on 11 July, *Formidable* was once again the only operational British fleet carrier in the Mediterranean. After the fall of Sicily, *Formidable* was the first aircraft carrier to enter the Grand Harbour at Malta since January 1941 and Operation Avalanche, the Salerno landings, followed in September. An unusual feature when supporting the landings at Salerno, and possibly earlier amphibious operations, was the adoption of the letter 'F' in a white circle. I know of no other time when this was done. After the Italian armistice, the ship was able to return to the Home Fleet and covered Arctic convoys to Russia until the end of 1943, when she went to Belfast to prepare for deployment to the Far East. This entailed upgrading her radars and other electronics, extending the deck and equipping her with Corsair and Avenger aircraft.

HMS FORMIDABLE Pennant 67

Illustrious class aircraft carrier 1944-5

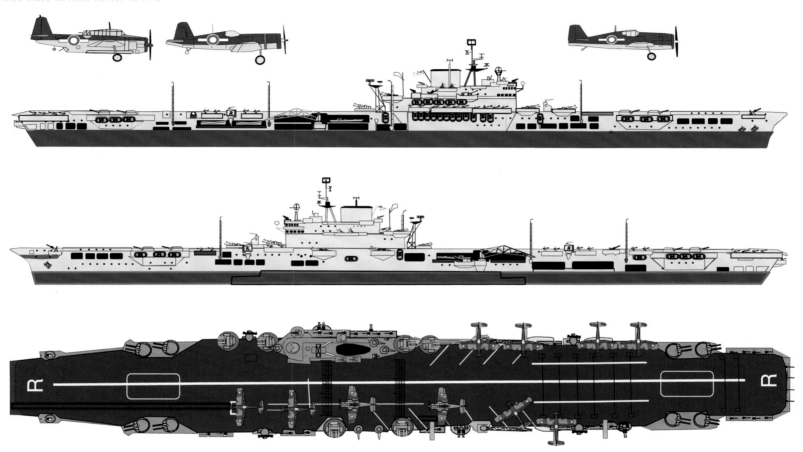

Formidable is shown in a scheme of MS4a overall with B15 deck and white lines. She replaced *Illustrious* as part of the BPF but was delayed by shaft trouble which reduced her speed to 26 knots. The problem was a left over from the severe damage suffered in 1941 and which continued to plague her centre propeller shaft. She was soon in action and on 4 May 1945 she was hit by a Kamikaze, which struck the flight deck opposite the island. The resulting fires destroyed eleven aircraft on deck but were quickly extinguished and, although the armoured deck was dented, it was patched with fast drying cement and the ship was operational again within fifty minutes. On 9 May, she was hit by another Kamikaze, without damage to the flight deck, but eighteen aircraft were destroyed. Once again, she was operational within fifty minutes. On 18 May, she suffered an accidental hangar fire, which damaged the ship and resulted in the loss of thirty aircraft. Nonetheless, she was back in action the same day and, despite few aircraft remaining, was able to fly combat air patrols for the fleet with her remaining Corsairs. Repairs were carried out in Sydney before she resumed operations with the BPF. Hellcat night-fighters were among the replacement aircraft and these proved extremely valuable. *Formidable* carried out the first British air strike on the Japanese mainland and flew many sorties as the war reached its final climax. Still having problems with her centre shaft, the ship returned home and was placed in reserve. She remained there until sold for scrap in 1953.

HMS INDOMITABLE Pennant 92

Modified Illustrious class aircraft carrier late 1941-mid-1942

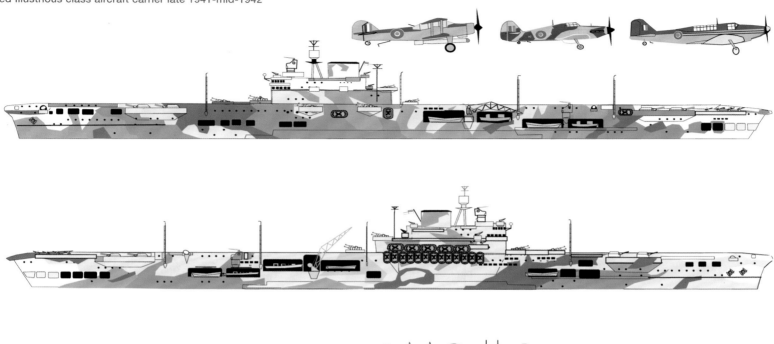

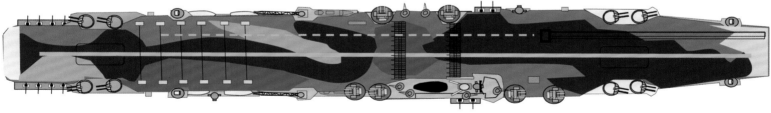

Indomitable is shown wearing an early version of the Admiralty disruptive scheme. It blended relatively pale colours with some patches of dark to produce a confusion effect – B5, B6, MS4a and white provided the lighter shades with 507a providing a contrast. All shades would have been readily available at the time the ship entered service. The deck is speculation based upon aerial photographs and practice with other carriers at this time. The general intent was to confuse where the lifts were to make it harder for attacking aircraft to aim for these vulnerable areas. After completion, this ship went to the West Indies to work up, after which she was to join Force Z bound for Singapore to provide air cover for the *Prince of Wales* and *Repulse*. However, she ran aground and had to proceed to the US for urgent repairs. Despite these being completed at an amazingly fast rate, *Indomitable* had only reached Cape Town by the time Force Z was sunk by

Japanese aircraft off Malaya. Her twenty-one fighters may have saved the day but, considering the large number of attackers, it is possible she may simply have become a casualty herself. Instead, *Indomitable* proceeded to Colombo via Aden, after which she was engaged in flying-off large numbers of fighters for the Dutch East Indies. There was a near miss with the Japanese main carrier fleet, which the British Eastern Fleet mostly avoided. After providing cover for Operation Ironclad, the occupation of Diego Suarez during May 1942, she was recalled to the Atlantic to join Force H based on Gibraltar. During the near miss with the Japanese main carrier force, she was carrying 12 Fulmars of 800 Squadron, nine Sea Hurricanes of 880 Squadron and twenty-four Fulmars spread twelve each between 827 and 831 Squadrons. For Operation Ironclad, 806 Squadron joined with four Fulmars, but 800 Squadron had been reduced to only eight Fulmars.

HMS INDOMITABLE Pennant 92
Modified Illustrious class aircraft carrier mid-1942-mid-1943

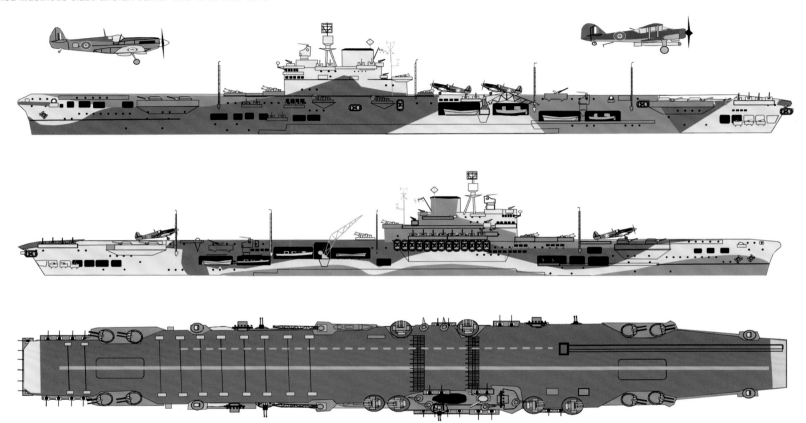

Indomitable is believed to have been repainted in this new Admiralty disruptive scheme prior to joining Force H, probably while in South Africa on transit from the British Eastern Fleet. The colours used were MS2, B5 and MS4a. The deck appears to be camouflaged in photographs, but these are not clear enough to be sure since carrier decks often showed the effects of wear due to aircraft operations. By this time, the light AA was heavily reinforced. There were now thirty-two single 20mm and two twin 40mm Bofors in addition to the original six octuple 2pdr mounts. The 4.5in heavy AA were controlled by four Mk V HACS with Type 285 radar. All 2pdr directors had Type 242 radar fitted. Unlike her sister ships, the forward searchlight was still carried. *Indomitable* was available for Operation Pedestal, a hotly-disputed convoy to Malta, during which she was hit by three bombs and badly damaged. Near misses also added to her damage. She was able to limp in to Gibraltar for temporary repairs, then proceeded to Liverpool for those to be completed. The air group embarked was made up of entirely British aircraft of only two types.

The air group retained Albacores as the main strike aircraft with twenty-one flown by 817 Squadron. For Operation Husky, she carried thirty Seafire fighters of 807, 880 and 899 Squadrons. Her duty for Husky was to provide air support for the fleet so land-based aircraft from Tunisia and other bases could attack invasion targets. On 10 July, the landings took place and the cover force stood some two hundred miles offshore ready to strike if the Italian Fleet sortied to attack the invasion force. On the evening of 11 July, a German Ju-88 aircraft came in very low, avoiding radar, and was not recognised as an enemy until it had penetrated the screen and dropped a torpedo. The enemy aircraft then flew out through the fleet without a shot being fired at it in return. The torpedo struck abreast the port torpedo room, causing serious flooding, but, despite the damage, the ship was able to make it to Malta under her own power. This time the damage was such that she was sent to the USA for repairs which took from September 1943 to March 1944.

HMS INDOMITABLE Pennant 92 (BPF Pennant R8)
Modified Illustrious class aircraft carrier April 1944 – Early 1945

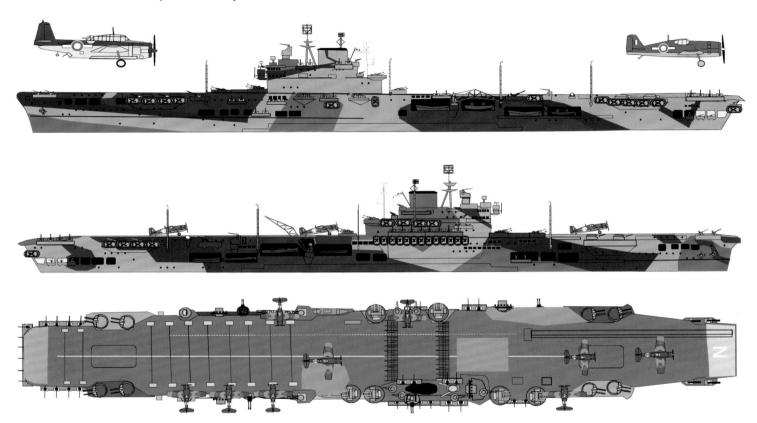

A new Admiralty Disruptive scheme was applied during April 1944, using G5, B55, B30 and B15. It was retained when the ship went to the British Eastern Fleet and for much of her time in the Pacific. Photographs seem to indicate that a square patch of deck near the island was always painted a slightly lighter grey and was possibly to trick enemy aircraft about where the aircraft lift was. *Indomitable* completed repairs in the USA and arrived in Rosyth on 2 May 1944. During seven months of repairs, many crew had been transferred and new air groups taken on. She left for the British Eastern Fleet on 12 June, with working up taking place during passage. The ship reached Trincomalee on 25 July 1944 and became very active with the fleet as it carried out operations against the Japanese. Operations against enemy targets in the Dutch East Indies and the Nicobar Islands were carried out until January 1945. *Indomitable* and others assembled at Fremantle, Western Australia to form the British Pacific Fleet (BPF). The Royal Navy crews had to learn the operating techniques of the USN in order to work with the Americans. But the greatest problem faced was

the lack of supply and support ships to enable the BPF to operate at sea for long periods of time. A fleet base was established at Manus Island in the Admiralty Islands group, but less than half the support ships needed were assembled there when the fleet finally arrived via Sydney. Much of this was due to the disgraceful demands of Australian trade unions, which held ships up with rolling strikes and go-slow actions. The situation was so bad that the USN found it much quicker to send ships all the way home for repair in US ports than to undergo ridiculous delays in Australian dock-yards. On arrival at Manus Island, the BPF became Task Force 57, as part of the US Fifth Fleet, under the command of Admiral Spruance. When US Task Force 58 had three carriers, *Wasp*, *Intrepid* and *Franklin*, badly damaged, the BPF was called on to help with the destruction of Japanese aircraft to prevent them interfering in Operation Iceberg, the invasion of Okinawa. During the resulting strikes, *Indomitable* was attacked by a Kamikaze, which hit the armoured deck and slid over the side with little damage caused. The ship was back in full operation within short time.

HMS INDOMITABLE Pennant 92 (BPF Pennant R8)
Modified Illustrious class aircraft carrier early 1945

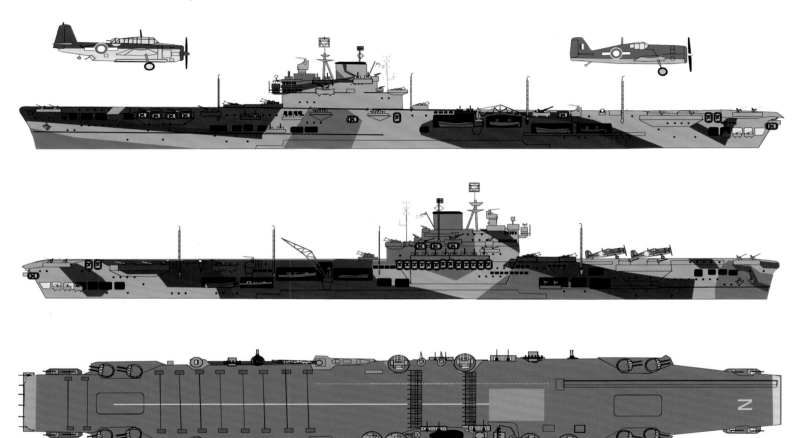

Indomitable received battle damage during operations with the British Pacific Fleet and was repaired by US fleet repair ships at Leyte Gulf. Her paintwork was somewhat battered and, although some Royal Navy paint was available, there was insufficient B30 so US Navy ocean grey 5-O was used instead. The other shades were Royal Navy codes, but it is possible that US Navy blue 5/N was used as well. The pattern remained mostly the same but there were some variations to the previous lines. The lighter grey square on the deck was apparently an attempt to fool Japanese attackers as to the real location of the aircraft lift. Unlike earlier in the war, the lifts were no longer outlined in white. Deck lines were in white but, in photographs, appear to be thinner and less pronounced,

which could also have been a camouflage measure. In many photographs, the areas painted in B55 appear almost white. It is possible that the grey used was MS4a, which was much lighter than B55. The usual deck letter A was changed to N while serving with the BPF. After considerable sea time and constant operations, the ship withdrew to Sydney for a refit and repairs. The original six octuple 2pdr AA mounts were strengthened with the addition of fourteen 40mm and twenty-four 20mm Oerlikons. However, it is possible that some of the singles had been exchanged for twin mounts as on other ships of this type.

HMS INDOMITABLE Pennant 92 (BPF Pennant R8)
Modified Illustrious class aircraft carrier mid-1945

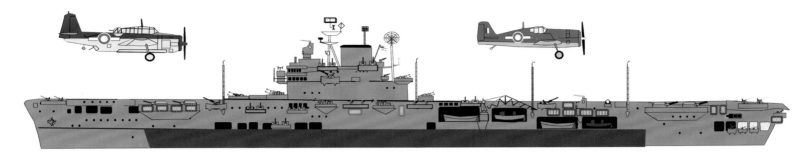

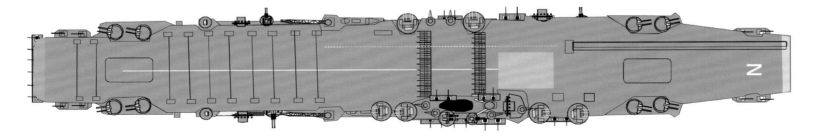

Indomitable went to Sydney for a refit, during which her previous camouflage was over-painted to the Admiralty standard pattern first introduced in 1944. This comprised a hull panel of B20 and G45 overall. The masts were painted white and the steel decks and flight decks G10. While refitting, the ship was provided with an American SM-1 radar, which was also known as CXBL. Although this radar was carried by most US fleet carriers, it was very heavy – the rotating mechanism alone weighted six tons. As a result, *Indomitable* was the only British carrier to be fitted with

it. By the time the refit was completed, the Japanese had surrendered. However, she joined the fleet in time for the relief of Hong Kong, after which she sailed for the UK via Sydney. After a few years of active service, and then a period in reserve, she was sold for scrap in 1955. Like most of her group, her main strength, the armoured deck, restricted the number of aircraft that could be carried and proved too expensive for post-war modification. Only her half-sister, *Victorious*, was modernised.

INDEFATIGABLE CLASS AIRCRAFT CARRIERS
HMS INDEFATIGABLE Pennant 10
Indefatigable class aircraft carrier May–August 1944

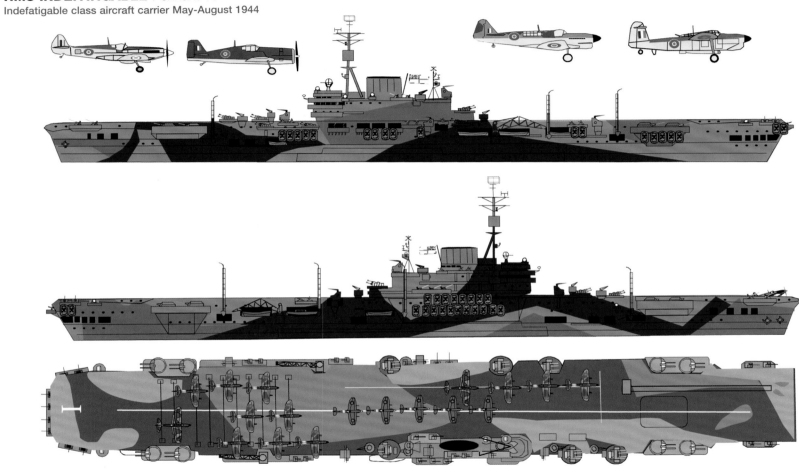

Indefatigable suffered many delays due to the pressure of war on British shipyards and the priority given to steel for escort vessels during the dark days of the Battle of the Atlantic. She did not enter service until May 1944, despite having been laid down in 1939. The Admiralty Dark Disruptive Scheme was one of the last ever designed for large ships with her sister ship being the last of all. It was well suited for her first operations with the Home Fleet, all of which were strikes in Norway, including attacks on the German battleship *Tirpitz*. The shades used were G45, G20 and G10, the combination of which resulted in a very dull overall scheme. The deck camouflage is estimated from photographs. The *Indefatigable* class had a heavier look than the *Illustrious* class and, with two

hangars, could carry more aircraft; but this was at the cost of the hangers having less height. This was a problem, as they could not accommodate Corsair fighters, which were serving in some numbers with the Royal Navy. In their place, the far shorter-range Seafire had to be carried. The US-built Hellcat was also suitable, but available in fewer numbers. Strike aircraft comprised the British Barracuda torpedo-bomber and the Fairey Firefly fighter-bomber, the dimensions of which had been kept to within the limited size of Royal Navy carrier lifts and low hangars. Although of much the same design, as earlier catapults, the model fitted was somewhat more powerful and could launch heavier aircraft with full loads.

HMS INDEFATIGABLE Pennant 10 (BPF Pennant R7)
Indefatigable class aircraft carrier mid-1945

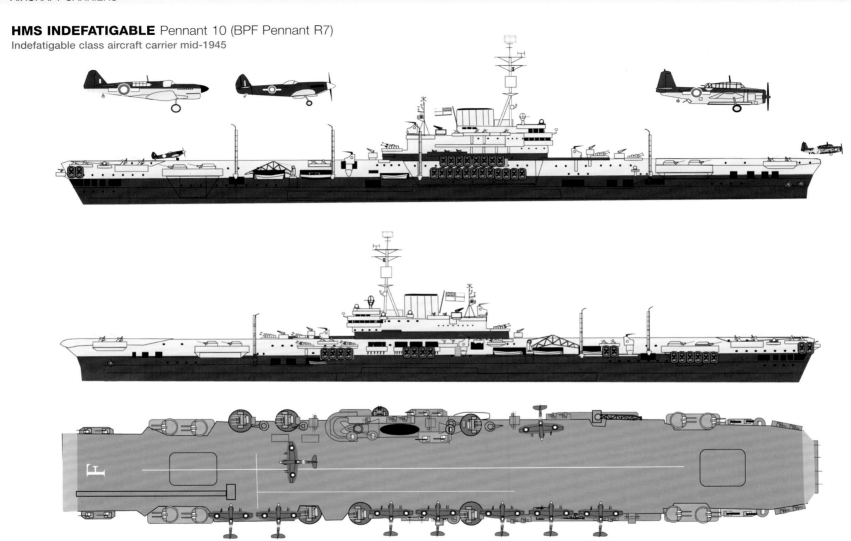

Indefatigable was repainted in Pacific camouflage while refitting in Sydney. The band of B15 was particularly high and the rest of the ship was painted MS4a. Rather unusually, there was also a band of B15 at the lower level of the island structure. At this time, the armament of the ship was sixteen 4.5in AA, six octuple and one quad 2pdr mounts, thirteen single 40mm, as well as fifteen twin and six single 20mm AA. On 1 April 1945, a Kamikaze hit the flight deck at the base of the island. The armoured deck resisted the impact and little damage was done. The ship was fully operational within an hour. *Indefatigable* took part in many strikes against Japanese targets including the carrier *Kaiyo*, which was left burning and with its back broken. This was the only time a British carrier attacked an enemy carrier. On 15 August, there had been no confirmation of the ceasefire and further strikes were launched. Avengers from *Indefatigable* were intercepted by twelve Japanese A6M fighters and, in the ensuing battle, escorting Seafires shot down eight of the enemy and damaged the rest with the loss of only one Seafire. This was the last fighter dogfight of World War II.

HMS IMPLACABLE Pennant 86 (BPF Pennant R5)
Indefatigable class aircraft carrier August 1944

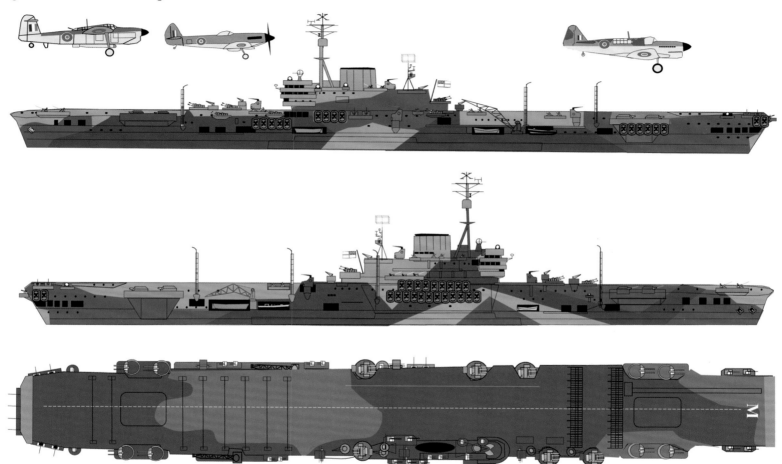

Implacable entered service in an Admiralty Dark Disruptive Scheme using G45, B10 and B30. In photographs, the light areas appear much lighter and could have been MS3. The scheme was short-lived and painted out after less than eight months. She was completed on 28 August 1944 and, after a brief work up, took part in six days of operations against shipping in Norwegian waters, between late October and early December 1944. Her aircraft accounted for U-boat *U-1060*, which was driven ashore, and coastal shipping of 40,000grt. These strikes were in preparation for the ship to transfer to the Pacific to join the BPF. Recognition features between this ship and her sister *Indefatigable* were that the ship's boats were carried one deck lower, the Type 281 radar aft of the

funnel and a MkV HACS director on the island, but forward of the light mast between it and the funnel. Type 291 radar was carried at the top of the main tripod mast. Some light AA were in slightly different positions. The low hangar roofs meant this class could only operate specific aircraft and could not accommodate the US-built Corsair. *Implacable* was the last British fleet carrier to transfer to the Pacific, leaving the Home Fleet without any vessels of the type, but this was no longer important as all major German fleet units had been sunk or severely damaged, leaving no Kriegsmarine threat to be countered.

HMS IMPLACABLE Pennant 86 (BPF Pennant R5)
Indefatigable class aircraft carrier May 1945

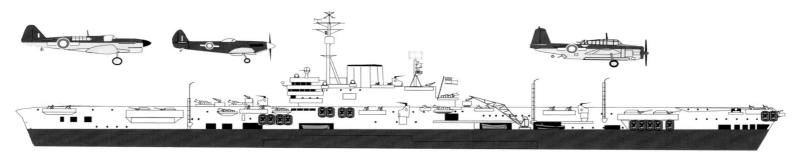

HMS IMPLACABLE Pennant 86 (BPF Pennant R5)
Indefatigable class aircraft carrier August 1945

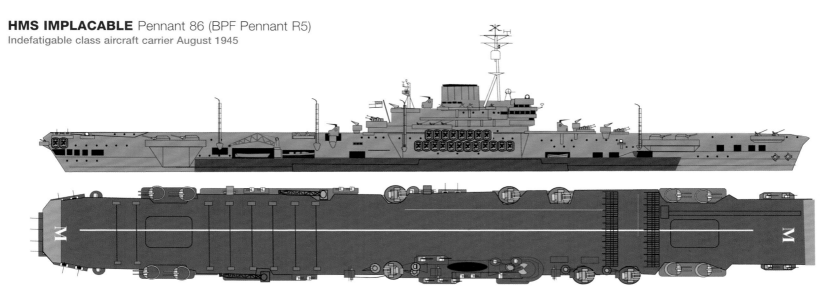

Implacable had her disruptive scheme painted out in May 1945 and adopted the Admiralty standard scheme then in use. The scheme was the same on both sides. This comprised a panel of B15 amidships and the rest of the ship in B45. Her joining the British Pacific Fleet had been delayed by engine trouble that necessitated repairs in Sydney. The ship was thus rather too late to see much service against Japan before the war was over – however, she took part in strikes on Truk and the Japanese home islands from June to August 1945. Then, in August, she returned to Sydney again with the majority of the BPF for additional work and refitting. Here, she was repainted in the light grey of 507c with a dark blue panel of B15 that ran from bow to stern. Masts were painted white. Photographs of the ship suggest the deck was dark grey while serving in the Pacific. The letter M was borne on the flight deck, but this was changed to C after the war had ended. The ship was refitted for training duty in 1948 and served in that role until 1954, when she was placed in reserve and sold for scrap shortly after. *Implacable* was broken up late in 1955.

LIGHT FLEET AIRCRAFT CARRIERS

HMS UNICORN Pennant F 72

Unicorn class light and maintenance aircraft carrier 1943

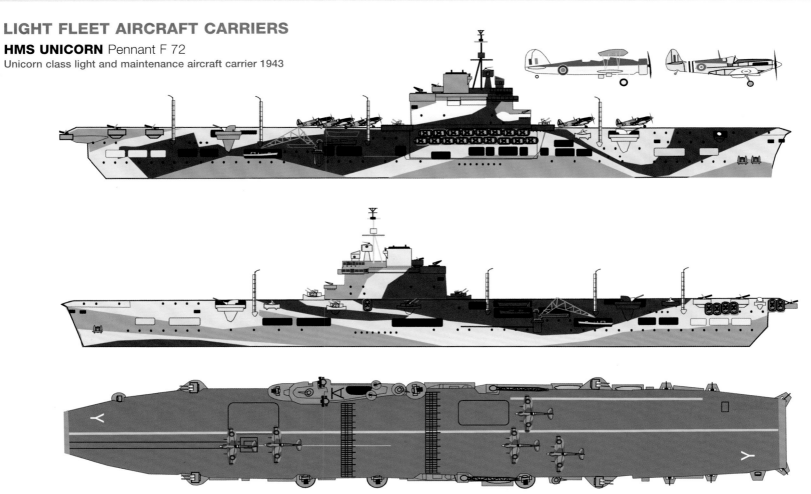

On entering service, this ship was painted in an Admiralty Disruptive Scheme. The colours used were B15 and MS30 on a base of MS4a. The deck was dark grey but the exact shade is not known. The flight deck does not appear to have been camouflaged in photographs of the ship at this time. The yellow line on the starboard side was apparently to guide aircraft using the aft lift. Unicorn was ordered as a specialist support ship for aircraft carriers. She was to carry spare aircraft for them, engines and other spares for their aircraft and, most importantly of all, specialist mechanics who could carry out major repairs. In this format, she was to be more like a depot ship than a carrier. However, soon after construction started, it was realised that it could be an advantage if the ship could fly-off aircraft as replacements and be able to land-on others in need of maintenance. The loss of carriers and damage to others led the Admiralty to the conclusion that it would be even

more useful if Unicorn could be used as an operational carrier if needed. Despite all these changes of intent, the ship progressed well and was ready for service by March 1943. There were two hangars and she was similar in appearance to Ark Royal, especially with the overhanging aft flight deck, yet was much shorter. As a result, she looked rather high and bulky, but was nonetheless a good steady sea platform. Her speed was based around that of a fast depot ship. Although unable to keep up with the faster fleet carriers, at 24 knots, her speed was more than adequate for operating with the older battleships. As it turned out, the ship barely had time to work up before being required to escort three troop convoys from the UK to Gibraltar. She then took on her designed role of aircraft maintenance and resupply. In September, she operated as a carrier for the landings of Operation Avalanche, providing fighter cover over the landing ships and beachhead.

HMS UNICORN Pennant F72 (BPF Pennant R018, then B312)
Unicorn class light and maintenance aircraft carrier 1944

HMS UNICORN Pennant F72 (BPF Pennant R018, then B312)
Unicorn class light and maintenance aircraft carrier 1945

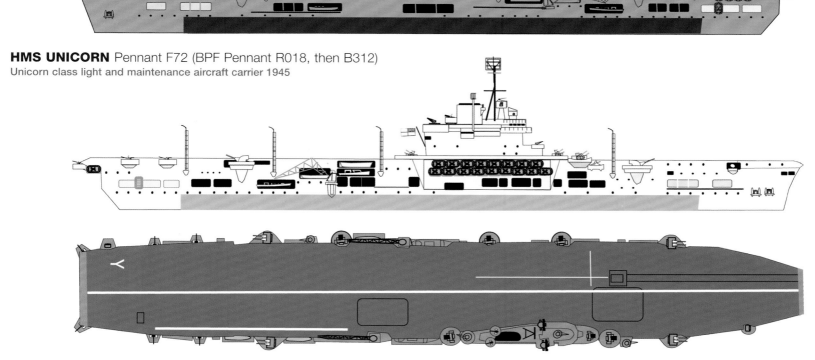

After operations in support of the Salerno landings, this ship was sent to the Indian Ocean and, eventually, to the British Pacific Fleet. During this time, she acted in her designed role as a maintenance and repair carrier, where her services were found to be extremely helpful. Replacement aircraft were supplied to fleet and escort carriers and they, in turn, transferred aircraft in need of overhaul and repair to *Unicorn*. The two hangars and large deck area provided plenty of space for the work to be carried out, while still leaving space for spare aircraft, many of which were carried crated and assembled as needed. Prior to deployment, the AA armament was increased. An additional quad 2pdr mount was placed forward of the island and another near the port side crane.

Some 20mm were increased to twins. The original British Type 72 DM aircraft homing beacon was replaced by the US YE beacon attached to the side of her funnel. Her service with the BPF included the invasion of Okinawa. This ship proved so useful that two light fleet carriers under construction were converted for a similar role, but without the ability to land aircraft on the deck. At the end of World War II, she assisted in the repatriation of prisoners of war. When not operating as a light carrier, she had plenty of spare accommodation and was often called on as a troop transport. She also served during the Korean War and was not broken up until 1959-60.

HMS COLOSSUS Pennant 15 (BPF Pennant R61)
Colossus class light aircraft carrier December 1944

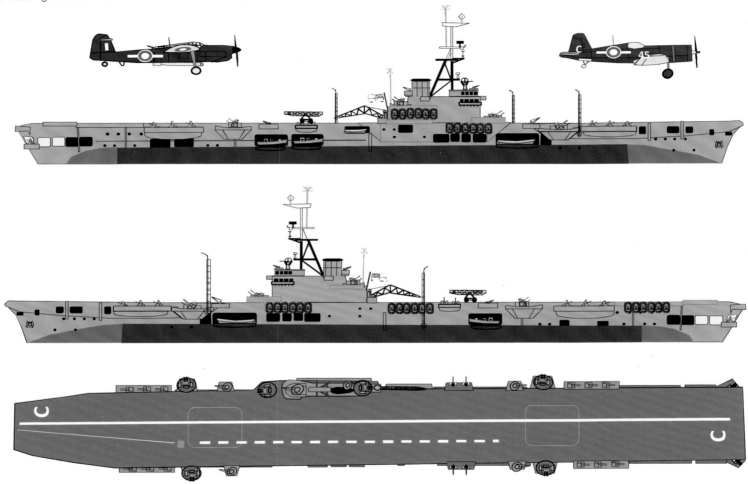

This ship completed in December 1944, entering service in a scheme designed especially for the class. The overall colour was G45, with a central panel of B20 or B15. The panel had curved sections of B30 or MS2 at each end. The exact ones used depended on availability and, as they were very close in shade, it is almost impossible to tell which was used when viewing black and white photographs. Admiralty instructions specified G10 for the decks. The armament was entirely made up of light weapons. Six quad 2pdr mounts were the heaviest and they were backed up by

thirty-two 20mm in fourteen twin mounts and four singles. This class adopted certain merchant practices in order to speed production and enable work to be done by yards not used to Admiralty standards. Weaponry and electronics fit thus varied from ship to ship according to what was available. They were never intended to be converted to merchant ships after the war as some sources have mistakenly stated.

HMS COLOSSUS Pennant 15 (BPF Pennant R61)
Colossus class light aircraft carrier 1945

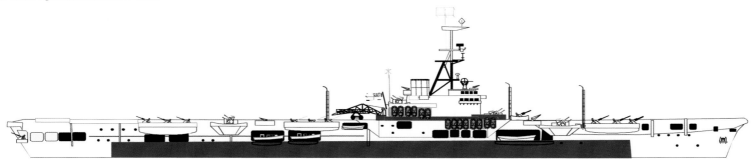

On arrival in Sydney, *Colossus* underwent modifications to enable her to cope with the Kamikaze threat. This involved replacing all twin and single 20mm mounts with single 40mm Bofors. The armament then became twenty-four 2pdrs and twenty-seven single 40mm Bofors. At the time, Japanese aircraft carriers were painted in a similar style to the Royal Navy Admiralty scheme. As a result, the new carriers were painted 507c overall with a dark panel of B20 amidships. By the time this work was completed, Japan had surrendered and the ship did not see combat in the Pacific. This ship was transferred to France as *Arromanches* in 1951.

TRIUMPH, WARRIOR, THESEUS
All these ships were completed post-war and entered service in peacetime colours. All three had 40mm Bofors instead of 20mm, with some twin mounts instead of quad 2pdr mounts.

MAJESTIC CLASS
All completed post-war

HMS VENERABLE Pennant 04 (BPF Pennant R63)
Colossus class light aircraft carrier January 1945

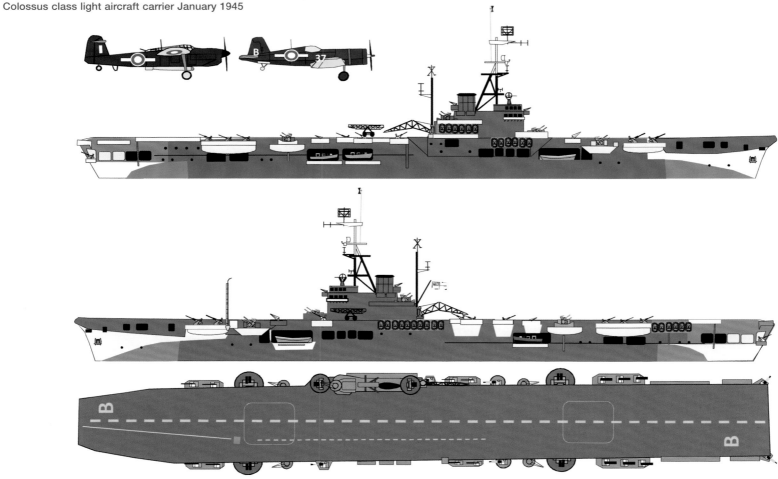

By the time *Venerable* entered service, most British carriers seem to have changed from yellow to white deck markings. However, photographs of the ship seem to indicate that the markings are quite strikingly dull compared to her sister ships. I have therefore shown the deck markings in dark yellow, as was common mid-war. At least two ships of this class wore an adaptation of the intended Admiralty standard scheme designed for them. The above scheme variation uses B30, G45 and 507c. The flight deck was specified as G10. The light AA of the ships in this class varied quite a lot, with many carrying 20mm in twin mounts. However, this ship completed with twenty-four 2pdrs, in six quad mounts, and twenty single 40mm Bofors. *Venerable* was intended to join the 11th

Aircraft Carrier Squadron for operations with the British Pacific Fleet, but the war ended before the ships could all assemble at Manus Island. She took part in various operations to reoccupy territory captured by the Japanese. The *Colossus* class carriers were externally almost identical to the *Majestic* class, which followed them. However, internally they were not as well laid-out as the later ships, with an older style of crew messing and accommodation facilities which made them less comfortable to serve in. Post-war, the ship was sold to the Netherlands in 1948 as *Karel Doorman* and underwent many changes in appearance. She was later sold to Argentina as *Veinticinco de Mayo* and took part in the Falklands War against Great Britain. She was scrapped in 1999-2000.

HMS GLORY Pennant 68 (BPF Pennant R62)
Colossus class light aircraft carrier May 1945

HMS GLORY Pennant 68 (BPF Pennant R62)
Colossus class light aircraft carrier August 1945

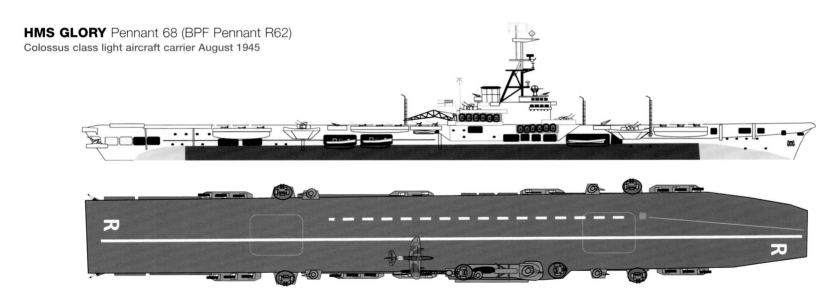

Glory spent some time in the Mediterranean in early 1945, during which she wore a rather strange modification of the Admiralty standard scheme, which was referred to by crew members as 'dazzle.' Prior to that, she worked up in the standard scheme as per *Colossus* and, as with that ship, changed to a Pacific style later. However, the curved areas on either end of the central panel were retained and appear to have been pale blue. Two of the *Colossus* class seem to have worn alterations to the Admiralty scheme while in, or passing through, the Mediterranean but the reason why is not clear.

It could have been to confuse identity, but Axis activity in the area was almost non-existent at the time. The colours appear to be 507c, B15 or B20, with MS3. The deck was 507a. The initial armament was six quad 2pdr mounts, fourteen twin 20mm and four single 20mm. Most of the 20mm mounts were replaced by single 40mm Bofors AA guns at Sydney in July 1945, for a final war armament of twenty-four 2pdrs and twenty-three 40mm Bofors.

HMS VENGEANCE Pennant 71 (BPF Pennant R62)
Colossus class light aircraft carrier January 1945

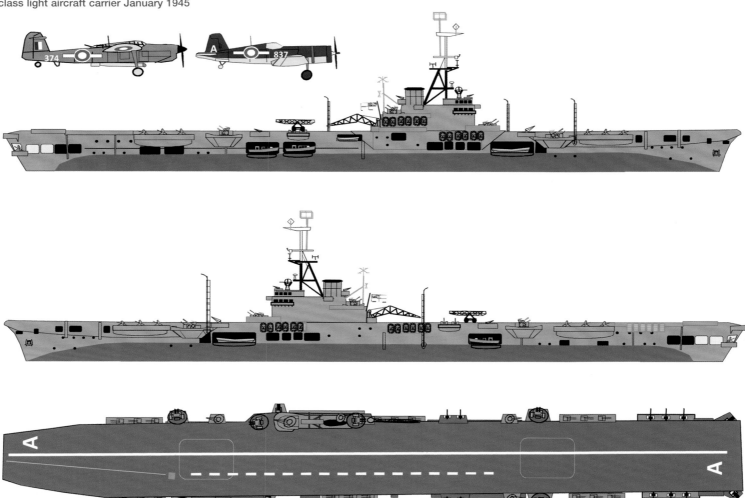

Vengeance wore the basic Admiralty scheme. The hull panel was 507a, with MS2 at each end. The overall colour was MS3. The flight deck was G10, which, by 1945, was the specified Admiralty shade. As with the rest of the class, this was changed to 507c pale grey with a dark hull panel after deploying to the Pacific. She carried twenty-two twin 20mm AA and ten single 20mm as well as sixteen 2pdr.

HMS OCEAN Pennant 68 (BPF Pennant R65)
Colossus Class Light Fleet Aircraft Carrier August 1945

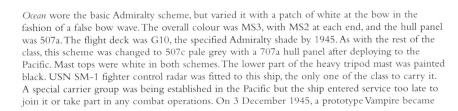

Ocean wore the basic Admiralty scheme, but varied it with a patch of white at the bow in the fashion of a false bow wave. The overall colour was MS3, with MS2 at each end, and the hull panel was 507a. The flight deck was G10, the specified Admiralty shade by 1945. As with the rest of the class, this scheme was changed to 507c pale grey with a 707a hull panel after deploying to the Pacific. Mast tops were white in both schemes. The lower part of the heavy tripod mast was painted black. USN SM-1 fighter control radar was fitted to this ship, the only one of the class to carry it. A special carrier group was being established in the Pacific but the ship entered service too late to join it or take part in any combat operations. On 3 December 1945, a prototype Vampire became the first jet aircraft to land on an aircraft carrier. She took part in the Korean War in 1952-3. In 1956, *Ocean* was at the Suez landings, where she acted as a commando carrier to put troops ashore by helicopter. The ship went into reserve in 1957 and was broken up in 1962. Although giving good service, and despite refits, the *Colossus* class was more crowded and less comfortable to serve on than the later *Majestic* class ships. This ship carried twin 40mm AA guns in place of the quad 2pdrs, as well as twenty-four singles for a total of thirty-six 40mm guns. Directors for the twin weapons were provided in the locations previously occupied by 2pdr directors.

HMS PIONEER Pennant D76
Colossus class light maintenance aircraft carrier February 1944

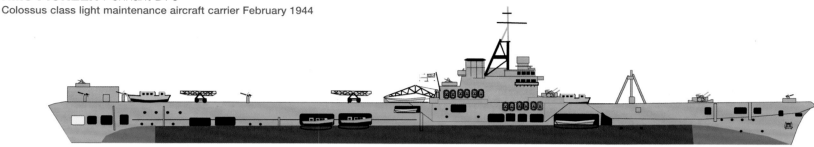

These ships had plenty of spare deck space and therefore carried all their AA weaponry there. The lack of sponsons enabled them to move closer to other carriers when exchanging aircraft and avoided unnecessary damage. The large sheer legs over the forward lift enabled the movement of heavy aircraft and equipment that was otherwise immobile. There were two mobile cranes on deck as well as the standard crane fitted to the light fleet carriers.

HMS PERSEUS Pennant 51 (BPF Pennant B346)
Colossus class light maintenance aircraft carrier October 1945

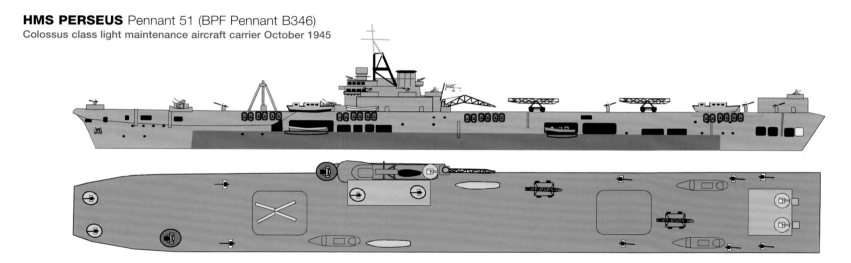

The versatility of the earlier maintenance carrier *Unicorn* was such that the Admiralty decided that, if it was to be operating squadrons of aircraft carriers, more such vessels would be needed. However, it was decided during their construction that, as a larger number of newly-built carriers were coming online, there was no need for them to necessarily be able to operate aircraft of their own. The *Colossus* class carrier *Mars*, which was under construction, was renamed *Pioneer* and her sister *Edgar* was renamed *Perseus*. Both were ordered to convert to the maintenance role. As such, they carried spare aircraft, engines, spare parts and had extensive workshops, which would enable them to carry out maintenance and repair of aircraft from other carriers. The intent was that such a ship would be attached to a carrier group to free the carriers up for more intensive operations, as it

would be able to supply replacement aircraft and carry out most of the repairs. The carriers, in turn, would provide air cover. *Pioneer* was the first to complete and wore the official version of the scheme intended for the *Colossus* class, with an all over G45 with B20 hull panel and sloping panels of MS2 at each end. The lower masts were black but, from the funnel up, they were white. *Perseus* is shown in another of the standard designs. She has a panel of B30 on an overall hull of B55. While there were a large number of carriers in service, they were very useful ships but, as the number of carriers declined, they went into reserve. *Pioneer* was scrapped in 1954. *Perseus* followed in 1958, after being the trials ship for the steam catapults developed after World War II.

HMS AUDACITY Pennant D 10
Audacity class escort aircraft carrier 1941

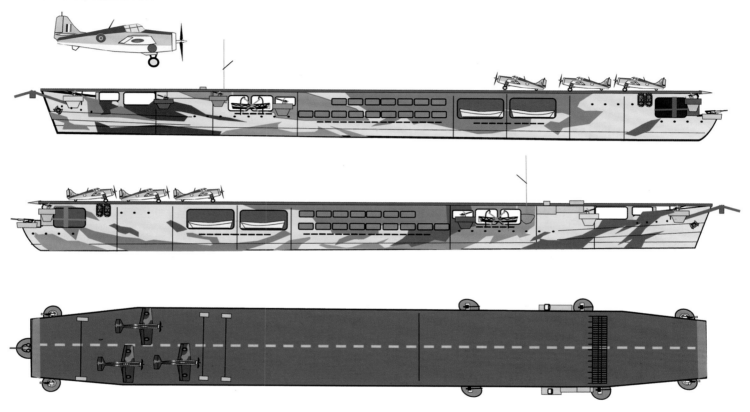

In 1940, German forces occupied French Atlantic bases, which enabled them to send more submarines to attack incoming British convoys and to also use aircraft for scouting and attacks on those convoys. Some British ships were fitted with a catapult and mostly a worn-out aircraft, which could be launched to chase enemy scouts and attackers, but with the disadvantage that they could not land back on the ship and would have to ditch if they could not make it to land. Clearly, a carrier was preferable but none could be spared and early experiments had shown the fleet carriers to be too vulnerable. A project was put forward to convert a merchant ship with a simple flight deck and minimum facilities specifically for convoy duty. *Audacity* was originally the German merchant ship *Hanover*, which was captured in the Indian Ocean and sent to the UK. The Admiralty obtained her for conversion as a trial for the idea, thus creating the very first escort carrier. She briefly carried the name *Empire Audacity*. There was no lift or hangar and all aircraft had to be serviced on deck. At first, it was intended she would only carry Martlet fighters, but it was found that Swordfish could operate from her to provide an ASW capability. Her career was short-lived as she was sunk by *U-751* while covering Convoy HG-76 on 20 December 1941. Although

she had made only two round trips between the UK and Gibraltar, her usefulness had been proved in the ability of her aircraft to spot U-boats near the convoy and force them to dive. Although most aircraft used were fighters, there was no way for a U-boat to tell if the attacking aircraft could sink them or not and therefore took the precaution of a crash dive. This was very useful in forcing U-boats shadowing and reporting the position of a convoy to break contact. The Martlets were also able to intercept Fw-200 long-range aircraft which had previously been able to shadow a convoy with impunity, by staying out of AA range. Despite the simplicity of her conversion as an aircraft carrier, the flight crews were very happy with their accommodation, as the previous passenger cabins were retained for their use. The armament was also very basic and comprised a single 4in gun aft, four single 2pdrs and four single 20mm. She could carry eight aircraft. They had to be moved aft during launching operations, and moved forward when aircraft were landing. *Audacity* is shown in a camouflage scheme often used in 1941. The base was MS4a overall, with irregular patches of G5, MS3 and B5. The deck appears to have been dark grey and possibly camouflaged. Her short career meant she carried no other paint scheme.

HMS ARCHER Pennant D 78
Archer escort aircraft carrier 1941

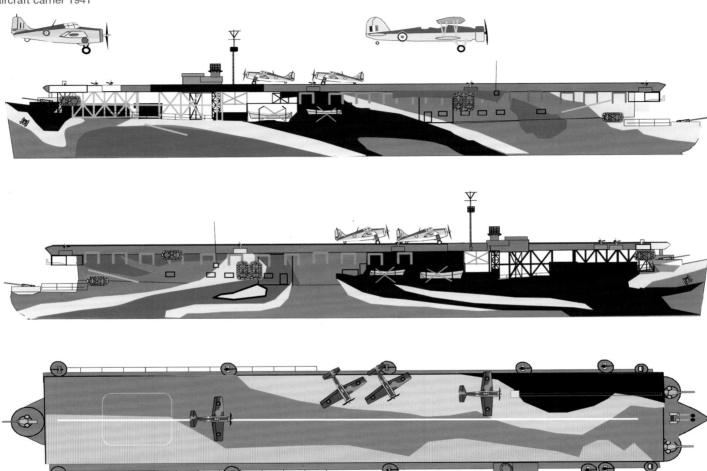

Archer was built in the USA and, although painted to an early Admiralty scheme, the paints used were all USN types. The paints used were navy blue, haze grey and ocean grey. No deck letter was carried. Unlike British carriers, the flight deck was made of wood and there were issues with the different way in which fuel was handled, which caused a delay in entering service. Unlike *Audacity*, she had a quarter-length hangar, serviced by a large lift, thereby doubling the number of aircraft that could be carried and enabling servicing to take place under cover. A catapult was also provided to enable aircraft to take off even when heavily laden. The original US pattern 4in guns were replaced by RN guns of the same calibre. Ten 20mm AA were provided and later a pair of twin 40mm were added. Unfortunately, this ship was plagued by continual engine problems and was reduced to a stores ship in August 1943. Prior to that, she had participated in Operation Torch and on Atlantic convoy escort duty. She was returned to the USA in 1945, repaired and then converted into a merchant ship. She served consecutively as *Empire Lagan*, *Anne Salem*, *Tasmania* and finally *Union Reliance* before being scrapped in 1962.

AVENGER CLASS ESCORT CARRIERS
HMS AVENGER Pennant D 14
Avenger class escort aircraft carrier 1942

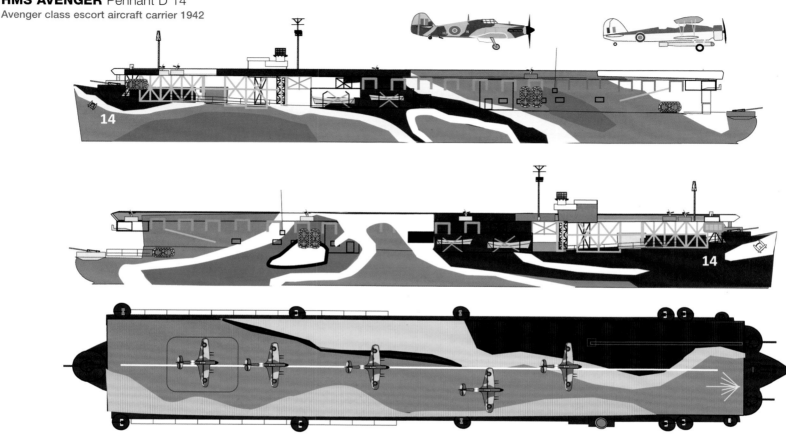

Avenger was built in the USA as an improvement over the mechanically unreliable *Archer*. There were three ships in the class and all were completed with USN paints. Ocean grey, haze grey, navy blue and light grey were used on the hull and flight deck. The patterns were painted on at time of delivery and paint for touch up supplied, which enabled the scheme to be retained for some time. As with *Archer*, the deck was constructed of wooden planks but these were painted to a camouflage scheme. The overall schemes for the class were similar, but nonetheless had distinct variations for each vessel. *Avenger* was of generally the same design as *Archer* and could operate up to fifteen aircraft for an operational cruise, but could carry up to eighty, folded and crated, when acting as a ferry ship. During normal operations, she usually carried six spare Sea Hurricanes in crated form. As completed, they had three US pattern 4in guns, but these were soon changed to British types to ease ammunition supply. There were ten 20mm AA but the ship was lost before this could be increased as in her sister ships. *Avenger* was first engaged escorting Convoy PQ18 to North Russia from the 2-21

September 1942. This proved to be a decisive passage as German aircraft repeatedly attacked the convoy. Five enemy aircraft were shot down by Sea Hurricanes and twenty-one others damaged. The poor firepower of the Sea Hurricane 1B was probably the reason for the large number damaged rather than destroyed. However, German records admit to forty-one aircraft that did not return. *Avenger* lost four Sea Hurricanes; one to the enemy and three to friendly fire from nervous merchant ships. Some of her Swordfish were also damaged by their own side. She took part in Atlantic convoy operations and then was part of the cover force for Operation Torch in November 1942. On 15 January 1943, she was torpedoed by *U-155* off Gibraltar and blew up with heavy loss of life. This was blamed on the different manner in which aviation fuel was carried on US-built ships and, from then onward, all escort carriers received from the USA were altered to British standards, which meant less fuel could be carried but it was stored more safely. This resulted in some friction between the US and the UK as it caused a delay in the ships entering service after they had been delivered.

HMS BITER Pennant D 97
Avenger class escort aircraft carrier 1942

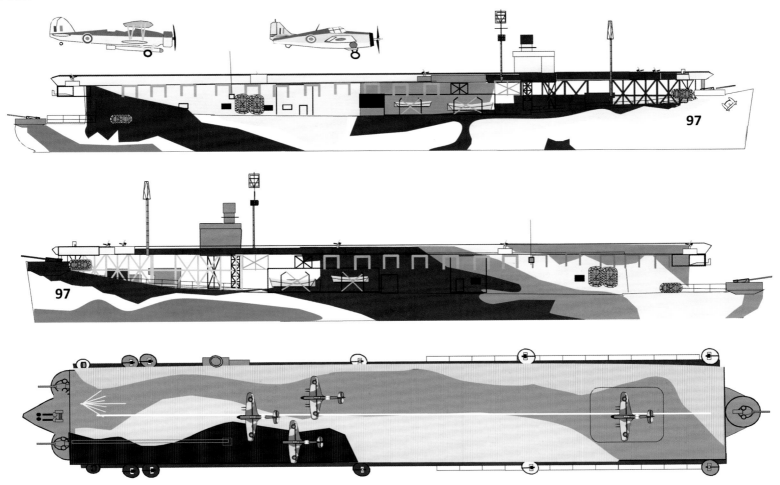

Biter was a unit of the *Avenger* class built in the USA for the Royal Navy. All ships of the class carried a similar camouflage scheme at first glance, but there were quite a few differences between them. All, however, used USN paint and were provided with a good supply in their paint lockers, enabling them to retain the schemes for some time. Ocean grey, haze grey, light grey and navy blue, with areas of white, formed the side pattern and the first three were used for the flight deck. Again, the flight deck had a pattern similar to the other ships of the class, but there were again distinct variations that enable each of them to be told apart. There were no deck letters carried but, as there were other escort carriers in service and more on order, it was decided they should carry their pennant number each side of the bow to enable them to be identified. This was a common USN practice but rare in the Royal Navy. This ship acted as air escort for sixteen trans-Atlantic convoys and was also engaged in anti-submarine hunts. It was normal for the ship to carry some crated aircraft as spares, as lack of room prevented them being carried assembled, and these could be assembled to replace losses. She was returned to US possession in April 1945 and transferred to France as *Dixmude*.

HMS DASHER Pennant D37
Avenger class escort aircraft carrier 1942

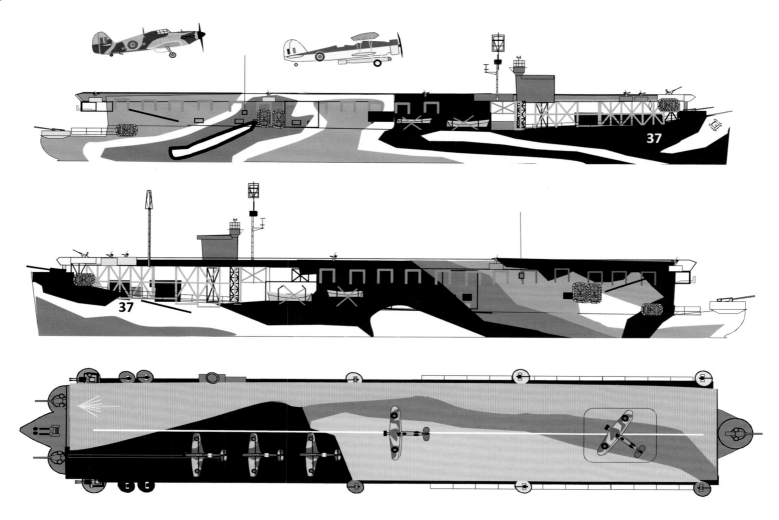

Dasher used the same USN paint colours for her own version of the scheme carried by her sister ships. Haze grey, light grey, navy blue and white were used but, unlike the others of the class, ocean grey was omitted. *Dasher* did not serve for long. She took part in some Atlantic convoys and Operation Torch before she was lost to an explosion and resulting fire while refuelling her aircraft in the Firth of Clyde on 27 March 1943. As with all ships of this type, the US type 4in guns were replaced with Royal Navy weapons. She had ten single 20mm and, just before her loss, had been fitted with two 40mm AA twin mounts.

HMS ACTIVITY Pennant D 94
Activity class escort aircraft carrier 1944

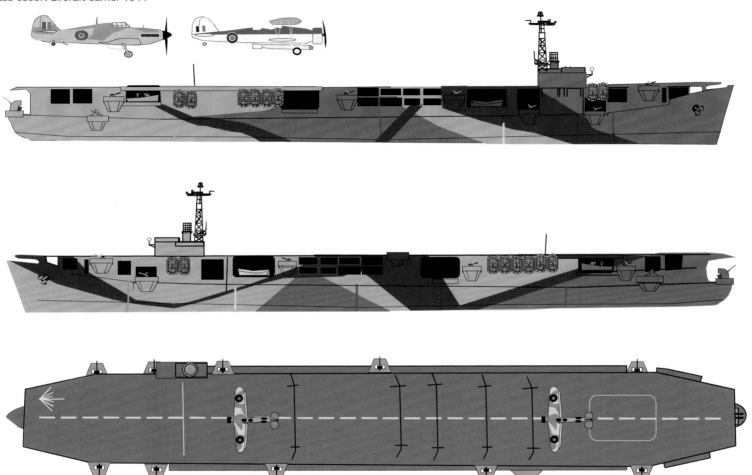

Activity was the smallest of the British escort carriers. She was converted from the fast refrigerated ship *Telemachus* and, although only able to carry a small number of aircraft, she was apparently quite successful. The ship is shown here in an Admiralty-designed scheme using B55, B30 and G5. At the time of her commissioning, the Admiralty had directed that most ships should have all horizontal decks painted with 507b and I have illustrated her accordingly. However, following the custom of the period, the flight deck may have been camouflaged. Armament consisted of a twin 4in dual purpose mount aft, plus ten single and two twin 20mm. Most service took place on convoys to

Russia and Atlantic convoys, as well as the UK-Gibraltar run, which she completed fourteen times. Additional oil could be carried to enable escorts to be refuelled at sea, thus extending their range. At times, she was used as a training ship for deck landings, which, considering *Activity* had the smallest flight deck in the Royal Navy, must have been quite an experience for new pilots. Late in the war, this ship was used to transport aircraft to the Far East. Post-war, she underwent conversion back to a merchant ship and was renamed *Breconshire*.

HMS CAMPANIA Pennant D48
Campania class escort aircraft carrier 1944

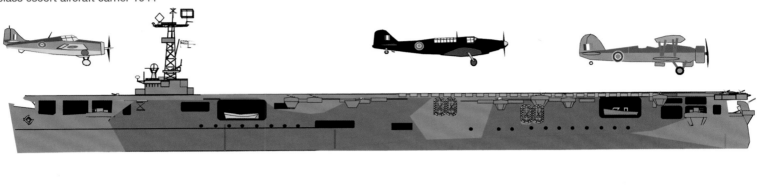

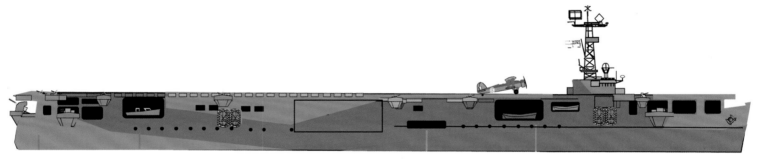

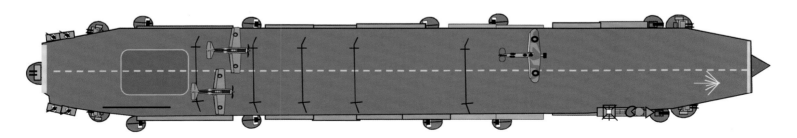

Green paint had been in short supply early in World War II, but, by 1944, was more available. *Campania* entered service in March 1944 and adopted a scheme prepared by the Admiralty for escort carriers. There were three colours: G10, G45 and B30. Some shortening effect seems to have been included by using the grey centrally. The deck was G10 with markings in yellow. Her armament was quite strong for a British-built escort carrier, comprising a twin 4in AA mount aft, four

quad 2pdr mounts and sixteen 20mm in twelve single and two twin mountings. This ship was generally similar to *Vindex* and *Nairana*, but was longer and had a greater beam. Most of her service was on convoys to Russia, for which her crew accommodation was insulated and heated. The ship's radar fit included a Type 277 radar, Type 281B, Type 291 and a HF/DF was also fitted.

HMS CAMPANIA Pennant D48
Campania class escort aircraft carrier 1945

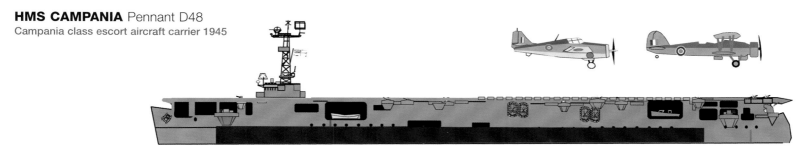

In 1945, *Campania* adopted the Admiralty standard scheme for Home Waters. It consisted of a B20 panel on a G45 overall hull.

HMS PRETORIA CASTLE Pennant F61
Pretoria Castle class escort aircraft carrier 1944

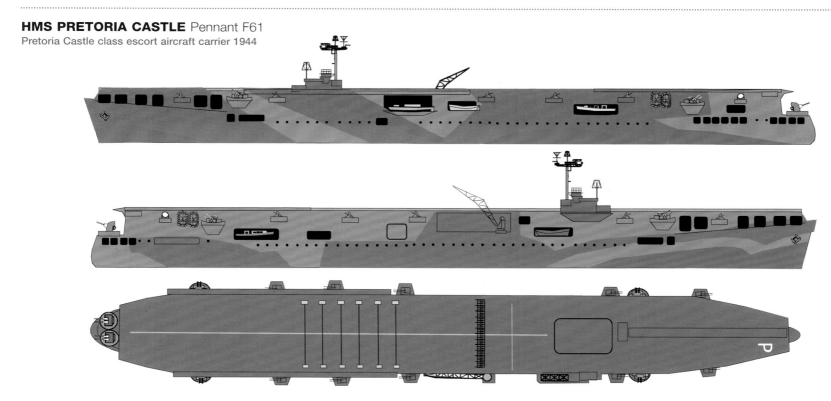

Pretoria Castle was the largest escort carrier built for the Royal Navy, but was mostly used for training new crew as well as for deck landing trials and training pilots. Her scheme was typical of some of the last Admiralty disruptive patterns with a combination of B30, G45 and G10. The steel flight deck was also G10 with markings in dull yellow. She had an armament of four quad 2pdrs and ten twin 20mm. Avengers and Hellcats could be carried for operations, but the actual aircraft varied considerably because of her training role and no permanent flight squadrons were attached to the ship. She could carry out operational patrols and won a Battle of the Atlantic honour.

VINDEX CLASS ESCORT CARRIERS
HMS NAIRANA Pennant D05
Vindex class escort aircraft carrier 1944

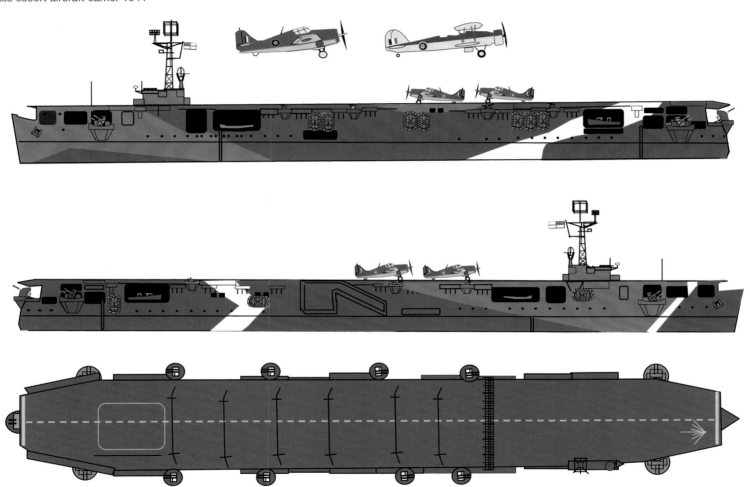

Nairana completed in 1944 and was one of the few escort carriers built in British yards. All horizontal steel decks were painted with 507b, including the flight deck, the markings on which were dull yellow. The first scheme worn was a late Admiralty disruptive type using G45, B30, white and G10. The ship was part of a Hunter-Killer Group operating in the Atlantic and took part in convoys to Russia. Type 277 radar and Type 281B radar were carried, as well as Type 293. The armament comprised a twin 4in mount aft, four quad 2pdrs and eight twin 20mm. The full operational capacity of this ship was twenty-one aircraft.

HMS NAIRANA Pennant D05
Vindex class escort aircraft carrier 1945

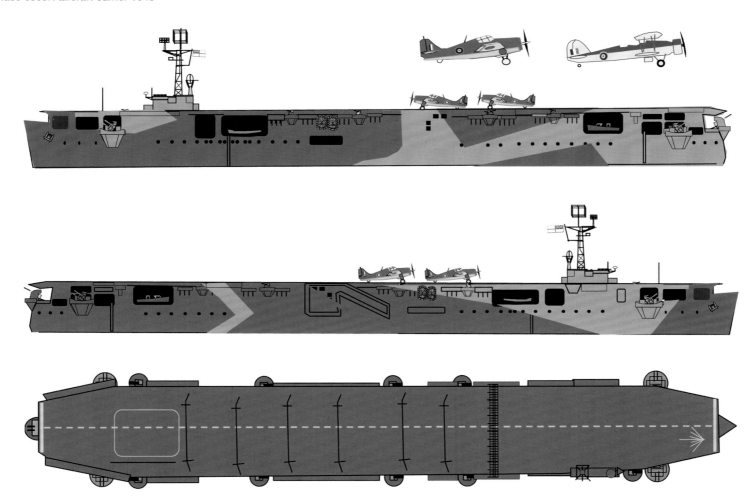

In 1945, all horizontal steel decks were painted with 507b, including the flight deck with the markings being dull yellow. The previous Admiralty disruptive scheme was simplified to B30, B55 and G10, with white discontinued. British escort carriers were generally smaller than those built by the USA and carried fewer aircraft, but this was because they were intended to operate in the Atlantic where the emphasis was on sea-keeping qualities and ASW aircraft, rather than long range and a higher complement of fighters. The full operational capacity of this ship could be varied according to her role. On some convoy duties there could be more fighters and, on others, more attack or ASW aircraft. After the war, she was sold to the Netherlands and was renamed *Karel Doorman*. She was decommissioned in 1948 and converted into the merchant ship *Port Victor*. Her replacement was also named *Karel Doorman* but she was the ex-British HMS *Venerable*.

HMS VINDEX Pennant D15
Vindex class escort aircraft carrier 1944

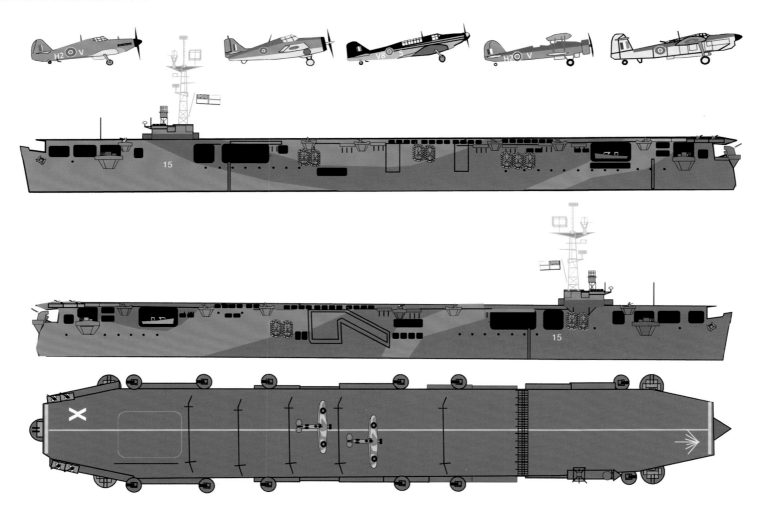

Vindex was completed in a scheme based on G10 and G45. All horizontal decks were painted 507b. Note the pennant number is carried on each side, but without the flag superior. This ship served on convoy escort duty with much of her service being in the North Atlantic. She was the first escort carrier to operate Firefly aircraft and she also had Fulmar night-fighters in her complement when serving on Russian convoys. Both ships of this class were fitted with an extensive suite of

radar and other electronics that would have been unimaginable only three years earlier. She and her sister ship *Nairana* were distinguished by tall lattice masts to carry all the electronics. There was only a single lift, but the hangar was much roomier than *Activity*, the previous British-built escort carrier. Armament comprised a twin 4in DP mount, four quad 2pdrs, twelve twin 20mm and four single 20mm.

ATTACKER CLASS ESCORT CARRIERS
HMS ATTACKER Pennant D02
Attacker class escort aircraft carrier 1942

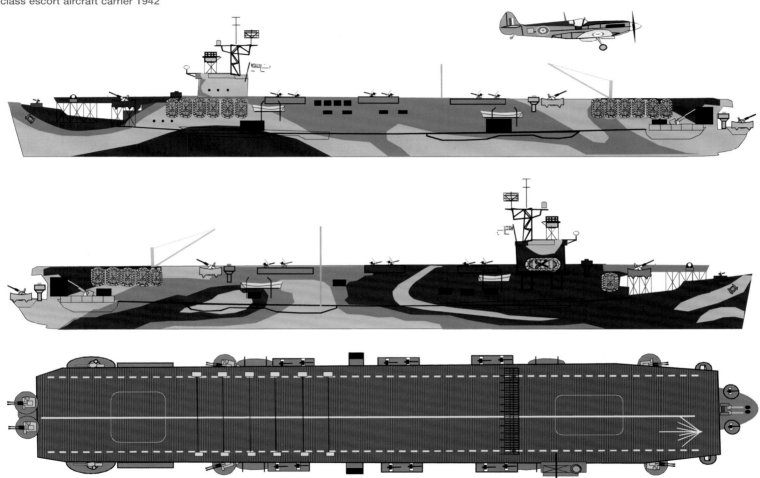

Attacker entered service in a disruptive pattern that was applied on completion using USN paint shades. The wood decks of most US-built carriers were stained blue with deck markings in yellow. The colours used for the camouflage scheme were ocean grey, haze grey and navy blue. She went to the Mediterranean as a fighter carrier and was involved in covering various amphibious landings. It appears she only operated Seafires and was not engaged in ASW or attack operations. On comple-tion, she was armed with two 4in guns of US pattern, which were changed to Royal Navy weapons later. There were six twin 40mm AA and fourteen single 20mm. The aircraft complement was offi-cially twenty, but she was able to operate more if a deck park was used. The main radar sets were Royal Navy types. There was a Type 271 radar lantern fitted on the bridge and Type 281 on the lattice mast. In addition, there was a US SL radar set on the lattice mast and a British Type 242 IFF.

HMS ATTACKER Pennant D02
Attacker class escort aircraft carrier 1944

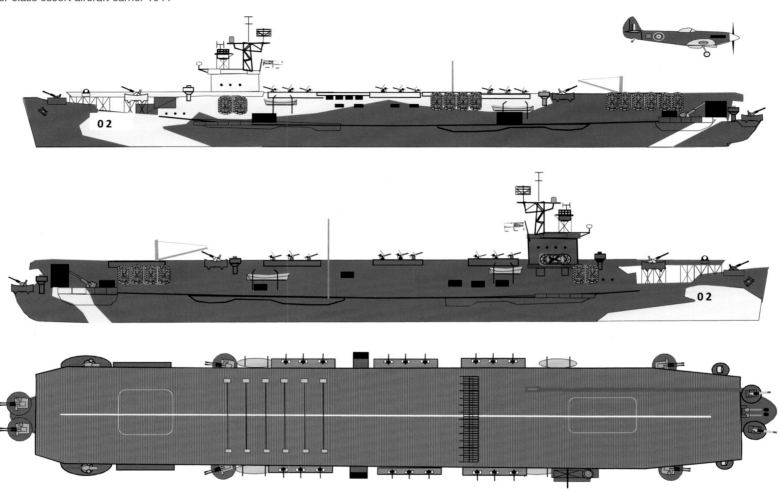

Attacker was eventually repainted in Royal Navy colours and is shown here in the scheme she wore for the landings in the south of France. G10, B30 and white formed a disruptive scheme much different than that worn when received from the US builders. The wood flight deck was repainted in mid-grey but the shade is uncertain. White markings were used on the flight deck from 1944. Most service was as a fighter carrier and the ship saw a lot of action in the invasions of Italy and the south of France and the Western Mediterranean in general. By 1945, the

Mediterranean was a backwater and *Attacker* was designated to transport aircraft to the British Pacific Fleet. It is probable that, for that service, she was repainted light grey with a dark blue panel on the hull. The armament was increased during 1945 with two single 40mm replacing the single 20mm in the bow. The number of 20mm singles was increased to eighteen. British Type 244 IFF was added to the Type 271 radar lantern. The pennant number is carried at the bow in black but without the flag superior.

HMS BATTLER Pennant D18
Attacker class escort aircraft carrier 1944

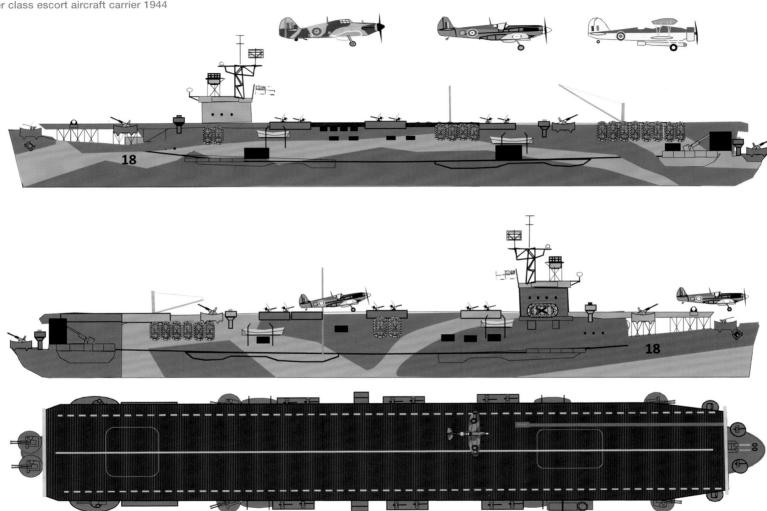

Battler was delivered in a US-applied scheme very similar to her sister *Attacker*. However, by 1944 she wore an Admiralty-designed scheme using B55, B30 and G10. The timber-planked flight deck was dark grey with markings in dull yellow. This carrier covered two convoys to Gibraltar from the UK before moving into the Mediterranean to take part in covering major amphibious operations

there. In 1944, the ship was active in mopping-up duties in the Aegean, before transferring to the British Eastern Fleet. The electronics outfit included Type 281 radar and a Type 271 radar in the distinctive lantern.

HMS BATTLER Pennant D18
Attacker class escort aircraft carrier 1945

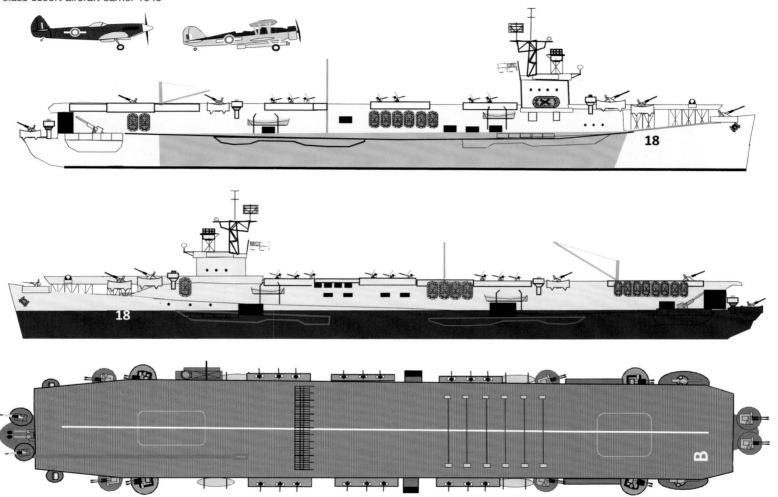

Battler went to the Indian Ocean after service in the Mediterranean. Unusually for so late in the war, she is listed as carrying Swordfish aircraft for that region. It is possible that this is a mistake or, alternatively, it was intended that the ship would only be used for convoy protection and ASW patrols. As she is not listed for any of the offensive operations carried out, convoy protection was probably her primary role. The pale 507c and mid-blue hull panel was typical of ships deployed to that region. By early 1945, there were large numbers of escort carriers available and some,

including this ship, were then used as jeep carriers, transporting new aircraft for use by the British Pacific Fleet. The decks and hangars could accommodate large numbers of aircraft with their wings folded. In this role, the ships had either no air group at all or carried a small number of aircraft for their own fighter and ASW protection. The original two 4in guns have been retained, but the light AA has been considerably strengthened. There are now a total of ten twin and two single 40mm as well as eighteen single 20mm.

HMS CHASER Pennant D32 (BPF Pennant R306)
Attacker class escort aircraft carrier 1942

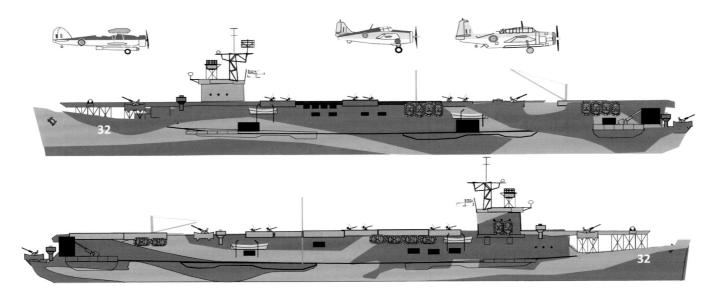

HMS CHASER BPF Pennant R306
Attacker class escort aircraft carrier 1945

Chaser completed in a scheme similar to her sister *Attacker* applied with USN paint and was engaged in escorting Atlantic convoys. By February 1944 she was engaged in escorting convoys to Russia, she had been repainted to an Admiralty scheme of G10, B30 and B55. The planked deck was dark grey with dull yellow markings. There does not seem to have been a deck letter issued and none was carried. Armament was standardised on a single 4in port and starboard, six twin 40mm and fourteen single 20mm Oerlikons. The armament does not seem to have been altered during her service. Her aircraft sank U-boats *U-366* and *U-973*, while the sinking of *U-472* was shared with the destroyer *Onslaught*. This ship was the first of the escort carriers to operate Avenger

aircraft. In late 1944, *Chaser* transferred to the Pacific where she acted as a jeep carrier, transporting aircraft for the fleet carriers, but was fitted to act as a fighter carrier if required. She is shown in a variation of the usual Pacific scheme. There is an overall hull of 507c, with a panel of B15, which unusually has irregular patches of 507c applied to it. The island is white and most of the deck edge fixtures are similarly white. It is presumed the port side was similar. The hull number R306 was probably carried to avoid confusion with USN ships while *Chaser* acted as an aircraft transport. It is unusual in having no gap between the letter R and the number.

HMS STALKER D 91
Attacker class escort aircraft carrier 1942-3

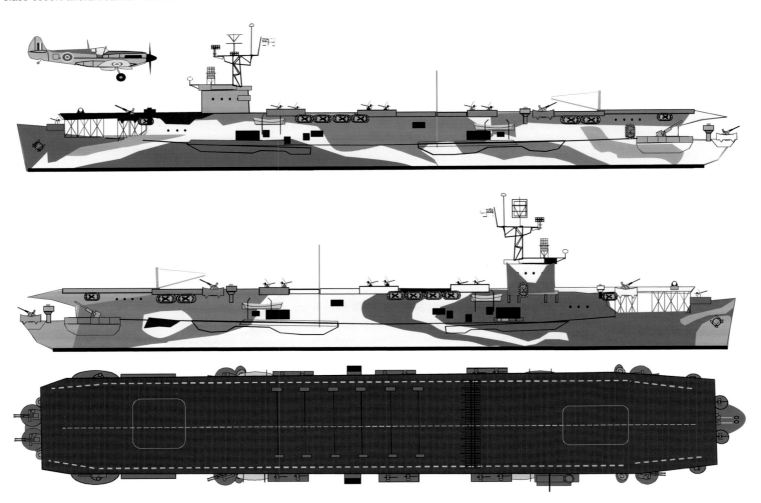

Stalker is shown here in the scheme she wore on delivery. USN paint was applied by the shipyard using ocean grey, haze grey, light grey and white, with a very small amount of navy blue. The deck was wood, stained blue, but was unusual in that the centre line was thinner than those each side. The side lines also followed the contours of the deck. All deck markings were in dull yellow. This ship was fitted as a fighter support ship and was present for the Allied amphibious landings in Italy in 1943, remaining in the region for most of 1944. The radar fit was mostly British, but a US YE homing beacon was carried. As a specialised fighter ship, this vessel was not engaged in convoy duty other than when on passage from point-to-point. Some single 20mm guns were replaced by twin mounts, but the bow guns remained singles.

HMS STALKER Pennant D 91
Attacker class escort aircraft carrier 1944

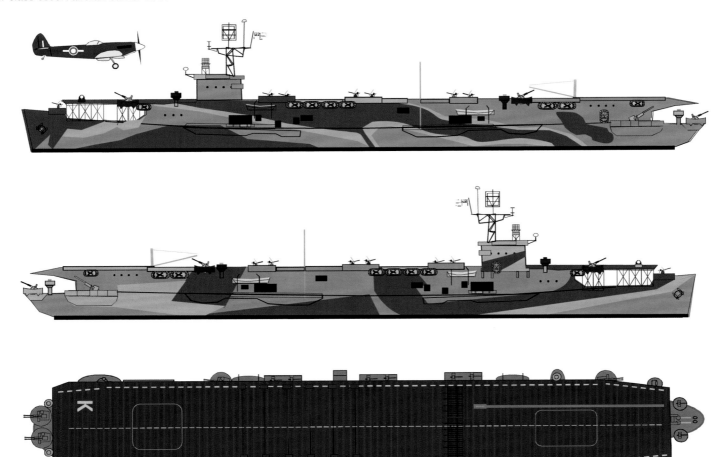

Stalker changed to Royal Navy colours in 1944. The overall colour was MS3, with areas of B55 and G5. The deck was dark grey and the non-standard deck markings were retained. The deck letter K was prominently displayed. This ship deployed to the Indian Ocean in 1945, where she took part in Operation Dracula, the amphibious attack on Rangoon. Later, she was involved in raids against Japanese forces in Sumatra and Burma as well as the Nicobar Islands. *Stalker* seems to have carried a larger number of aircraft than some of her sister ships. At some point, the scheme of this ship was altered to an overall pale grey with blue panel. Some single 20mm guns were replaced by twin 20mm mountings. Unlike other ships of this class, *Stalker* does not seem to have been used as an aircraft transport.

HMS TRACKER Pennant D 24
Attacker class escort aircraft carrier 1943

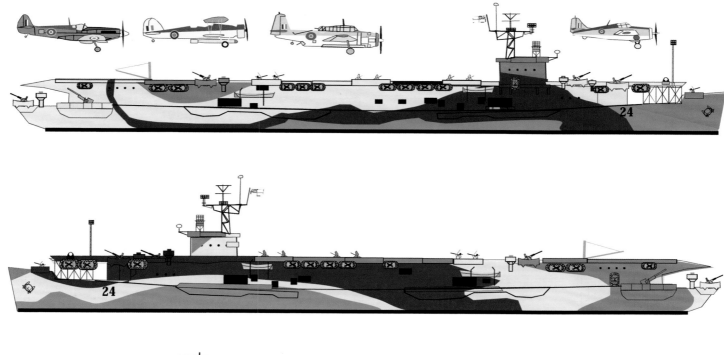

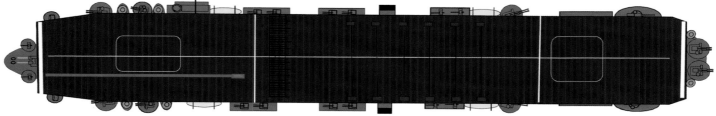

This ship spent most of her service on Atlantic and Russian convoys. The scheme was an Admiralty design that used B5, G5 and MS2 on a base of 507c. The flight deck was dark grey with white markings in a fashion that differed from earlier ships of the class. No deck letter appears to have been issued to this ship. A mix of British and USN electronics was carried, which included a pole mast for a US YE homing beacon forward of the bridge on the island. Although initially equipped with older aircraft, the complement was soon upgraded to US types with greater range and capacity. *Tracker* took part in the sinking of two U-boats and the damaging of at least three others. Her fighters shot down six Luftwaffe aircraft. After 1944, she was used to ferry aircraft in the Pacific.

HMS FENCER Pennant D 64 (BPF Pennant R308)

Attacker class escort aircraft carrier 1943-5

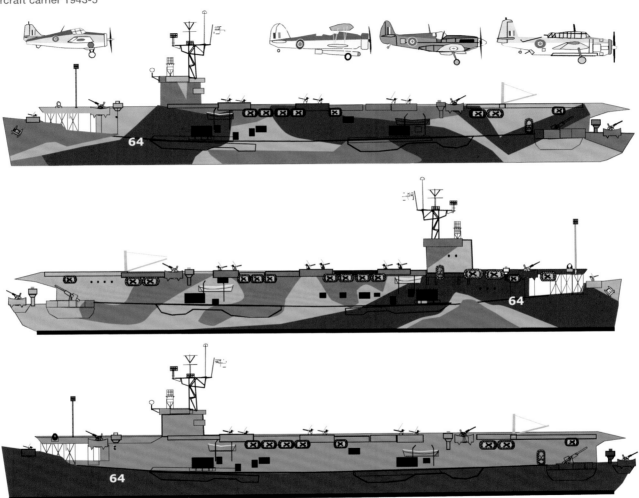

Fencer wears an Admiralty disruption scheme using G5 and MS2 on an overall base of B55. The pennant number without flag superior was carried rather larger, and in bold, than on other escort carriers. In 1945, the ship was repainted in Admiralty Standard Scheme A using B20 and G45. The duties of this ship included covering the establishment of an Allied base on the Azores soon after entering service. Her other duties included acting as a fighter carrier to cover the strike force during Operation Tungsten, an attack on the German battleship *Tirpitz*. Other duties were as a convoy escort carrier on Atlantic and Russian convoy runs. She took part in twelve trans-Atlantic convoys and two ASW sweeps. She sank U-boat *U-666* during those operations and her fighters shot down one Fw-200. On Russian convoys, she took part in the sinking of U-boats *U-277*, *U-674* and *U-959* and her aircraft shot down a Luftwaffe Bv-138 flying boat. Although transferred to the British Pacific Fleet in 1945, her duties seem to have been limited to transporting aircraft.

HMS STRIKER Pennant D 12 (BPF Pennant R315)
Attacker class escort aircraft carrier 1944

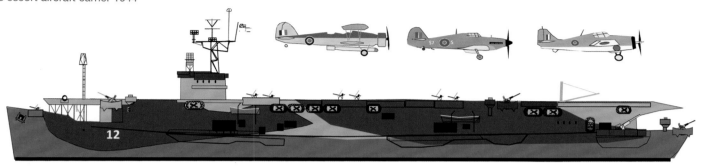

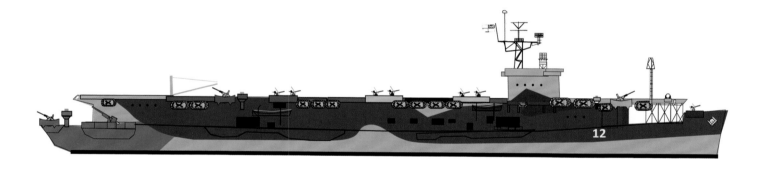

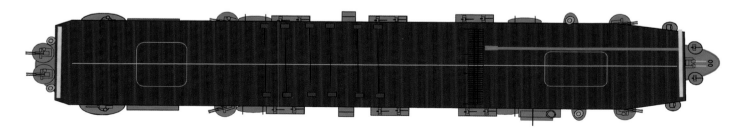

Striker received a disruptive camouflage where G5 provided a dark contrast to MS2 and MS3 with B55. The flight deck was standard dark grey, probably G5, with simple markings as shown. There was no deck letter assigned to this ship, but she carried her pennant in white, without flag superior, prominently on each side. There is a HF/DF mast forward of the bridge. During operations off the Norwegian coast in 1944, this ship was mostly engaged in ASW protection of attack carriers and in providing local fighter cover. She also took part in nine convoys to Gibraltar and one to Russia. She shared the sinking of U-boats *U-354*, *U-344* and *U-394* and her fighters shot down three Luftwaffe Bv-138 patrol planes.

HMS HUNTER Pennant D 80
Attacker class escort aircraft carrier 1943

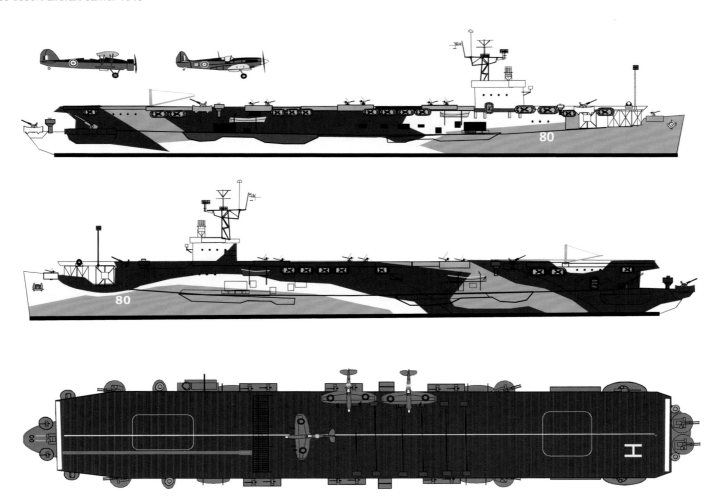

This ship was originally to be named *Trailer* in Royal Navy service and for the USN as *Block Island*. However, she was renamed and commissioned as *Hunter* on 11 January 1943. The camouflage appears to have been in Royal Navy colours from the start. The colours used were MS1, MS3 and white. The deck was the usual G5, with the deck letter H. She was completed as a fighter carrier and was present for the Allied landings in Italy and later Operation Dragoon, the landings in the south of France. There were also some convoy protection duties completed, but the main role of the ship remained fighter protection of other forces during amphibious operations.

HMS HUNTER Pennant D 80
Attacker class escort aircraft carrier 1944

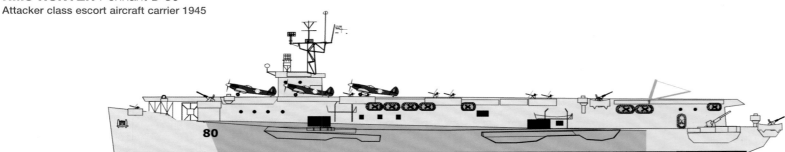

HMS HUNTER Pennant D 80
Attacker class escort aircraft carrier 1945

The original camouflage scheme was altered in 1944 during repainting. The starboard side followed much the same lines as previously, but with the addition of more MS1 forward. The port side was altered to an almost completely different style. This scheme was worn during the last part of her service in the Mediterranean. On transfer to the British Eastern Fleet, the scheme of this ship was altered to an overall 507c with mid-blue panel, which was common to that command. She was to have been part of a strike on Penang but, when the Japanese surrendered, *Hunter* became part of the force that took the surrender.

HMS SEARCHER Pennant D 40
Attacker class escort aircraft carrier 1943

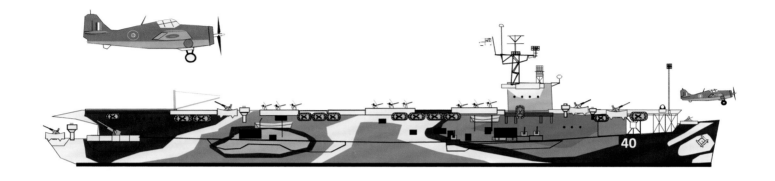

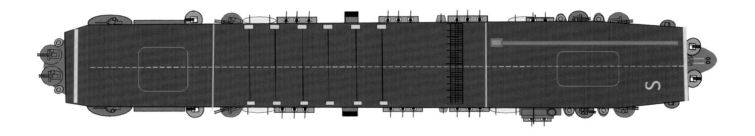

Searcher was completed in April 1943 with a US-applied camouflage scheme using USN paints. The four shades were ocean grey, haze grey, light grey and navy blue. The port side scheme is unknown. The deck was wood stained with blue dye in US fashion. At delivery, she was more heavily-armed than her sisters and more in line with the *Ruler* class. There were two single 4in guns, eight twin 40mm, four twin 20mm and twenty-four single 20mm. Her role was as a fighter carrier, but she did support two convoys to Gibraltar.

HMS SEARCHER Pennant D 40
Attacker class escort aircraft carrier 1944-5

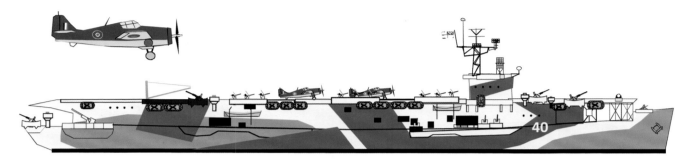

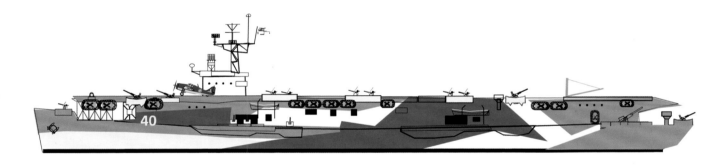

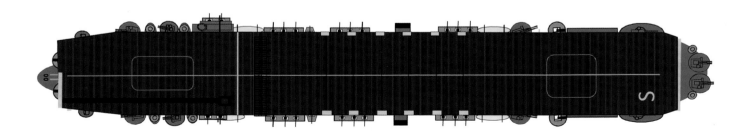

The scheme of this ship was changed from the original USN paint style to Royal Navy colours in 1944. Areas of white were applied with B30 dark olive and MS3 slate green. She continued to serve as a fighter carrier on many operations. Fighter cover was provided for Operation Tungsten and she also took part in carrier strikes against other German shipping in Norwegian waters. This ship did not transfer to the Far East or Pacific, remaining in European waters as the war there concluded and mopping-up operations were carried out.

HMS RAVAGER Pennant D 70
Attacker class escort aircraft carrier 1943

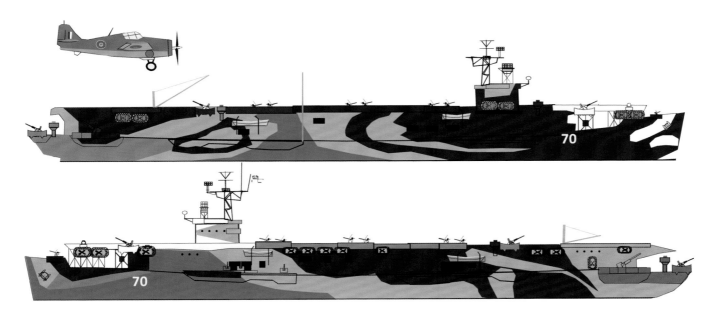

HMS RAVAGER Pennant D 70
Attacker class escort aircraft carrier 1944

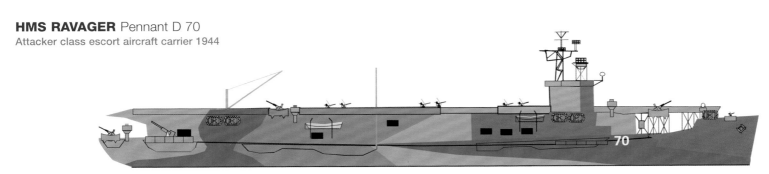

Ravager entered Royal Navy service in April 1943 wearing a pattern applied by the ship builder using USN paints. These included ocean grey, haze grey, light grey and navy blue. The irregularly-shaped enclosed patch on the starboard side was common to many of these schemes. In 1944, she was repainted using Royal Navy paints and is shown in G10, B30, MS3 and G45. The number 70 was carried prominently in white. The port side camouflage pattern is unknown. Her deck scheme was the same as *Searcher*. This ship was designated for training purposes and also took part in some aircraft ferry operations. Apart from that, she was not involved in any convoy or offensive operations and was returned to the US in 1946.

HMS PURSUER Pennant D 73
Attacker class escort aircraft carrier 1943

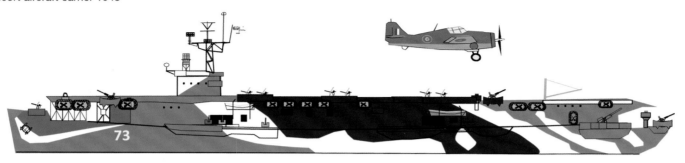

Pursuer was another ship delivered in a US dockyard-applied paint scheme, which was retained until mid-1944. The colours used here are USN navy blue, haze grey, a touch of ocean grey and white.

The starboard side is not known. She was designated a fighter carrier, but did escort two Gibraltar convoys during which her aircraft shot down one Fw-200, one He-177 and one Ju-88.

HMS PURSUER Pennant D 73
Attacker class escort aircraft carrier 1944

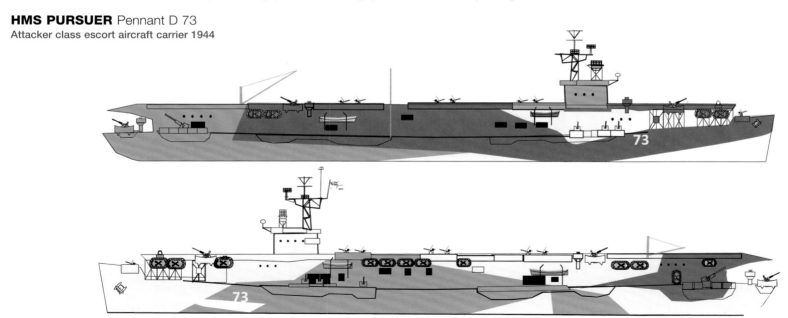

Pursuer took part in operations mostly in home waters and the Mediterranean. Her role included fighter cover for attacks on the German battleship *Tirpitz* and Operation Dragoon. She did not go to the Far Eastern or Pacific fleets at the end of the war in Europe. She was returned to the USA

in 1946 and sold for scrap the same year. She is shown here in an Admiralty scheme applied in 1944. It was of a simple style using a white base with MS3 and G10. The flight deck was probably similar to her sister ship *Searcher*, with which she frequently operated.

RULER CLASS ESCORT CARRIERS
HMS TRUMPETER Pennant D 09
Ruler class escort aircraft carrier 1943-5

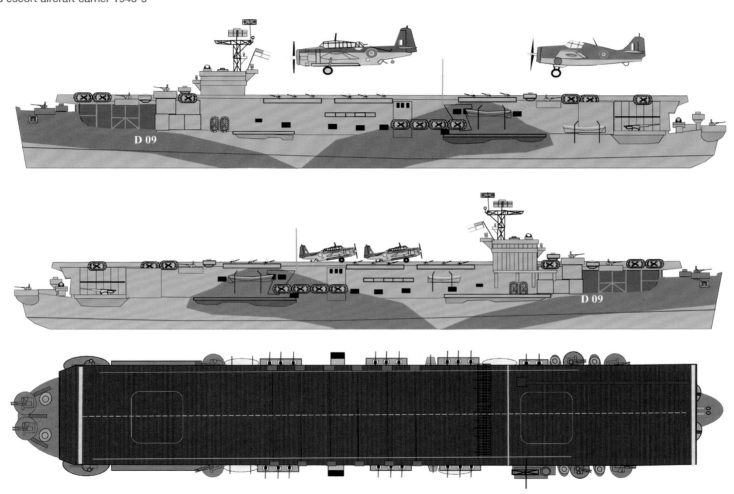

Trumpeter is shown here in B55 overall with areas of G10 to provide one of the less dramatic camouflage schemes. From the air, the *Ruler* class were very similar to those built before them, but were recognisable by the squared-off forward flight deck and two lifts of the same size. The catapult was more powerful than that fitted to earlier classes and the class was a general improvement over the preceding escort carrier classes. This ship took part in Operation Goodwood, a strike on the battleship *Tirpitz*, where she provided ASW support for the task force. There was also considerable activity during air strikes on German shipping in Norwegian waters 1944-5 and a convoy to and from Russia.

HMS AMEER Pennant D 01 (BPF Pennant R302)
Ruler class escort aircraft carrier 1944

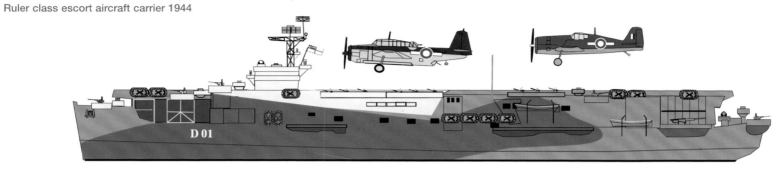

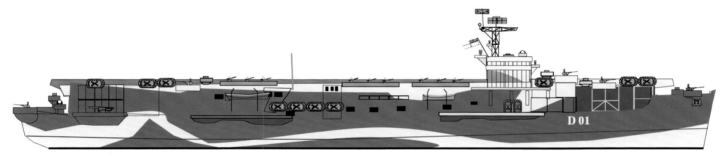

HMS AMEER Pennant D 01 (BPF Pennant R302)
Ruler class escort aircraft carrier 1945

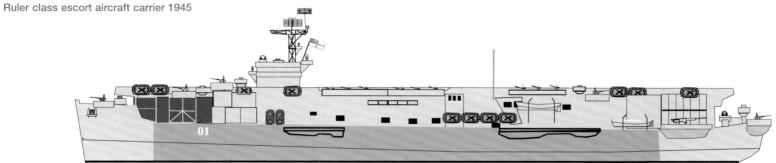

Ameer is shown in the top two illustrations in an Admiralty scheme based around three colours: MS3, G10 and white. The deck was as *Trumpeter*. The ship worked up in UK waters but was then transferred to the Indian Ocean as part of the British Eastern Fleet where she took part in many strikes against Japanese targets. She suffered some damage from a Kamikaze hit off Phuket, Thailand, but was quickly returned to service. She was part of the cancelled strike against Penang in August 1945, which instead became an occupation and acceptance of the Japanese surrender of that port. During the last part of her service in the region, she adopted an overall 507c with mid-blue panel. She originally carried her full pennant number D 01 but, by the end of the war, the flag superior had been removed and only the number was carried.

HMS ARBITER Pennant D 31 (BPF Pennant R303)
Ruler class escort aircraft carrier 1943-5

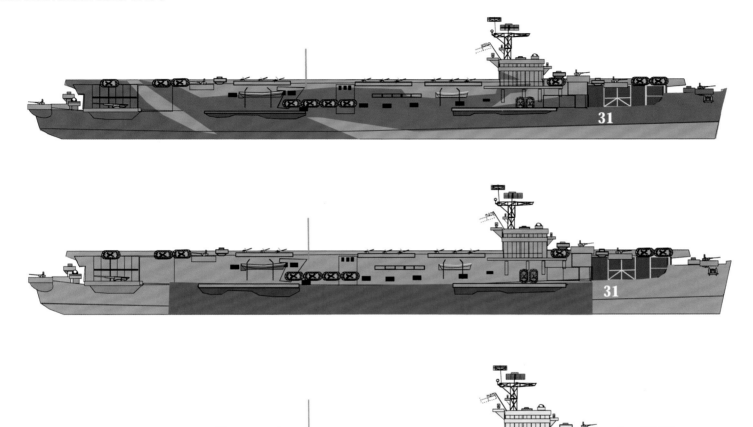

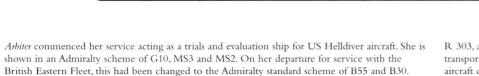

Arbiter commenced her service acting as a trials and evaluation ship for US Helldiver aircraft. She is shown in an Admiralty scheme of G10, MS3 and MS2. On her departure for service with the British Eastern Fleet, this had been changed to the Admiralty standard scheme of B55 and B30. Later, in 1945, she became an aircraft ferry for the British Pacific Fleet, carrying the number R 303, and adopted a B20 blue hull with 507c upper works. Her duties were mostly as an aircraft transport and she did not take part in any offensive operations but, from time to time, available aircraft did carry out combat air patrols in support of transport operations. In July 1945, this ship had four single 40mm Bofors guns added.

HMS ATHELING Pennant D 51 (BPF Pennant R304)
Ruler class escort aircraft carrier 1943

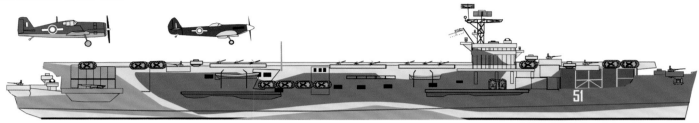

HMS ATHELING Pennant D 51 (BPF Pennant R304)
Ruler class escort aircraft carrier 1944

HMS ATHELING Pennant D 51 (BPF Pennant R304)
Ruler class escort aircraft carrier August 1945

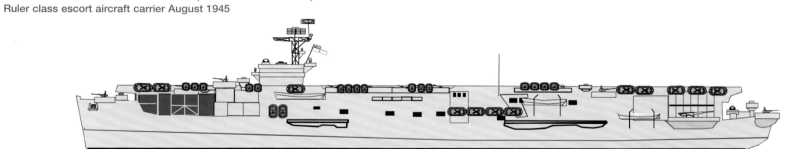

Atheling is shown at top in an Admiralty scheme of 507a, 507c and MS3. The port side is unknown. However, she was sent to the British Eastern Fleet after working up, during which time her camouflage was altered to an unusual variation of the scheme common to that region. The overall colour was white with a centre panel of B20 dark blue, but with patches of white. At some point in 1945, the blue panel was changed to the standard solid one. She was designated as a fighter carrier, but as a relatively late arrival only took part in one major operation before taking on trade protection duties and aircraft transport. Around August 1945, she was further altered to become a troopship. She was then painted in overall 507c and a considerable number of extra Carley rafts were added on the flight deck and over some of the AA positions. There was not time to remove the AA weapons, so frames were led up over them with the rafts on top, so they could be slid off in an emergency. Her duties involved taking troops to garrison areas surrendered by the Japanese, the liberation of POWs and the transport of troops back to the United Kingdom. The hangar was divided into accommodations with numerous bunks. No aircraft were carried in her troopship role.

HMS EMPEROR Pennant B 98 (BPF Pennant R307)
Ruler class escort aircraft carrier 1943-4

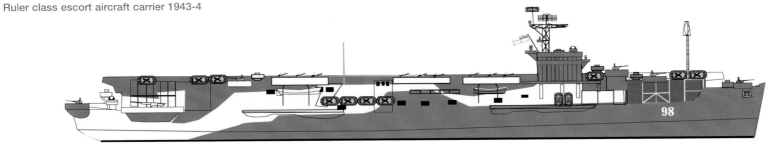

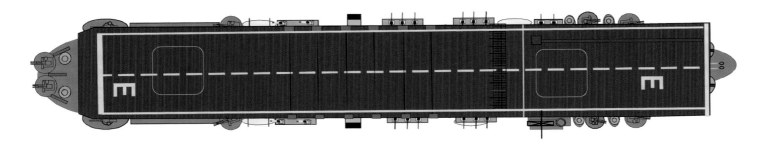

HMS EMPEROR Pennant B 98 (BPF Pennant R307)
Ruler class escort aircraft carrier 1945

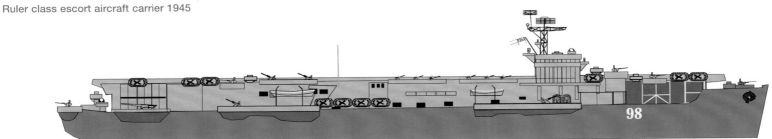

Emperor was designated as a fighter and strike carrier. She took part in a large number of operations, starting with assisting in strikes against the German battleship *Tirpitz* and operations against German shipping off Norway. During these operations, she wore the scheme shown at the top, which comprised G10, B30 and white. The flight deck was grey, as shown above, but with all fore and aft lines broken. On transfer to the British Eastern Fleet, she wore the Admiralty standard scheme using B55 and B30. The flight deck was as above but, rather unusually, had a large letter E

forward and another aft. It is probable that, while serving in the Indian Ocean, her grey may have been lightened and the green hull replaced with a blue panel. During her service with the British Eastern Fleet, she was a very busy ship – being allocated to several strike operations as well as reconnaissance and protection of amphibious forces. Note that the light AA has been altered, with some 20mm replaced by single 40mm and four more singles added.

HMS BEGUM Pennant D 38 (BPF Pennant R305)
Ruler class escort aircraft carrier 1943

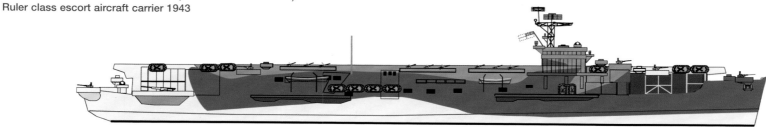

Unlike most other escort carriers, *Begum* does not seem to be carrying a visible pennant number on the hull in any photograph I can find. She went straight to the British Eastern Fleet on completion of alterations and working up in UK waters. She wore an Admiralty camouflage similar to several of her sister ships, utilising white with 507a and MS3. The flight deck was similar to the other ships in her class.

HMS BEGUM Pennant D 38 (BPF Pennant R305)
Ruler class escort aircraft carrier 1944-5

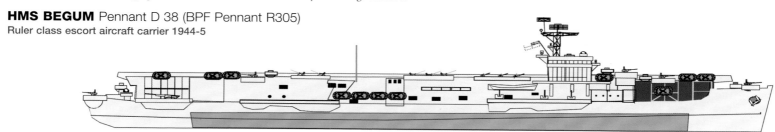

While serving in the Indian Ocean, *Begum* adopted a scheme typical of ships in that region. However, the mid-blue panel was quite low, passing well beneath the side sponsons, whereas most other ships carried it at the level of the lower sponsons. Like other ships of her class, her AA was strengthened with additional 20mm and 40mm weapons. Her duties centred on commerce protection and convoy escort and *Begum* shared in the destruction of U-boat *U-198* during an Indian Ocean ASW sweep. She carried the deck letter B.

HMS PATROLLER Pennant D 07
Ruler class escort aircraft carrier 1943-5

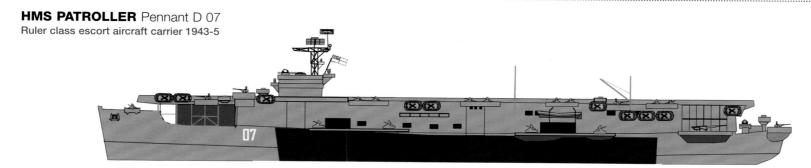

Patroller was used as an aircraft transport. She is shown here in a late Admiralty standard scheme of B15 and B55. This ship was one of the last five completed, all of which had twin 20mm mounts instead of singles. There were also twin 20mm at the bow instead of 40mm. Her armament therefore comprised sixteen 40mm in eight twin mounts and twenty-six 20mm AA in twin mounts. At the end of the war, she was further converted and turned into a troop carrier for the repatriation of British personnel that were stationed all over the world.

HMS KHEDIVE Pennant D 62
Ruler class escort aircraft carrier 1943-5

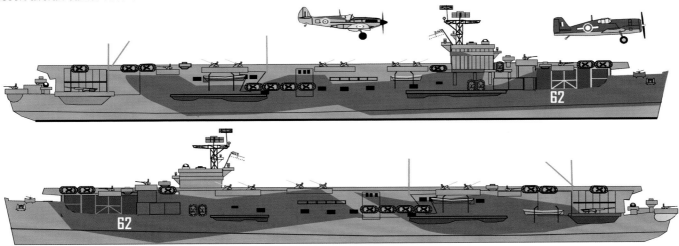

Khedive was designated an assault and fighter protection unit on completion. She is shown here in a similar scheme as her sister ship *Trumpeter* based on two colours – B55 and 507a – to provide a contrast but easy maintenance. A rather unusual recognition feature is that, at the bow, she has single 20mm instead of the twin 40mm mounts specified. This sort of difference was usually due to shortages of weapons at the time the ship was completing and, rather than delay her entry into service, she was fitted with what was available. Once mounts were available, they would be retro-fitted at the next refit. Along the flight deck edge, the usual single 20mm were all replaced by single 40mm guns for a total of twenty-eight 40mm altogether. Records are sparse, but some ships had the low-angle US 5in guns aft replaced by single L38 weapons, which were dual purpose. She took part in Operation Dragoon and mopping-up in the Aegean region. As with others of her class, she was transferred to the British Eastern Fleet in 1945 where she took part in other operations.

HMS EMPRESS Pennant D 42
Ruler class escort aircraft carrier 1943-5

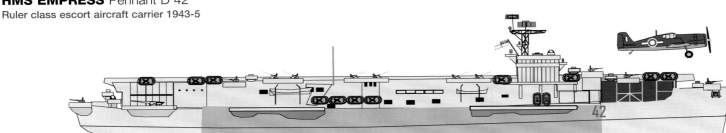

This ship was a latecomer to the British Eastern Fleet but nonetheless had a busy service. She is shown here in 507C overall, with mid-blue panel. The pennant number was carried in white for a time when the ship wore the standard Admiralty 1944 scheme of B15 and B30. However, when it was lightened to the above, the number was painted up in red so it was easier to see. This ship was designated as an assault carrier, but usually acted in the fighter support role. She was involved in extensive photo-reconnaissance operations in preparation for amphibious landings and covered ships sweeping mines off Phuket. She was allocated to the force intended to invade Penang but instead covered the forces that reoccupied Penang when the Japanese surrendered.

HMS NABOB Pennant D 42
Ruler class escort aircraft carrier 1943-5

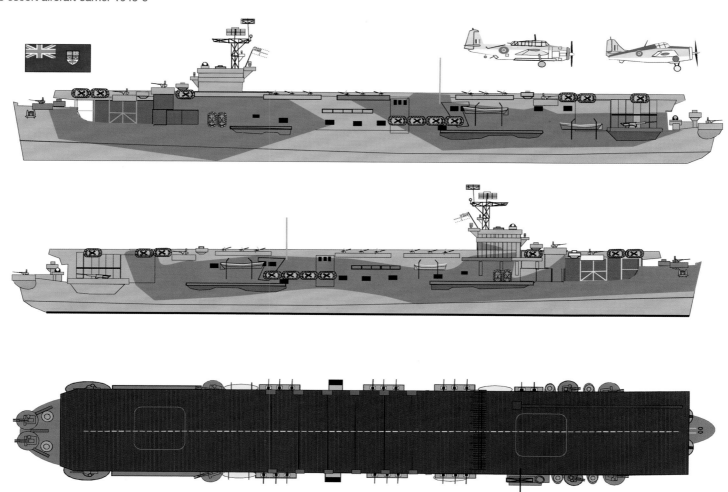

Nabob was Canadian-manned, although she remained a Royal Navy-owned ship. Her camouflage scheme was based on B55 and G10, which was common on escort carriers used for Atlantic operations. Her deck markings were very simple with a single white dashed line down the centre of the flight deck. The lifts were not outlined. No deck letter was issued or carried. *Nabob* was torpedoed by *U-354* on 22 August 1944, and came very close to sinking due to a 152 foot-long hole in her side, but her engines were workable and a journey of over 1,000nm to port was successfully carried out. Once in port, the ship was considered not worth repairing as there were many other escort carriers entering service and the war was obviously winding down. Nonetheless, she was converted for merchant service post-war and was not broken up until 1977.

HMS REAPER Pennant D 82 (BPF Pennant R324)
Ruler class escort aircraft carrier 1944-5

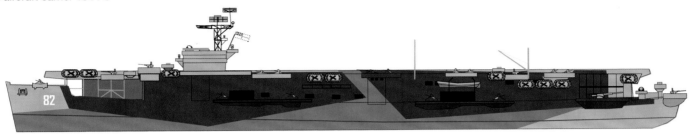

Reaper was also used as an aircraft transport. As with *Patroller*, she received twin 20mm AA mounts. She is shown above in an Admiralty scheme of B15, B30 and MS3. After numerous ferry operations, she was sent to the British Pacific Fleet as a ferry carrier for the 11th Aircraft Carrier

Squadron, operating from Manus Island. However, the war ended before the squadron was fully activated. Her duties continued as a transport, but also included troop transport and repatriation duties.

HMS SLINGER Pennant D 26 (BPF Pennant R313)
Ruler class escort aircraft carrier 1944

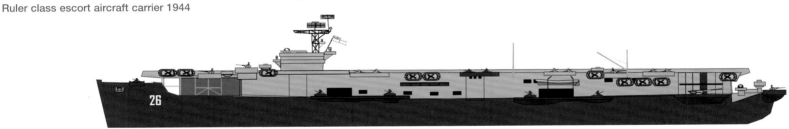

Slinger had the misfortune to be damaged by a mine in February 1944, just after entering service, and was out of action until 1945. As a result, she was mostly used on aircraft transport duties, despite having originally been intended as a fighter carrier. The ship was sent to join the British

Pacific Fleet to support the fleet carriers with spare aircraft. She is shown here in an Admiralty 1944 standard camouflage scheme of B20 and MS3. It is not known if this ship used any other camouflage and, as her active service was so short, there are very few photographs of her.

HMS SLINGER Pennant D 26 (BPF R313)
Ruler class escort aircraft carrier 1945

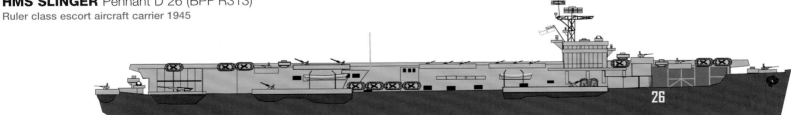

Slinger was also an aircraft transport and she, too, received twin 20mm AA mounts. She is shown above in an Admiralty scheme of B15 and MS3. She was sent to the British Pacific Fleet as a ferry carrier for the 11th Aircraft Carrier Squadron operating from Manus Island. Her duties continued

as a transport after the war ended but, like her sister ships, she also took part in troop transport and repatriation duties.

HMS TROUNCER Pennant D 85
Ruler class escort aircraft carrier 1943-5

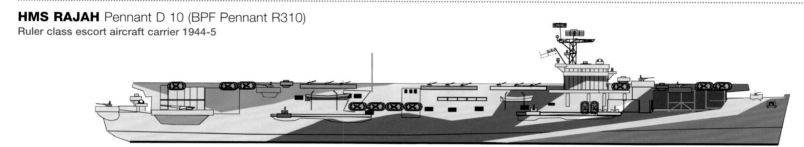

Trouncer was an aircraft transport. She is shown here in a late Admiralty standard scheme of G10, B30 and 507c. Her AA armament was altered after entering service. Many of the 20mm were removed and replaced by a total of fourteen 40mm singles. She operated in support of Royal Navy forces in the Indian Ocean and Pacific, survived the war, was returned to the USA and converted to a merchant ship.

HMS RAJAH Pennant D 10 (BPF Pennant R310)
Ruler class escort aircraft carrier 1944-5

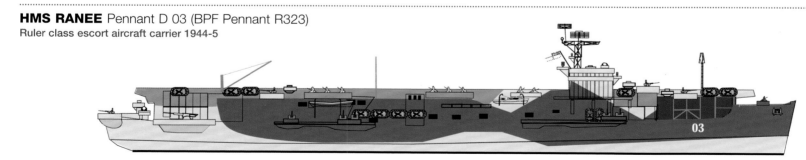

Rajah was also used as an aircraft transport. She is shown in the Admiralty scheme frequently used for the period using G10, B30 and 507c. She transported spare aircraft from the UK to the British Eastern Fleet and remained in that command until the war ended. Her duties were restricted to the transport of replacement aircraft for the other carriers operating in that region, as well as for land bases. She was returned to the USA after the war, converted to a merchant ship and sold.

HMS RANEE Pennant D 03 (BPF Pennant R323)
Ruler class escort aircraft carrier 1944-5

Ranee was completed as an assault carrier but, in the end, spent her service as an aircraft transport for the British Eastern Fleet. She is shown here in a similar scheme to her sister ships, above, and using the same range of colours. This scheme was applied in dockyards and, although basically similar, did vary from unit to unit, as can be seen. She was also converted to a merchant ship after the war and sold as the *Friesland*. Later renamed *Pacific Breeze*, she was broken up in 1974.

HMS SHAH Pennant D 21 (BPF Pennant R312)
Ruler class escort aircraft carrier 1944

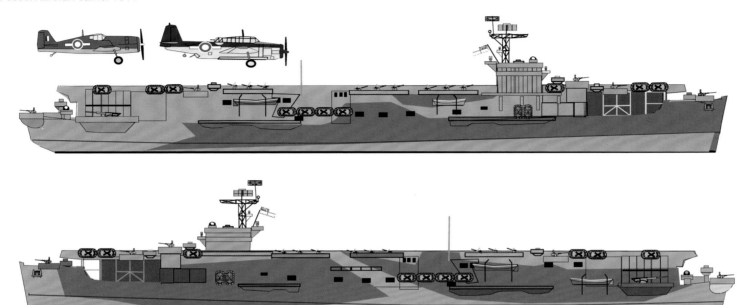

HMS SHAH Pennant D 21 (BPF Pennant R312)
Ruler class escort aircraft carrier 1944-5

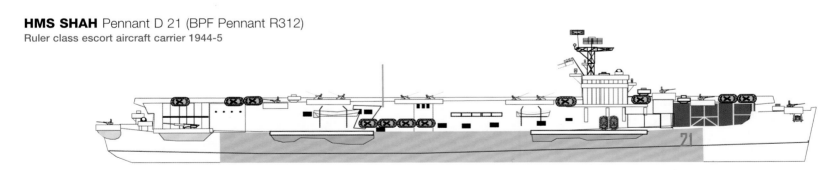

Shah was designated as an escort carrier for commerce and convoy protection. She entered service in the scheme as above with G10, B30 and B55. The hull number was carried in red. The lower section of B30 had originally been painted right to the bow but it seems to have been badly done and quickly wore to something short of the bow – it was apparently left that way until she received her first refit. The ship then went to the British Eastern Fleet, where she was used in several strike operations as well as convoy, ASW and transport duty. In the lower illustration, she is shown in overall white with a mid-blue central panel. Aircraft from this ship attacked and then kept track of the Japanese cruiser *Haguro*, which was eventually sunk in a torpedo attack by British destroyers. She was handed back to the USN in December 1945 and was then converted to merchant service. The ship was finally broken up in 1967.

HMS **SPEAKER** Pennant D90 (BPF Pennant R314)
Ruler class escort aircraft carrier 1943-5

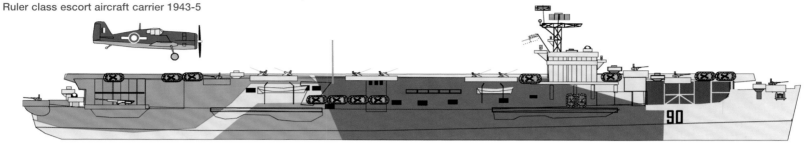

Speaker was completed as a fighter and assault carrier and initially carried out those duties for the British Pacific Fleet. However, the need for replacement and additional aircraft was high and she was soon allocated to the role of aircraft transport. She operated from Manus Island and was frequently employed in the important duty of keeping the front-line carriers fully stocked with aircraft and, occasionally, in providing fighter cover. She is shown here in the usual G10, B30 and 507c scheme but was soon repainted to overall 507c with a panel of B20. By the end of the war, this ship was painted 507s overall.

HMS **PREMIER** Pennant D 23
Ruler class escort aircraft carrier 1944-5

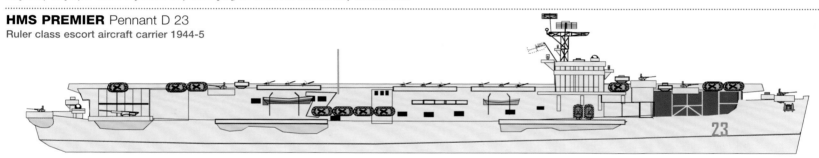

Premier was designated an escort carrier for convoy and trade protection. Her original scheme was similar to *Trouncer* but, by mid-1945, she was painted in 507c overall with pennant number in red. She took part in operations off Norway between November 1944 and March 1945, after which she was transferred to the British East Indies Fleet. However, hostilities ended shortly after her arrival.

HMS **SMITER** Pennant D 55 (BPF R321)
Ruler class escort aircraft carrier 1944-5

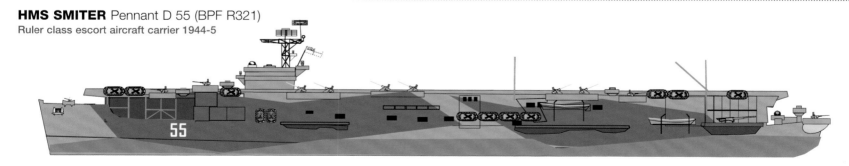

Smiter was late entering service and saw only some convoy duty in the Atlantic during 1944 before being converted to an assault carrier and sent to the Far East. However, the war ended on her arrival in August 1945. It is probable that for the Pacific she was repainted to overall 507c with blue panel.

HMS RULER Pennant D 72 (BPF Pennant R311)
Ruler class escort aircraft carrier 1944

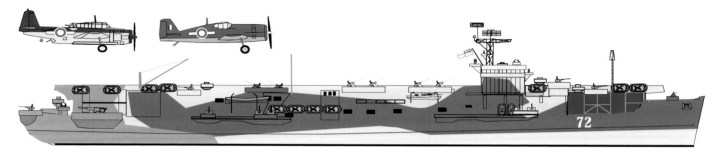

HMS RULER Pennant D 72 (BPF Pennant R311)
Ruler class escort aircraft carrier 1945

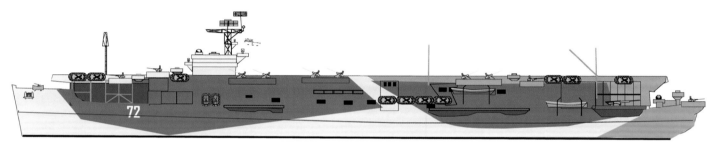

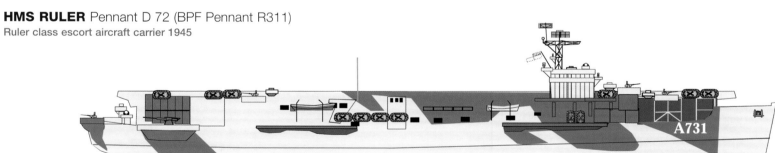

Ruler was designated as an assault and fighter carrier after she finished her final fitting out in Canada. The Royal Navy was not satisfied with the fuel storage of this class and always had their own modifications carried out. This often took some months and was a cause of friction between the US and Britain, as the Americans expected them to enter service more quickly. She is shown here in the typical scheme for the class using MS3, G10 and 507c. Most of the class had this type of scheme on completion but it was changed to a light hull with blue panel when they were sent to the Far East. *Ruler* joined some of her sister ships in the Indian Ocean late in the war but then moved on to the British Pacific Fleet almost immediately. The hull number became A731 in her

late Pacific service. Her duties were to cover the fleet train with fighters and to be available to assist the fleet carriers with cover while they refuelled and stored. She was covering *Implacable* when that ship carried out strikes against Japanese forces at Truk. This was to give the crews of both ships combat experience and be fully worked up before strikes against Japan itself. At the end of the war, she was engaged in aircraft transport and troop repatriation before being returned to the US in 1946. For an unknown reason, she did not undergo conversion to a merchant ship and, despite being so new, was sold for scrap.

HMS THANE Pennant D 83 (BPF Pennant R316)
Ruler class escort aircraft carrier 1944-5

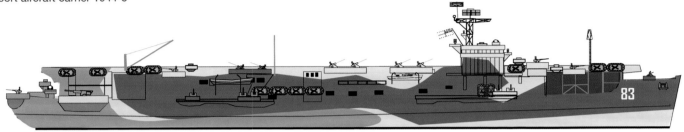

Thane was designated as an assault and fighter carrier. She underwent the usual modifications to suit the Royal Navy practice for the handling of fuel and ammunition. After working up, she proceeded to the UK and was intended to be transferred to the British Eastern Fleet. However, on 15 January 1945, she was torpedoed by U-boat *U-482*. The damage was severe but she managed to make port.

However, on examination of the damage, it was considered that she was so badly damaged as to be not worth repair and she was declared a constructive total loss. The ship was in such a state that she was unable to be returned to the US and was therefore scrapped in the UK.

HMS QUEEN Pennant D 19 (BPF Pennant R320)
Ruler class escort aircraft carrier 1944-5

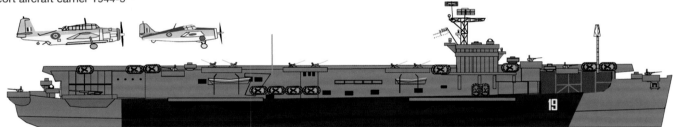

Queen was another ship that arrived toward the end of World War II. She was in time for the last Royal Navy offensive sweep of Norwegian waters, after which her role was to accompany convoys to Russia. At the end of the war, she was retained for use on various aircraft transport and troop

repatriation duties until late 1946. On return to the US, she was converted to a merchant ship and served in that role until 1972, when she was scrapped in Taiwan.

HMS PUNCHER Pennant D 79
Ruler class escort aircraft carrier 1944-5

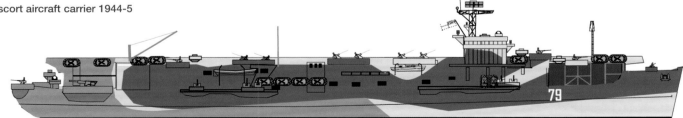

Puncher only took part on convoy duty during her passage to the UK. Mostly, her role was training pilots in deck landing, despite her designation being as a convoy escort carrier rather than a

training ship. On return to the US, she was converted to a merchant ship and was last recorded as the *Ben Nevis* in 1959.

SEAPLANE CARRIERS
HMAS ALBATROSS Pennant I 22
Seaplane carrier 1928

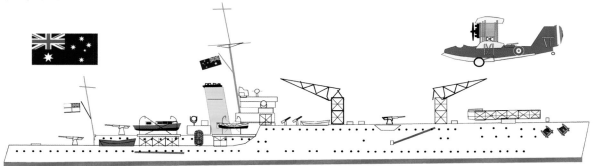

HMAS ALBATROSS Pennant I 22
Seaplane carrier 1929

Albatross was purpose-built for the Royal Australian Navy in the Cockatoo Australian dockyard. At top, she is shown not long after completion wearing typical Far East colours of white hull and upper works, with buff funnel and brown boats. In the lower illustration, the ship wears a pale grey, similar to 507c, which she wore for most of her service with the RAN. The decks were mostly dark grey metal with areas of brown Corticene. With a top speed of over 22 knots, she was the largest and fastest seaplane carrier in British Commonwealth service. The large roomy hangar forward enabled her to operate up to six Seagull III amphibian aircraft with ease and more could be carried on deck if needed. However, only four were usually carried, with another two spare aircraft being kept ashore. The catapult was of the compressed air type. Armament comprised four British 4.7in AA

gun, four Vickers machine guns and five twin Lewis machine guns. In 1929, two single 2pdr AA were also added. This heavy concentration of AA was because the ship was expected to operate alone in areas where no land-based aircraft or other warships would be available to provide additional defence. During the Great Depression, she was placed in reserve to save manpower and money. The speed of this ship and the designed intention for it to operate independently is believed to have influenced the Japanese navy, which produced a range of fast seaplane carriers prior to World War II. In the late 1930s, the ship was attractive enough to the Royal Navy for her to be accepted as part payment for the cruiser HMAS *Hobart* (ex–*Apollo*) and was transferred accordingly. At the time, the Royal Navy had no comparable ship and her usefulness on remote stations was recognised.

HMS ALBATROSS Pennant I 22 then D 22 (1940)
Seaplane carrier 1942

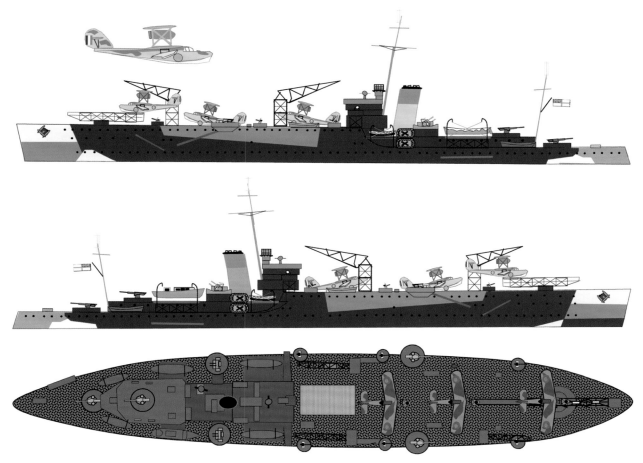

Albatross adopted an unofficial camouflage scheme in 1942. It was almost certainly designed aboard ship or locally where she was serving. It had a clever element to it as the result was to make her look like a small freighter of an older design. Colours used were B5, G5, B55 and white to produce this visually effective disguise. After her transfer to the Royal Navy, the old Seagull III amphibians were replaced by more modern Walrus aircraft. The original compressed air catapult was replaced by a more powerful type. During World War II, two quad 2pdr mountings were added, along with six single 20mm guns. She was stationed in the South Atlantic for some time, using her Walrus aircraft to search for German submarines, blockade runners and raiders. After a refit in the USA, she went to East Africa in April 1942 for further patrol duty. April to May 1944 saw the ship converted to a repair ship for landing craft and she took part in the Normandy operations. During her war service, she was hit by a German Dakel slow-running torpedo but survived. *Albatross* was decommissioned in June 1945, sold into commercial service as the migrant transport *Hellenic Prince* and was not broken up until 1954.

INDEX